Desperate Hours

Desperate Hours

The Epic Rescue
of the *Andrea Doria*

Richard Goldstein

John Wiley & Sons, Inc.

Published by John Wiley & Sons, Inc.
Published simultaneously in Canada

This publication is designed to provide accurate and authoritative information in regard to the subject matter covered. It is sold with the understanding that the publisher is not engaged in rendering professional services. If professional advice or other expert assistance is required, the services of a competent professional person should be sought.

Library of Congress Cataloging-in-Publication Data:

Goldstein, Richard.
    Desperate hours : the epic rescue of the Andrea Doria / Richard Goldstein.
       p. cm.
    Includes bibliographical references.
    ISBN 0-471-38934-X (cloth)
    1. Andrea Doria (Steamship). 2. Stockholm (Motorship). 3. Shipwrecks—North Atlantic Ocean. I. Title.

    G530.A244 G66 2001
    363.12'3'09163—dc21

                                                    2001024233

Printed in the United States of America

10 9 8 7 6 5 4 3 2 1

For Nancy

Acknowledgments

I'm grateful to the men and women—the rescued and their rescuers—who shared their memories of an extraordinary summer's night on the North Atlantic.

For providing photographs or helping me obtain documents and other materials, a special thank you to Commander David Corey, Norman Cubberly, Richard Faber, Joe Griffith, Linda Morgan Hardberger, Dr. William Homan, Carol and William Johnson, Captain Robert Meurn, Leonardo and Giovanna Paladino, Lennard Rambusch, Jerome Reinert, and Francesco Scotto. Don Bowden of AP/WideWorld Photos and Tom Gilbert of TimePix smoothed my research in their photo archives.

Lennart Angelmo, Robert Bierman, Lars Hemingstam, Mary Kirson, Henrik Ljundstrom, Captain Robert Williamson, and Dr. Preston Winters helped me locate people whose lives were touched by the collision of the *Andrea Doria* and the *Stockholm*. Henrik Nordstrom translated correspondence in Swedish.

George J. Billy, chief librarian at the U.S. Merchant Marine Academy, and Richard Corson, chief librarian at the State University of New York Maritime College, provided pointers for my research there.

I benefited greatly from the support and guidance of Stephen S. Power, senior editor at John Wiley & Sons, and Emily Loose, who first saw the possibilities in this story at Wiley, and from the efforts and enthusiasm of Jim Hornfischer at The Literary Group International.

My wife, Dr. Nancy Lubell, was there as always with love and encouragement.

Contents

Introduction

She was the most lovely ocean liner of her day, a fantastic blend of aesthetics and technology, a symbol of Italy's revival from the ravages of World War II. But more than four decades later, the enduring image of the *Andrea Doria,* viewed in the old black-and-white newsreels, is that of a funnel inexorably tipping closer to the sea as a summer's dawn gives way to a sun-splashed morning.

On the fogbound night of July 25, 1956, the *Andrea Doria* collided with the Swedish ocean liner *Stockholm* 45 miles south of Nantucket Island. The *Stockholm*'s bow ripped a massive hole in the *Doria*'s starboard side, causing her to list severely. Eleven hours later, she was lying on her side at the bottom of the North Atlantic.

It was forty-four years since the "unsinkable" *Titanic* had been sliced by an iceberg. The *Doria,* too, had been deemed the ultimate in safety on the seas—her radar the most modern, her hull divided into eleven watertight compartments. The *Stockholm* also possessed radar for the most impenetrable of nights. And yet, as on that April night in 1912 off the Grand Banks of Newfoundland, the impossible came to pass.

The death of the *Doria* retaught a lesson that speaks to the world of today: The most modern of technological wizardry guarantees nothing without a respect for its limitations and sound judgment. A series of miscalculations on the bridges of the *Andrea Doria* and the *Stockholm* brought the two ocean liners together as if they had been destined to converge.

And the loss of the *Doria,* renowned for her silhouette and her artwork, also told of the fragility of life. One moment we may have everything, in the next all can be lost.

This was underscored when a woman evacuated by one of the lifeboat crews that saved almost seventeen hundred people—history's greatest peacetime rescue at sea—was interviewed for the newsreels upon arriving at a Manhattan pier.

"I was a happy bride ready to set up home with all my belongings," the woman said. "I had beautiful clothes, beautiful family jewelry, beautiful silver. I am destitute. I've got nothing else, not even a handbag. I lost all my documents. I've got my husband, that's all. I hope America will welcome me and help me because physically and morally, I'm wrecked."

In the era of the *Doria* and the other great liners, travel proceeded at a leisurely pace. Passengers dressed splendidly for dinner. Fine food was coveted and frequent-flier miles unimagined. Ocean liners possessed distinct personalities evoking a sense of place. "Airplanes come off the assembly line by the dozen—a ship is much more of a human thing," Commodore Harry Manning, who guided the liner *United States* to an Atlantic speed record in 1952, observed in the aftermath of the *Doria*'s sinking. "A ship is the property of a nation, a symbol of a nation. It is not only the ship of a company, it is the ship of a people."

The sinking of the *Doria* symbolized the waning of a graceful approach to travel. Two years later, the advent of commercial jetliners transformed week-long transatlantic journeys into seven-hour hops.

The *Andrea Doria* retains her allure today. She is known as the Mount Everest of the deep, a magnet for divers seeking adventure or perhaps a sampling of her elegant china. But the arrival of high tech in deep-sea diving, enabling hundreds to explore the *Doria* each summer at depths of up to 250 feet, carries its own peril. The skill and judgment of some divers have evidently failed to measure up to the wondrous equipment, and so the *Andrea Doria* has continued to claim victims more than forty summers after she departed from the venerable harbor at Genoa for the last time.

PART I

The Voyage

CHAPTER 1

"Brace Yourself"

What a strange tune for a Swedish band to be playing.

A puzzled Carol Johnson picked up the strains as she peered into the North Atlantic night through the porthole in her cabin—No. 112 on the motorship *Stockholm,* en route from New York to Copenhagen and then its home port of Göteborg, Sweden.

Carol and her husband, Bill, each aboard an ocean liner for the first time, were eagerly anticipating immersion in their Swedish heritage. Carol, a slim, blond woman, had just turned twenty years old. She was Brooklyn-born, but all four of her grandparents were Swedish immigrants. Her maiden name was Lundquist. Bill Johnson, a lanky twenty-three-year-old with a crew cut, was the son of a former Swedish-American Line seaman who had come to America as a young man. His father, Charles Johnson, had considered Sweden to be God's kingdom on earth. Now the son was going to be studying Swedish on a Fulbright fellowship at the University of Lund, having completed graduate studies at Drew Theological Seminary in New Jersey. Although he was a minister with two small congregations in New Jersey, he had joined the Stockholm crew as a glasswasher to obtain free passage for his wife and daughter.

Crewmen were not normally allowed to have their families with them, but G. Hilmer Lundbeck, New York manager of the Swedish-American line, had quietly permitted Carol and the couple's five-week-old daughter, Karin, to come along. Bill was required, however, to sleep in the crew cabins. At this moment—a bit past eleven o'clock on the night of Wednesday, July 25, 1956—he was chatting with a fellow seaman named Alf Johansson in their quarters near the bow.

Karin, having just been fed, was lying beside her mother in the lower bunk of a two-tiered berth when Carol heard music. She recognized the popular tune, of course, but could not fathom why it had been selected for the dancing pleasure of all those Carlsons and Olsons traveling to Scandinavia. Especially on their first day at sea.

Why "Arrivederci Roma"?

Then Carol saw the lights—row after row of them. The glare mingled in a confusing few seconds with the sounds of the band. And Carol knew the music was in no way resonating from the lounge of the *Stockholm*.

Earlier that evening, Horace Pettit, a doctor from Bryn Mawr, Pennsylvania, traveling with his wife, Jane, and twelve-year-old daughter, Barbara, had walked the *Stockholm*'s deck with compass in hand, checking it against the ship's course. Pettit loved the sea. He had made twenty-six crossings of the Atlantic on ocean liners and had long plied the Atlantic coast in his 45-foot schooner *Heron*.

He was reading in the family's cabin when he heard a sharp whistle blast. It had not come from the *Stockholm*. He, too, looked out his porthole, and he saw the night aglow.

"Brace yourself," he shouted to his wife. "We're going to crash."

Martin Sejda, a fifteen-year-old from Pennsylvania, had been strolling on the otherwise deserted deck of another ocean liner, a ship unsurpassed for the beauty of its lines and the elegance of its decor. His parents, Dr. and Mrs. Martin Sejda Sr., and his twenty-four-year-old sister, Dolores, were partaking of some eleventh-hour partying on the pride of the Italian nation, the steamship *Andrea Doria,* due in New York the next morning after a nine-day journey from Genoa. Then the teenager became sleepy and decided to join the rest of his family. He was about to turn from the rail when he saw something that froze him: The night air had suddenly lit up. Something huge was speeding directly at him. He would remember how this form was "coming in at an angle like it was trying to keep from hitting us." He began to run.

Dun Gifford was chatting with friends on a couch in a lounge. His father, Clarence, chairman of a Providence, Rhode Island, bank; his mother, Priscilla; two brothers, Chad and Jock; and his sister, Bambi, had returned to their first-class cabins following a little party, a glorious conclusion to a European vacation. Dun happened to look out a plate-glass window. "A lighthouse in the middle of the ocean?" he wondered.

Frances Aljinovec and her friend from Cleveland, Mary Marsich, were returning from a two-week tour of Europe. Their last day in Italy had been so much fun that they had almost missed the *Andrea Doria*'s departure.

Mary had put on her pink pajamas and slipped into her lower berth. Frances climbed into the top bunk and glanced out the porthole to check the weather. The fog that had engulfed the *Andrea Doria* for

The *Andrea Doria*, renowned for her graceful lines and magnificent artwork.
(Richard Faber Collection)

the past eight hours had been pierced. Night had become day. "A ship is going to hit us," she cried out.

Nick de Franetovich, a Californian sitting at the bar of the *Doria*'s Belvedere Observation Lounge, sipped a final highball before turning in. He looked out the large observation-deck windows. Then he turned to the bartender. "What the hell . . ."

CHAPTER 2

"A Floating Art Gallery"

For Piero Calamai, Italy's premier man of the sea and the only captain the *Andrea Doria* would ever know, the festivities had begun with a smile, a wave, and a greeting: "Hello, New York," all coaxed from him by newsreel men as he stood in his dress blues, braving an icy wind on a pier at Manhattan's West Forty-fourth Street.

Three and a half years later, almost to the day, all would be shattered. But on this sunless winter Friday—January 24, 1953—the Italian nation, only beginning to emerge from the devastation of World War II, could justly celebrate. At noon the *Andrea Doria,* pride of a resurgent Italian maritime service, had eased into New York Harbor under the guidance of Captain Calamai on her maiden voyage from Genoa. Her upper works were festooned with pennants, a helicopter having escorted her in.

A crowd of twenty thousand and a host of politicians, headed by New York's mayor, Vincent Impellitteri, accorded a spectacular welcome to Italy's flagship, the first new Italian liner to arrive in New York since the war and a beauty to behold.

"With her decks gracefully terraced down toward the stern and her single stack, part solid, part grilled, striped in the splendidly daring colors of the Italian flag, you get a sense of a pleasure craft intended to sail under Mediterranean skies, blue as the Madonna's robe," the art critic Arlene B. Loucheim observed in the *New York Times.*

"Her name is *Andrea Doria,* and she is as beautiful a new piece of marine construction as I ever saw," Robert Ruark would marvel in a column. "It is ladies like the *Andrea Doria* that I kiss in print."

The hoopla surrounding the *Doria*'s arrival underlined the glamour still attached to the North Atlantic ocean liner. The era of the elegant liners was nearing its end—one third of transatlantic travelers having chosen to fly by the early 1950s—but dozens of liners still embarked from New York, Southampton, and Le Havre every week.

Thousands of persons—passengers, family members bidding *bon voyage,* curious New Yorkers savoring the atmosphere of sailing day—might be at the great West Side piers on a weekend morning. Reporters and photographers assigned to the shipping "beat" interviewed the arriving world-class celebrities—movie stars or an occasional royal or statesman—hoping for a quote and a picture beside a life preserver labeled *Queen Mary* or *Ile de France.*

The duke and duchess of Windsor, traveling with a hundred pieces of luggage, were the most photographed of the celebrity set, favoring the Cunard ships and the liner *United States.* Marlene Dietrich was partial to the *Queen Elizabeth,* Lana Turner the *Mauretania.* Greta Garbo preferred to be left alone. Once, upon learning that a horde of reporters had massed in ambush, she slipped off the *Queen Mary* on a lower-deck crew gangway, disguised as a Cunard stewardess.

So the reception for the *Andrea Doria* was truly grand. And yet, the *Doria*'s maiden trip had hardly been unblemished. The evening before she entered the harbor, a mountainous sea had sent her rolling precipitously. Dining room tables flipped over, chairs flew, and 20 of her 794 passengers were injured. And a pratfall punctuated the *Doria*'s arrival. Grover Whelan, New York City's official greeter, became wedged briefly between the stack and wheelhouse of the Coast Guard cutter *Manitou* when it took the mayor's party to the quarantine station for a transfer to the liner.

None of this, of course, occasioned foreboding. The *Doria* was equipped with the most modern of safety devices, and her care was, by all accounts, in exceedingly good hands.

Captain Calamai, a sturdy six-footer at home on the high seas since graduating from the Genoa Nautical Institute in 1916, belonged to the first family of Italy's nautical life. His father, Oreste, had founded the prestigious publication *The Italian Navy,* and his younger brother, Admiral Paolo Calamai, commanded the Italian naval academy at Leghorn.

Piero Calamai had been a junior officer in the Italian Navy during World War I, then served as staff captain on the ocean liners *Conte Grande, Augustus,* and *Conte di Savoia.* Rejoining the navy in World War II as a lieutenant commander, he won the Italian War Cross for saving the battleship *Caio Duilio* by running it aground on a sandbar when it was torpedoed by the British in the harbor at Taranto in November 1940. After the war Calamai served as master of three new Italian Line vessels in the South American service, then alternated with another captain aboard the *Saturnia* on its North Atlantic run before being named captain of the *Andrea Doria* in December 1952. At age fifty-five, he was one of the youngest officers ever to command a major Italian ocean liner.

Calamai was essentially a quiet man, his composure ruffled only rarely, and a teetotaler not wholly at ease in fulfilling his social obligations. He would have preferred taking meals in his cabin to presiding over the glittering dinners at the captain's table.

"He was an old-style gentleman, ambitious but modest, almost shy," Guido Badano, his third officer senior on this maiden voyage, would remember.

When not in command on the seas, Calamai lived with his wife and two teenage daughters in Genoa, the seaport city of hills that had produced Italy's towering maritime figures Christopher Columbus and Admiral Andrea Doria, the Mediterranean's preeminent warrior-statesman of the sixteenth century.

Admiral Doria fought for and against Italian princes, for and against France, and consistently against the Turks and the Barbary pirates. He commanded warships that were perhaps 150 feet long, rigged with two and sometime three large sails, powered by captured slaves or criminals shackled to rowing benches, making 4 or 5 knots while hundreds of men massed on the upper deck to do battle with cannons and swords.

In 1528, at age sixty-two, Andrea Doria directed an amphibious assault that drove a French garrison out of Genoa and reestablished the republic after more than a century's domination by foreign powers. He refused to become Genoa's head of state, but his homeland would never again fall under foreign control in his lifetime.

By the time he died in November 1560—five days short of his ninety-fourth birthday—Admiral Doria had gained a niche as one of the great sea captains of history. Two centuries later, an American brig was named in his honor. That *Andrea Doria* was the first American ship to receive a salute in a foreign port, having been greeted with an eight-gun tribute upon calling at St. Eustatius in the Dutch West Indies in 1776.

The admiral's name would resonate again in the decade following World War II with the design of a ship that inaugurated the rebirth of the Italian Line.

The major liners pressed into wartime service by Mussolini—the *Conte di Savoia,* the *Rex,* the *Augustus,* and the *Roma*—had all been sunk. The Italians were left with four prewar liners—the *Saturnia,* her sister ship the *Vulcania,* the *Conte Biancamano,* and her near sister the

Captain Piero Calamai
and the opera star Renata
Tibaldi visiting the statue
of Admiral Andrea Doria
in the first-class lounge on
one of the *Doria*'s hundred
North Atlantic crossings
between 1953 and 1956.
(Richard Faber Collection)

Conte Grande—all of them seized by the United States, converted to troopships, then returned by 1947.

Italy began a huge rebuilding program with the *Giulio Cesare* and the new *Augustus,* completed in 1951 and 1952, respectively, for the Genoa–South America run. Then the Italians turned to the U.S. market—the Genoa, Cannes, Naples, Gibraltar, New York run.

The *Andrea Doria,* designed by the Italian architect Minoletti, built at a cost of $29 million, and launched in June 1951, was Italy's largest new liner—697 feet in length and 29,100 gross tons—and her fastest one as well. Her two sets of steam turbines driving twin screws made more than 25 knots in her final trial runs in the Gulf of Genoa although designed for a maximum of 23 knots for her transatlantic trips.

She also was a symbol of America's massive effort to rebuild the war-torn European economy, having been constructed at the Ansaldo Company shipyards at Sestri, a suburb of Genoa, with help from Marshall Plan loans.

By certain measures, the *Doria* was outstripped by other liners. The *Queen Elizabeth* and twelve other passenger ships were longer. The

990-foot liner *United States,* which entered service in 1952, could cross
the Atlantic in three and a half days, having been designed not only for
the burgeoning postwar passenger trade but also as a potential troop
carrier for the Korean War and future Cold War crises. But the *Doria*
was uniformly regarded as the most gorgeous ocean liner of her day,
both in her exterior lines, which evoked an illusion of movement even
while in port, and in her decor.

The Italian Line hailed the *Doria* as "a living testament to the
importance of beauty in the everyday world" and "a floating art gal-
lery." Hyperbole aside, she blended modern technology (air conditioning throughout) and modern artistic touches such as exotic blond wood
panels and surrealist murals with works reflecting Italy's artistic heritage, drawing on the efforts of the nation's leading painters, sculptors,
ceramists, and designers.

Her 31 public rooms (15 first class, 9 cabin class, 7 tourist class)
were adorned with handwoven tapestries, original oil paintings, statu-
aries, murals, and rare woods. Each class had its own bar, library, gym-
nasium, shops, and accommodations for dancing and movies. She was
the first ocean liner with three outdoor swimming pools, and each of
them featured a lido deck with colorful beach umbrellas, lounging
chairs, and bar service. Even her plumbing paid homage to art, several
bathrooms adorned with designs of blue fish, in tribute to the baths of
imperial Rome.

On the Boat Deck—the fourth highest of the ten decks—the Belvedere Observation Lounge, directly below the bridge, offered an elegant and intimate first-class spot for nighttime dancing.

The Promenade Deck, the *Doria*'s social center, one level below the
Boat Deck, featured a dazzling array of artwork in the lounges and
ballrooms. Near the bow, two 1,000-pound ceramic panels designed by
the potter Guido Gambone of Florence, self-taught but one of Italy's
most renowned craftsmen, graced the Winter Garden.

The first-class lounge on this deck was one of the most beautiful
public rooms, dominated by *The Legend of Italy,* an eight-wall mural
covering 1,600 square feet and eight walls. Designed by Salvatore
Fiume, the son of a Sicilian coffinmaker, it re-created works by Michelangelo, Raphael, Cellini, Donatello, da Vinci, and Titian and depicted
the best of Italian architecture. A life-sized bronze statue of Andrea
Doria by Giovanni Paganin, portraying the admiral in armor and bran-
dishing his sword, provided the centerpiece for the lounge. A silver
family crest that had once hung in the admiral's Genoese mansion,
donated by a descendant, Marquis Giambattista Doria, and a mural

Even the *Andrea Doria*'s card room employed decorative touches. (Richard Faber Collection)

depicting a street in Genoa where a similar statue had been placed, served as backdrops.

The children's dining room also offered artistic flourishes—a kangaroo surprised to see a pineapple top emerging from her pouch, smoking frogs, and flower-eating pelicans peering from murals.

Each dining room had its own china pattern. The first-class china, designed by Italy's premier porcelainmaker, Richard Ginori, featured a red and gold pattern, while the second-class pattern was trimmed in blue and gold.

The Catholic Chapel (it had a single entrance for all classes) held paintings depicting the twelve Stations of the Cross, and a magnificent silver chalice and candlestick holders.

Surrounding the chapel were four deluxe suites, among them the double cabin 174–176 that was known as the Zodiac Room, its stars and astrological signs designed by Fornasetti. Reflecting a more contemporary note was the so-called Rita Hayworth apartment, its walls lined with quilted satin, the beds covered with satin spreads, and the windows adorned with satin drapes, evocative of a satiny photo featuring the sultry actress in *Life* magazine.

The *Doria*'s glamour extended even to its fifty-car garage, which on a certain trip in July 1956 would house the Norseman "car of the future," designed by Chrysler in accord with the latest aerodynamic principles at a reported cost of $200,000, handbuilt by the Ghia sports car company of Turin, Italy, and bound for final testing in Michigan. More mundane, but impressive nonetheless, was the Rolls-Royce entrusted to the garage on that journey by a socialite from Miami Beach named Edward Parker, returning from a honeymoon in Paris.

Captain Piero Calamai was superbly equipped to safeguard his ship from the bridge on the Sun Deck, one level below the slot where the single white funnel, banded with a thick red and a thin green line, rose 37.5 feet.

Since the loss of the *Titanic* in 1912, few nautical experts were willing to brand a ship "unsinkable." But the *Doria* was known for an attention to safety that complemented its quest for unmatched beauty.

Captain Calamai and his senior officers employed two radar screens to scan the seas for anything from a fishing boat to another ocean liner. They had loran (long-range navigation equipment) and a radio direction finder to determine the *Doria*'s location at all moments.

The *Andrea Doria* was divided into eleven watertight compartments by steel bulkheads. In accord with requirements of the 1948 International Convention for the Safety of Life at Sea, she was designed to remain afloat even with two adjacent compartments flooded, as long as she did not list more than 20 degrees to either side, an almost unimaginable calamity that would open the tops of the compartments to seawater and lead to progressive flooding of the entire ship.

Fireproof insulated partitions divided the ship into thirty-three safety zones, each isolated by automatically operated doors. The hull's double bottom, storing fuel oil, lubricating oil, fresh water, and ballast water, provided enhanced protection against an obstacle scraping the ship from below. A double hull that was created through the placement of bulkheads parallel to the engine rooms afforded protection in the highly unlikely event of a collision.

Eight aluminum lifeboats were housed on each side of the Boat Deck. Operated by electric winches, they were slung from davits that they would slide along in accord with the principles of gravity. They could hold a total of 2,008 persons, almost 200 beyond the *Doria*'s capacity for passengers and crew.

A glance at the pronouncements of the Transatlantic Passenger Conference, representing the steamship companies of the North Atlantic,

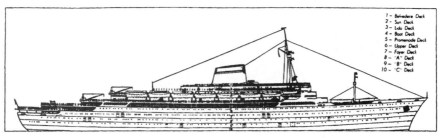

1 – Belvedere Deck
2 – Sun Deck
3 – Lido Deck
4 – Boat Deck
5 – Promenade Deck
6 – Upper Deck
7 – Foyer Deck
8 – "A" Deck
9 – "B" Deck
10 – "C" Deck

The ten decks of the *Andrea Doria*.

would have provided immense comfort to anyone still nervous about sailing. The *Titanic* had gone down with the loss of 1,513 lives when she hit an iceberg at full speed off the Grand Banks south of Newfoundland. But since World War I, the conference noted, ocean liners had carried more than 26 million passengers between America and Europe without a single casualty from a collision or a shipwreck.

CHAPTER 3

"Take the *Doria,*
You'll Never Forget It"

When the *Andrea Doria* departed Genoa on its 101st crossing of the Atlantic on the afternoon of Tuesday, July 17, 1956, Captain Piero Calamai was embarking on a personal farewell. Forty-two months after guiding the *Doria* on her maiden voyage to New York, Calamai was to make his last round trip before taking command of her sister ship, the *Cristoforo Colombo.*

The *Doria* stopped at Cannes on the French Riviera, then picked up passengers at Naples, departing at 4:00 P.M. Wednesday under sunny skies from the international port, separated by a fence from a major U.S. naval base. Now the *Doria* headed for the Tyrrhenian Sea toward Gibraltar, where the Mediterranean meets the Atlantic.

On Thursday morning, a blast of the ship's horn signaled the passengers picked up at Naples to take their life jackets and proceed to the muster stations listed on their cabin doors for the obligatory evacuation drill.

En route to a new life in America, the De Girolamo family from the village of Ischia in the south of Italy—the father, Francesco; the mother, Anna, and their five children: sons Antonio, 17; Nicola, 14; Mario, 8; and Biagio, 3; and daughter Maria Rosaria, 18—gathered with fellow tourist-class passengers in a ballroom near the stern.

Antonio would remember long afterward how efficient it all seemed. Many passengers in their group had put on their life jackets, but an officer in a white shirt with gold bars instructed them—first in English and then in Italian—to take the vests off, hold them at their left side, and await a recorded announcement at 7:45. At precisely that moment, a long whistle sounded, and another message, again in English and Italian, provided instructions on how to don the life vests and proceed to lifeboats if the order to abandon ship should ever come. The drill took about 20 minutes, and then the loudspeaker sounded a more welcome note: breakfast would soon be served.

But at another muster station, where Pastor Ernest LaFont gathered with his family, efficiency was hardly the byword.

LaFont, a missionary with the Church of God, returning with his wife, Grace, and eleven-year-old son, Leland, from his duties in Egypt, and bound for a furlough at church headquarters in Anderson, Indiana, was none too happy this particular morning. The Italian Line's reservation officials had already botched his accommodations. The LaFonts had booked a cabin together, but when they boarded in Naples, father and son had been placed in one cabin and Mrs. LaFont in another.

The LaFonts' agitation was about to grow. When they reported with twenty others to their evacuation station, not an officer was in sight. Nor would anyone in a white uniform and epaulets arrive over the next few moments. The passengers stood around for a while, then left without their drill.

At midday Friday, the *Doria* weighed anchor off Gibraltar to pick up its final complement of passengers from small boats. While the new arrivals were processed, the passengers already on board were given an hour's time for shopping. Ten boats crammed with watches, perfume, blankets, and T-shirts approached from the dock, vendors lofting the items to the *Doria*'s decks in baskets and calling out their asking prices. If a bargain was struck, the passenger lowered money in the basket. If not, the goods were returned.

As she prepared to board, Kathy Kerbow, returning to Park College in Missouri after a year's study at the University of Madrid, thought the scene idyllic. The water was so blue, the *Doria*'s black and white hull so sleek, the day so sunny, she seemed to be viewing a picture postcard.

With the last of the passengers finally aboard and the haggling with the merchants concluded, the *Doria* sounded a horn signaling it was time to head into the Atlantic. Captain Calamai took inventory for his logbook. The *Doria* carried 1,134 passengers—190 in first class, 267 in cabin class, and 677 in tourist class. The crew numbered 572—officers, seamen, stewards, waiters, chambermaids, and engine-room personnel. The cargo holds and garage carried 401 tons of freight, 9 automobiles, 522 pieces of baggage, and 1,754 bags of mail.

A glance at the manifest for first class revealed a few men and women who would be expected to provide a word and a smile for the reporters and photographers assigned to meet the great ocean liners when they arrived at the Port of New York.

The "star" of the *Doria* was a daughter of immigrants—not Italians, but Lithuanians—the shapely, dark-haired actress Ruth Roman, at age thirty-two a veteran of box-office successes of the 1940s and '50s.

A native of Lynn, Massachusetts, her father a carnival barker who died when she was a child, Roman had quit high school to pursue an acting career. Her first film role had been a bit part as a Wave in *Stage Door Canteen* in 1942. Her breakthrough came seven years later, when she played opposite Kirk Douglas in Stanley Kramer's *Champion,* an adaptation of Ring Lardner's short story about a manic prizefighter. That success prompted Warner Brothers to give her nine starring roles in the following two years.

When she tried out for a part in *Champion,* she thought she might be chosen to play the boxer's gold-digging girlfriend, and accordingly wore a tight-fitting black dress and heavy makeup to Kramer's office. But an air of wholesomeness stood out. Kramer picked her to play the loyal wife of the prizefighter. The part of the gold-digger went to Marilyn Maxwell.

The actress, who had crossed previously on the *Doria,* was traveling with her three-year-old son, Richard Roman Hall, known as Dickie, from her marriage to her former husband, Mortimer Hall, a broadcast executive. A slim, gray-haired nanny named Grace Els would be watching over Dickie. They were booked for Cabins 82 and 84, on the starboard side of the Upper Deck.

The actress Betsy Drake, traveling alone on the *Doria,* could not compete with Roman in terms of star quality, but she was married to one of the film world's biggest names, Cary Grant. That marriage had, however, been battered on a European film set, prompting Drake to return home without her husband.

The daughter of Carlos Drake, whose family had founded the Drake and Blackstone Hotels in Chicago, Betsy Drake, a slender five feet, six inches with short hair and sparkling blue eyes, was a model turned actress with an adventuresome mind. She loved books and was fascinated by psychology and intrigued by hypnotism.

She caught Grant's eye in August 1947 when he saw her performing at Wyndham's Theatre in London in the imported Broadway hit about racial prejudice *Deep Are the Roots.* In September, returning to America on the *Queen Mary,* Grant learned that Drake was also on board. While having tea in the lounge with fifteen-year-old Elizabeth Taylor, who was accompanied aboard ship by her mother, Grant spotted Drake going to a telephone. He followed her, pretending to be making a call in a nearby booth.

Ruth Roman and Admiral Andrea Doria during an uneventful trip the actress previously made on the *Doria*. (Richard Faber Collection)

When Drake left the booth, the ship was caught by a wave and she stumbled. Grant grabbed her to break her fall. A more formal introduction came the next day, when Grant prevailed upon the actress Merle Oberon, returning to America after filming *Berlin Express,* to arrange a buffet lunch for the three of them. Drake would soon be living with Grant in Beverly Hills, and the following year she was cast in her first film, playing opposite Grant in *Every Girl Should Be Married.* Christmas Day 1949 brought their own marriage.

In the summer of 1956 Drake had joined Grant at a movie location on the Spanish plains near Ávila, only to be humiliated by him. While filming *The Pride and the Passion,* based on C. S. Forester's novel of the Napoleonic Wars *The Gun,* Grant had romanced his virtually unknown costar, twenty-year-old Sophia Loren, proposing marriage over dinner one evening. Loren, however, already had a married lover, the director (and her future husband) Carlo Ponti. She said she needed time to think things over.

Drake departed Spain before the press learned of the romance. She drove to Gibraltar, where she boarded the *Doria,* a ship she had once sailed on with Grant, and took a first-class single cabin on the Boat Deck.

A marital spat of far less consequence—or so it seemed at the time— had brought a pair of refugee Hungarian ballet stars to a cabin on the port side of the Upper Deck.

Istvan Rabovsky, twenty-six, and his wife, Nora Kovach, twenty-five, returning from their performance at an open-air festival near Genoa, had originally booked Cabin 56, on the starboard side, a room with a shower and a bathtub. That seemed a bit excessive for Istvan. "Let's save some money," he told Nora. A cabin with just a shower would be sufficient.

Most of the time, as Istvan would remember, his wife won out when they had an argument. This dispute went on for two or three days, and finally Istvan prevailed. The couple gave up Cabin 56, which went to Thure Peterson, a chiropractor from New Jersey, and his wife, Martha. The ballet stars took the portside Cabin 77, containing a shower but no bathtub.

Though their travel arrangements were relatively modest, Rabovsky and Kovach were flourishing artistically, their earnings far beyond anything they could have imagined just a few years earlier.

Born to an unwed mother in the Hungarian city of Szeged, Rabovsky had shuttled among Gypsy foster parents and his own grandparents before being reunited with his mother. At age eleven, he saw a motion picture for the first time, a Fred Astaire film. It would change his life. Trying some dance steps for the amusement of his fellow students, he caught the attention of a teacher who discerned a hint of talent in the spindly youngster and helped him enroll in the Royal Hungarian Opera's ballet school in Budapest.

It was there that Istvan sat beside Nora Kovach, whose family placed her in a social world beyond the boy's grasp. Nora's mother was a teacher, her father a civil servant, while Istvan was a poor boy from the slums. But they began to dance together and fell in love before they had reached their teens.

In the decade following World War II, Rabovsky and Kovach were among the premier ballet stars of Hungary, and they performed in the Soviet Union, East Berlin, Romania, and Bulgaria. They were married in 1952, to the consternation of Nora's mother, who hurled a flower pot at Istvan's head (she missed) when they arrived to live at the Kovach family's apartment until they could find a place of their own.

As renowned artists, Rabovsky and Kovach were part of the Communist world's privileged class, but they felt crushed by the lack of personal freedom and yearned to test their talents in the vast cultural world of the West. While performing in East Berlin in May 1953, they slipped away from the secret police watching over their troupe and boarded a subway for West Berlin, the Berlin Wall not yet in place. Had a conductor checked them for identity papers, they would have been seized, the ballet stage presumably exchanged for jail cells. But they were not checked. They simply rode the train until the first subway stop in West Berlin. They were free.

The American impresario Sol Hurok, who had been in Salzburg, Germany, for its music festival, heard about their escape, signed them for a $3,000 advance, took them on a European tour with the London Festival Ballet, then brought them to America. They were soon appearing with major dance companies and became repeated guests on TV's *Ed Sullivan Show,* their careers ascendant.

Cabin 80 on the Upper Deck, adjoining the cabins booked by Ruth Roman, belonged to a rising star in the political world, Philadelphia's new mayor, Richardson Dilworth, and his wife, Ann.

The son of a Pittsburgh businessman, Dilworth would be a major presence in Philadelphia politics for two decades, as city treasurer, district attorney, mayor, and school board president. He was a reformer who attracted scores of talented people to public service and a patrician with sensitivity to the needs of the poor. And he had long before weathered many tests of his courage.

Fighting with the Marines at Belleau Wood in World War I after quitting Yale, Dilworth was struck by an artillery shell that nearly tore off his left shoulder. He underwent half a dozen operations, then returned to Yale, playing end on the football team and rowing for the varsity although his left arm had lost 70 percent of its motion and strength. He reenlisted in the Marines in World War II although he had six children, and served as an officer on Guadalcanal.

After the war, while in private law practice, Dilworth faced a very personal crisis—a drinking problem that threatened to kill his considerable political ambitions. He overcame his addiction only after being hospitalized, and in 1949 was elected Philadelphia's city treasurer. He later became district attorney, and in November 1955 was elected mayor, succeeding his fellow reformer Joe Clark, who would go on to the U.S. Senate the following year.

Dilworth and his wife were returning to America from a vacation in the Middle East and Europe that had concluded in Monaco with a visit to a former Philadelphian. After meeting the newly married Princess Grace and Prince Rainier in Monaco, the Dilworths had gone to Cannes, where they boarded the *Doria*.

Dilworth faced stormy political times back home, having come under fire over extensive concessions to patronage-hungry Democratic Party leaders in his first months as mayor. With his fifty-eighth birthday a month off and combat in two world wars behind him, he could hardly have anticipated any further tests of his fortitude beyond the political wars.

The newspaper world was represented as well aboard the *Doria*.

One of the liner's four deluxe suites surrounding the chapel had been booked by a family with a venerable name in American journalism.

Ferdinand Thieriot, thirty-five, the circulation manager of the *San Francisco Chronicle,* a younger brother of Charles de Young Thieriot, the newspaper's publisher, had been planning to fly home with his wife, Frances, also thirty-five, and the oldest of their four sons, thirteen-year-old Peter, after a visit with relatives in Spain. Thieriot's aunt, Helen Cameron, the widow of the former *Chronicle* publisher George Cameron, had wanted the Thieriots to spend time with her while she was staying in Paris, but Ferdinand phoned her to report a "lucky break." He was canceling the plane reservations, since space had become available on the *Andrea Doria.* Peter was eager to experience a trip on a magnificent ocean liner, and now he could. They would board at Gibraltar.

The Thieriots wanted the two-room suite, No. 180, on the starboard side of the chapel, but its sitting room had been taken by a Denver businessman named Max Passante and his wife, Theresa. Mr. and Mrs. Thieriot settled for the bedroom in the suite, arranging for Peter to take a single cabin a few doors down, toward the bow.

Obtaining the finest accommodations on the era's most beautiful ship seemed a natural fit for the Thieriots, members of the business and social elite of San Francisco. Ferdinand Thieriot indeed had impeccable credentials as a Phi Beta Kappa graduate of Princeton. But his roots were in the brawling days of the Old West.

Ferdinand was a grandson of Michael de Young, who with his brother, Charles, had founded the *Chronicle* in 1865 with a $20 gold piece borrowed from Michael's landlord. They made the *Chronicle* the dominant paper of San Francisco, but then the bullets began to fly.

In 1879, Charles de Young shot and wounded a mayoral candidate, Isaac Kalloch, who had insinuated that the brothers' mother ran a brothel. The next year, Kalloch's son, Milton, burst into the *Chronicle*'s newsroom and gained revenge, fatally shooting Charles. In 1884, Michael de Young, who had become known as M. H. de Young, was shot and wounded by a sugar baron named Adolph Spreckels, who had been attacked in the pages of the *Chronicle*. Since then, editorial disputes had been settled in a calmer manner, and now the Thieriots were hoping for a good week's rest at sea.

Like the Thieriot family, Camille Cianfarra, the *New York Times*'s correspondent in Madrid, had boarded the *Doria* in Gibraltar. Returning to New York with his family on home leave, he had sought an earlier passage on the *Cristoforo Colombo,* but it had no space available. Cianfarra and his wife, Jane, a freelance writer, took Cabin 54 on the Upper Deck, next to the cabin that Istvan Rabovsky and Nora Kovach had switched from. Their daughter, Joan Cianfarra, age eight, and Mrs. Cianfarra's daughter, Linda Morgan, fourteen, from her previous marriage to the American Broadcasting Company commentator Edward P. Morgan, settled into Cabin 52, directly above the suite taken by the Thieriots.

The forty-nine-year-old Cianfarra—known as Cian—was among the *Times*'s star reporters. Born in New York City but educated in Rome, where his father had been a correspondent for the *New York American* and United Press, he was ribbed by friends as a man who spoke Italian with an American accent and English with an Italian accent. He was a worldly man, comfortable in the social circles of the powerful. He had been with the *Times* since 1935, reporting from Mexico City, Rome, and Madrid, and had a wide network of news sources. He was best known for reporting exclusively a few years earlier how Vatican archaeologists had uncovered the tomb of St. Peter.

In the *Doria*'s cabin-class section on A Deck, a twenty-three-year-old songwriter named Mike Stoller was returning with his wife, Meryl, twenty-five, from a three-month trip to Europe financed by an unexpected royalty check. Stoller's introduction to music came as a tuba player at Forest Hills High School in New York City. He had moved with his family to Los Angeles as a youngster, and at age seventeen had begun to write songs with another teenager, Jerry Leiber. Their "Black Denim Trousers and Motorcycle Boots" had been recorded in France by Edith Piaf, bringing a $5,000 payment for European rights. Mike and Meryl, having been married for a year, were planning to start a family. They decided to use the royalty payment for an extended trip before undertaking the obligations of parenthood.

The Stollers had obtained tickets for a flight from Los Angeles to Copenhagen and had planned to return home from Naples on the Greek liner *Olympic.* But when Mike went to the Automobile Club office in Los Angeles to inquire about car rentals in France, the travel agent said he could switch him from the *Olympic* to the *Andrea Doria,* which he assured Mike was "very nice." The Stollers had obtained their booking on the *Olympic* from a friend who was a travel agent and felt badly about making a change. But their friend encouraged them to switch. "Oh, take the *Doria,*" he said, "you'll never forget it."

On Decks B and C, below the waterline, the men, women, and children traveling in third class—or tourist class, as the Italian Line called it—were lodged four to a cabin. But they were hardly traveling in what was once known as steerage. They partook of the fine food, savored the glorious artwork, and enjoyed their own swimming pool and lido deck. These passengers, mostly Italian immigrants, were, however, journeying on a bittersweet note. They were seeking a better life in America, but leaving behind extended families and the towns and farms beyond which most had never ventured.

Leonardo Paladino, a tailor from the southern Italian city of Bari, had heard an incredible story one day from a man who came into his shop to have his pants pressed. The customer had recently lived in America, working as a clerk. For pushing a pencil, he earned $250 a week—or so he said.

Paladino mused: "This man doesn't even have a trade and he's making a fantastic salary. If a man has a skill, like a tailor, imagine what he could earn."

His wife, Giovanna, came from a large family and could hardly bear leaving her brothers and sisters. When she would see them again, who knew? But the Paladinos would try America. Less than two years after hearing that tale of streets paved with the proverbial gold, Leonardo booked passage on the *Andrea Doria* with Giovanna and their daughters, Maria, 4; Felicia, 3; and Tonya, 2. Upon arrival, the family would stay for a while in Queens with Leonardo's sister, Antoinette Masciagna.

The weather remained lovely as Captain Calamai took the *Doria* into the Atlantic. The morning after the ship passed the Azores, a wind— perhaps 20 miles an hour—came up, the ship rolled some, and more than a few passengers skipped dinner. But then the sun returned, the winds died down, and it was time to relax once more. For the first-class passengers, there would be a dress ball. Along the lower decks, the Italian youngsters busied themselves with impromptu games of soccer. New York City was three days off.

CHAPTER 4

"A Picture of Scandinavian Efficiency"

A haze hung over the Manhattan skyline as the motorship *Stockholm* sounded her horn, then eased into the Hudson River from Pier 97 along West Fifty-seventh Street en route to Scandinavia.

It was 11:30 in the morning, Wednesday, July 25, the beginning of the 424th transatlantic crossing for the *Stockholm*'s captain, Harry Gunnar Nordenson, a veteran of more than three decades at sea. Some 450 miles to the east, the *Andrea Doria* was cruising toward New York. Making a top speed of 23 knots under sunny skies, the Italian liner was well into her voyage's last full day.

Nordenson's ship was the fourth Swedish liner to be called the *Stockholm,* a name that bore a troubled history.

The first *Stockholm,* a 547-footer built in Germany at the turn of the century, had an inglorious ending. She was sold to interests that converted her into a whaling factory vessel and renamed her the *Solglimt.*

In November 1914, the Swedish-American Line was founded to carry immigrants to America. Swedish shipping interests had missed out on the great emigration from Sweden to the farmlands of America's upper Midwest in the late nineteenth and early twentieth centuries, those immigrants having traveled largely on English ships.

The line began its North Atlantic operations on December 11, 1915, with the maiden voyage of the second *Stockholm,* formerly the Holland America Line's ship *Potsdam.* But by the end of World War I, the Swedish immigration to America had sharply declined, so this *Stockholm* had no useful mission. The Swedes turned to cruise ships, building the *Gripsholm* and *Kungsholm,* which were designed for great comfort with ample decorative touches.

During the late 1930s, the Swedish-American Line set out to build its largest ship ever, placing an order with the Monfalcone shipyards in Italy for a 28,000-ton liner with a capacity of 1,350 passengers that would be the third *Stockholm*. That ship was launched on May 30, 1938. But on December 20, when she was almost ready for her maiden voyage to New York, she was gutted at her dock in Trieste, Italy, by a windswept fire. It had evidently been touched off by an oxyacetylene torch carelessly left by a workman on a cork-covered deck. The liner was rebuilt at the Monfalcone yards and launched on March 10, 1940, but soon afterward the Mussolini government seized her for conversion to a troopship renamed the *Sabaudia*. An Allied air attack on Trieste in July 1944 destroyed her.

When the Swedes decided to build a fourth *Stockholm* at war's end, they scaled down their designs, fearing that the emergence of airline travel would make another huge ship uneconomical. This *Stockholm*, too, would be plagued by ill fortune, the laying of her keel at the Gotaverken yards in Sweden delayed for several months by shipworkers' strikes.

Finally launched on September 9, 1946, as the first North Atlantic liner of the postwar years, the fourth *Stockholm* was a vision in white except for a light yellow funnel that bore the blue shield adorned with the three golden crowns of the Swedish-American Line. Her most distinctive feature was a sharply angled bow reinforced with steel to penetrate the icy Scandinavian waters.

The favored image of the *Stockholm* was a cross between a sleek yacht and a warship, although a less flattering view was voiced by the British naval architect R. C. Barnaby, who wrote how she "looked more like an overgrown cargo liner with her 'goal post' foremast, cargo derricks and heaped-up superstructure."

"Her single, squat funnel seemed too small for the rising series of totally enclosed decks," observed Peter Padfield, a former British merchant officer and writer on maritime history. "But she had graceful lines, a fine clipper bow too, and with her all-white paintwork was a picture of Scandinavian efficiency and cleanliness."

The postwar *Stockholm* had no grand pretensions. Her cabins (50 in first class and 314 in second class) and her public areas were more functional than charming, and she lacked the large public spaces featured on the Swedish ships of the prewar years. She was the largest liner ever built in Sweden, but at 524 feet and 11,650 gross tons, she was the smallest liner operating on the North Atlantic run. Her two diesel engines could manage only a modest 19 knots.

But she had her points. The staterooms and crew cabins on her seven decks all had a view of the sea through at least one porthole, evidently a "first" for Atlantic liners. She offered saltwater baths and massages, a typical Scandinavian touch, and her swimming pool was indoors, a concession to her northerly routes.

On the *Stockholm*'s maiden voyage to New York in the winter of 1948, trouble came quickly—a heavy storm brought severe rolling that fatally injured one passenger. But when she arrived in New York on March 1, she was accorded the traditional whistle-tooting salutes from ships in the harbor and the spraying of minigeysers by fireboats.

The *Stockholm* basked in a moment of glory on February 20, 1950, when she responded to a distress call from the small Danish steamer *Kronprins Olav,* which had been swept by fire in the fog-shrouded Kattegat Strait between the North and Baltic Seas. Other ships were unable to find the steamer, but the *Stockholm* picked her up on a 12-inch radar viewing scope—a large-sized set for its day—and plucked 108 passengers from lifeboats. She even helped put out the fire.

But the *Stockholm* was gaining a reputation as one of the North Atlantic's worst "rollers." The Swedish-American Line placed 3,000 tons of stone in cargo holds designed for express goods, hoping that the additional weight would enhance stability. But it seemed that the design of the liner's bottom was ill-adapted for North Atlantic winters.

In November 1953, the *Stockholm* underwent a modicum of overhaul. She was brought to a shipyard in Bremen, Germany, where her superstructure was enlarged. Her passenger capacity was increased to 586 and her volume to 12,165 gross tons.

She resumed her regular runs in February 1954, setting out for New York. But just as in 1948, her maiden voyage brought misadventure. This time, while backing out of her berth in Halifax, Nova Scotia, she brushed a British freighter, the *Starcrest,* but came away undamaged.

The *Stockholm* underwent another face-lift early in 1955, when her first-class accommodations were cut to twenty-four berths on the Sun Deck and the second-class space was radically increased to meet the needs of budget-minded travelers. And early in 1956, she was fitted with stabilizers, finally correcting her tendency to roll.

The *Stockholm*'s Captain Nordenson, a portly, balding man, soft-spoken but considered a stickler for discipline, was, at age sixty-three, a consummate man of the sea.

Born in Quincy, Massachusetts, to Swedish immigrants from the Varmland region who returned there with him when he was five years old, he grew up in the Swedish town of Edane, then went to sea at age eighteen. He spent two years as a crewman on a three-masted Norwegian sailing vessel that cruised around the world, then worked on an English merchant ship. After studying at the Swedish Navigation College at Malmö, he received his master's license in 1918. He sailed for the Swedish shipping company Transatlantic, then joined the Swedish-American Line in 1920, serving on several ocean liners in the years between the world wars.

Nordenson gained notice beyond the world of the Swedish maritime service when he became the captain of the *Gripsholm,* known as the White Mercy Ship, during World War II. Sailing under charter to the United States on behalf of the Red Cross, flying the yellow and blue flag of neutral Sweden and so granted safe passage by the Germans, the *Gripsholm* transported thousands of refugees and brought home sick and wounded Allied prisoners of war.

Early in the morning of September 11, 1944, the *Gripsholm* was en route from Göteborg to Liverpool, England. She was repatriating a thousand ailing and wounded POWs. Escorted through Nazi-controlled waters by a German minesweeper, she was forcibly stopped and ordered into Kristiansand, in occupied Norway. German officials boarded her, making demands in violation of her safe-conduct guarantees, but Nordenson stood up to them, and the ship and its passengers were released. In March 1945 the U.S. Department of State issued a commendation to Nordenson for his conduct that day and for his overall role in commanding the *Gripsholm.*

Nordenson returned to the Swedish-American Line's passenger service following the war and in 1954 served briefly as captain of the *Stockholm.* Then he transferred to the liner *Kungsholm,* taking it on a round-the-world cruise, before returning to the *Stockholm* in 1955. As he took the liner out of New York Harbor on a humid Wednesday morning for its final run of July 1956, he was expecting to soon see his wife, Ruth, a nurse, and his two sons and daughter back home in Göteborg. With the *Stockholm*'s reputation for rolling now merely a footnote to an unhappy past, the captain was looking forward to a sunny and comfortable journey.

CHAPTER 5

"The Times Square of the Atlantic"

The *Andrea Doria* had proved to be everything Robert Young envisioned, and Young was not an easy man to please. He was director of West European operations for the American Bureau of Shipping, which set standards that ocean liners had to meet to obtain insurance.

Looking back on eight days at sea as he idled away the afternoon hours of Wednesday, July 25, Young felt far removed from his family's pretrip anxiety. The voyage on home leave with his wife, Virginia, and their children, Madge, fourteen, and David, eleven, had been thoroughly splendid despite their unease over cabin assignments. Considering the *Doria*'s reputation, it was no wonder the Youngs had had trouble getting the cabin locations they wanted even though they had begun planning their vacation early in the year. They had reluctantly agreed to take a pair of adjoining rooms on the Upper Deck starboard side, although these cabins were toward the forward end and so might be uncomfortable for Virginia Young, who sometimes suffered from seasickness. The Youngs had informed the Italian Line that if there were any cancellations, they would prefer something closer to amidships. A week before sailing, they were allowed to switch to a pair of Upper Deck portside cabins, almost in the middle of the ship. One of the cabins they were initially given was No. 56, the cabin forsaken a few days later by the budget-minded ballet star Istvan Rabovsky.

The Young family's new cabins were luxurious, like everything else on the *Doria,* and the evenings were splendid as well. The Youngs had attended a fancy dress ball, appearing as a desert sheikh and his favorite wife, and were startled to have won a prize, a lovely Italian tool-leathered jewelry box. During the afternoons, the family had spent pleasant hours lounging on the lido deck next to the swimming pool and enjoying the buffet lunches.

Robert and Virginia Young had been invited to the captain's farewell dinner on Tuesday evening. Normally the dinner would be held on the final night, but the *Doria* was due to arrive in New York at 9:00 A.M. Thursday. That meant the passengers had to have their bags packed by Wednesday afternoon, so stewards could take them to the starboard side of the Promenade Deck for transfer ashore as soon as the ship docked. Farewell evening or not, the farewell dinner had been exquisite, the *Doria*'s excellent food enhanced by vintage French and Italian wines.

As for the professional aspect of his trip, Young felt the evacuation drill had been organized efficiently. He had received permission to inspect the engine room and navigating bridge and found them well maintained.

But now Robert Young was becoming uneasy.

Wednesday morning had been sunny, the seas calm, but soon after lunch, fog began rolling in. Young was not surprised, since he knew the *Doria* was approaching the southern border of Nantucket Shoals, where fog was common during July and August.

The Weather Bureau called it "advection fog," formed when warm, humid air from the East Coast of the United States moved over the ocean, then came in contact with the cooler waters of the Labrador current. Over the previous fifty-two years—the span in which the Weather Bureau had been keeping records for the Nantucket area—an average of 45 percent of July days had been foggy. And conditions this day were ideal for fog. Water temperatures were in the mid-60s, but the moist air masses above were about 10 degrees warmer.

While his wife and children packed, Young remained on deck during the afternoon, watching the fog. He noticed that it was vertically stratified, meaning that the *Doria*'s course alternated between dense fog and clear air, a common phenomenon off Nantucket arising from small changes in water temperatures as a result of eddy effects and variations in the current. Young considered that kind of fog far more hazardous than continuous fog, since it left the captain uncertain over conditions.

The *Doria* had been sounding its foghorn, and at one point Young picked up the sound of another foghorn on the starboard side. It grew louder and louder. Then the *Doria* emerged from the fog and Young saw the other ship, a large freighter. It crossed the *Doria*'s stern. The passage was too close for Young's liking, but he took comfort in the certainty that the *Doria*'s officers were scanning their radar screens on the bridge.

Captain Calamai was indeed attending to the required precautions—at least most of them.

The captain arrived on the bridge about 3:00 P.M. and oversaw the routine for fog. Carlo Kirn, the first officer, switched on the Decca radar, one of the two screens. The fog whistle was activated and would sound for 6 seconds at 100-second intervals. A lever on the bridge activated a hydraulic control panel that closed the twelve watertight doors, creating eleven watertight compartments below A Deck. Twelve red lights shone in the wheelhouse, indicating the doors were shut.

The crow's nest lookout repositioned himself at the peak of the bow so he could spot an oncoming ship before the lookouts on the bridge might, and he had a phone connected to the bridge at the ready. Extra men were placed in the engine room in the event the *Doria*'s turbine engines had to be reversed quickly to avoid another ship. The steam pressure in the boilers was reduced, taking the *Doria*'s normal speed of 23 knots down to 21.8.

The International Regulations for Preventing Collisions at Sea, the rules of the road that all mariners were expected to follow, stated: "Every vessel . . . shall in fog . . . or any other conditions similarly restricting visibility, go at a moderate speed, having careful regard to the existing circumstances and conditions."

This was construed as maintaining a speed that allowed a ship to stop in half the distance of the visibility. If two ships approaching each other in fog each stopped in half the distance between them, in theory there would never be a fogbound collision.

But few ocean liners followed that yardstick, since time pressures were enormous. Ships timed their journeys so they could arrive at slack tide to minimize the chances of a mishap in docking amid strong currents and tides. And the economic consequences of a late arrival were considerable. Tugboats, refueling barges, longshoremen, merchants restocking ocean liners, and cleaning gangs would have to be paid for time spent waiting for a ship that was late.

While no steamship company would tell a captain to risk his ship and the lives of the passengers to arrive on time, the understanding was there—a captain perennially late would not keep his job for long.

It was Calamai's custom to slow down when encountering fog only if he were in crowded waters. He considered the area around Ambrose Light, the entrance to New York Harbor, such a spot. But the lanes near Nantucket Island were not, in Calamai's view, so crowded that a considerable slackening of speed was mandated in fog. If he hadn't had radar, he would have had to slow to about 12 to 14 knots. But with radar, only a token speed reduction while well out in the Atlantic would suffice.

Calamai left the bridge at 4:00 P.M. for paperwork in his cabin, returned for a while, and then, as evening approached, went to his cabin again to change from his summer whites to his evening blue uniform and beret. The second radar screen, this one a Raytheon, was switched on at 6:00 P.M. Calamai took a light meal on the bridge at 7:30.

A half hour later, when the *Doria*'s watch changed, the second officer senior, Curzio Franchini, took over the watch. The third officer junior, Eugenio Giannini, manned the Raytheon radarscope, set to a 20-mile range. Three yellow pips glowed, representing ships going in the same direction as the *Doria*, two of them some nine miles ahead and well off the line of the *Doria*'s course, the third perhaps six miles behind her.

Captain Calamai walked the bridge wing, occasionally glanced at the radar, and entered the chartroom to check the ship's position.

At about 9:30 P.M., Giannini noticed a new pip on his radar screen, estimating it as 17 miles away and practically dead ahead. Franchini entered the chartroom and fixed the ship's position by loran, a device that picks up pulses sent out by transmitters at fixed points on shore. By measuring the relative time of arrival of these pulses from four transmitters, a navigating officer could determine the location of his ship.

The loran reading, and a subsequent check via radio directional finder, confirmed that this pip was *Nantucket Lightship*, 43 miles south of Nantucket Island. The *Doria* was heading straight for her. When the *Doria* reached a point 14 miles away, Franchini took over the radar duties and Captain Calamai ordered a shift to the left, from 268 degrees to 262 degrees. By now the fog had grown thicker, the visibility essentially nil.

At 10:20 P.M. the *Doria* passed the unseen lightship, running about a mile to its south.

Nantucket Lightship was a red-and-white 130-foot boat with a crew of twelve. Guarding the treacherous Nantucket Shoals, it sent out electronic signals enabling ships to fix their positions and also provided fog reports, serving as one of the most important aids to navigation along the East Coast. On this night it had been sounding its foghorn— 12 seconds on, then 40 seconds off. Val Robbins, a Coast Guard electronics technician manning the lightship's loran equipment and radio beacon, would remember how each time the horn sounded, it was so piercing that shock waves killed birds flying by. Robbins and his fellow crewmen worked with their mouths open when the horn was sounding, seeking to equalize the pressure on their inner and outer ears.

Duty aboard the lightship, anchored in waters 190 feet deep, proved a daunting task. The history of Nantucket was replete with storms and high seas that had torn the lightships from their moorings, and of fog that threatened disaster.

In January 1934 the ocean liner *Washington,* the largest ship that had ever been built in the United States, emerged from a fog and side-swiped the lightship, carrying away her wireless rigging and part of her mast. Early on the morning of May 15, 1934, the White Star liner *Olympic,* moving through a dense fog as she honed in on the radio beam of *Nantucket Lightship,* rammed her, and sank the vessel, killing seven of the boat's eleven crewmen.

Back in January 1909, a fog-shrouded collision in the waters south of Nantucket Island had produced a landmark in the history of maritime communications.

The White Star liner *Republic,* sailing from New York with 461 passengers and 300 crewmen, was struck in the predawn hours by the Italian ship *Florida,* carrying some 800 people. The *Republic's* young wireless operator, Jack Binns, began pounding the key of his newfangled radio set. "CQD," he radioed. "We are cut to the waterline." This was the signal for "Seeking you, danger," the three dots, three dashes, and three dots of "SOS" yet to be standardized. The Marconi wireless operator on Nantucket relayed Binns's message to ships in the area, and 12 hours later the White Star ocean liner *Baltic* arrived and picked up the more than fifteen hundred survivors. The *Florida* continued on to New York, but the *Republic* sank. Five people died—three crewmen on the *Florida* and two passengers on the *Republic*—but the heroic actions of the *Republic's* radio operator, who stayed at his wireless set for many hours despite intense cold, had averted a huge death toll.

That was the first time wireless had been used in a major rescue operation. And in the summer of 1956, Jack Binns was a living reminder of the perils of the Nantucket waters. He was still active, serving as president of a New York electronics company.

Fogbound accidents off Nantucket were hardly confined to the dustbin of nautical history. On the night of October 2, 1954, the Holland America Line passenger ship *Maasdam,* bound for England from New York with 523 passengers, collided with the French freighter *Tofevo,* bound for New York from Montreal, just south of *Nantucket Lightship.* The *Maasdam's* captain said he had the freighter on radar when it shifted course without explanation. The collision left the *Maasdam* with a smashed bow and the *Tofevo* with a 60-foot-wide gash in its port side, but no one was injured. The *Maasdam*'s passengers presumably were grateful for escaping unscathed, but more than two hundred of them staged a sit-down strike in the liner's lounge upon its return to New York when they learned that the Holland America Line would provide only minimal reimbursement for their layover while they awaited alternate travel arrangements.

While the *Andrea Doria* was a little more than three days' sailing time from New York, a fogbound collision occurred in the main channel southeast of New York Harbor, 3 miles from Ambrose Light and 23 miles from the tip of Manhattan. The Panamanian tanker *San José II,* though equipped with radar, rammed the American freighter *Fairisle* on her port side at 1:10 in the morning. The Coast Guard picked up thirty-nine people from the listing freighter's lifeboats and escorted the ship into Gravesend Bay off Brooklyn, where she turned over two days later while attempts were made to right her. The freighter's captain had his license suspended by the Coast Guard for excessive speed.

Like the waters in the Ambrose Channel approaching the Lower Bay of New York Harbor, the Nantucket area was a bustling shipping zone, traversed by thousands of ships each year. It was known as "The Times Square of the Atlantic," notwithstanding Captain Calamai's feelings of security in guiding his liner through these foggy waters at nearly top speed. Ships sailing between the Port of New York and European and Canadian ports, as well as ships in and out of Philadelphia, Baltimore, and Norfolk, all passed through there. Some sixty oceangoing vessels, including perhaps six to eight passenger liners, were entering and leaving New York Harbor each day in the summer of 1956. Perhaps fifty of them took routes placing them in the Nantucket area.

But Calamai could hardly have been dwelling on disasters as the *Andrea Doria* passed *Nantucket Lightship,* 200 miles from New York. He was a veteran of more than a hundred crossings of the North Atlantic and numerous trips across the South Atlantic and was accustomed to fog. In contrast to the *Olympic,* the *Republic,* and the *Florida,* which had relied on a crow's-nest lookout, he had an array of electronic navigational equipment, most notably two radar sets. They were state-of-the-art and evidently working to perfection.

CHAPTER 6

"Each Shall Alter Her Course to Starboard"

At 8:30 Wednesday evening, the ocean liner *Stockholm* was running in clear weather, 150 miles out of New York Harbor, on the first leg of its route to Copenhagen and Göteborg. The *Andrea Doria* was 90 miles farther east.

On the Swedish ship, it was time for a change in the bridge watch. Captain Gunnar Nordenson had already retired to his cabin. The senior second officer, Lars Enestrom, turned the bridge over to the third officer, Johan-Ernst Bogislaus August Carstens-Johannsen.

Enestrom chatted with Carstens—as he was known to his colleagues—before relinquishing his duties, wanting to be sure that Carstens adapted himself to the darkness on the bridge before taking command.

Carstens was twenty-six years old, a husky, ruddy-complected 6-footer, his dark, curly hair tumbling to his forehead at a peak. He came not from a seafaring, but upper-class family. Born in Lund, a small manufacturing town in southwestern Sweden, he was the youngest child of a physician. His sister was a dentist and his brother was the legal counsel to the bishop of Linkoping.

Neither medicine nor the law had beckoned for Carstens. He had gone to sea at age sixteen, had later planned minesweeping operations for the Swedish Navy, and after training at Swedish nautical schools had served on five ships, three of them cargo boats, before coming to the *Stockholm*. He held master's papers, meaning he could serve as a captain on any type of ship. Carstens was earning $230 a month, less than half of what an officer on an American merchant ship would be paid, but ample enough to start a family. He had been married the previous December, and his Alsatian-born wife, Lileane Martel, was at the apartment they had just taken in Göteborg, awaiting the birth of their first child in October.

Carstens was making his fourth crossing as a third officer on the *Stockholm*, having been transferred two months earlier from the liner *Kungsholm* with the initial assignment of a second mate junior.

When he took control of the bridge, fortified for the night by a hearty dinner and steam bath, he was told to keep the *Stockholm* on its course of 90 degrees true—due east.

Most ocean liners had two officers on the bridge at any given time— one for lookout, the other for checking the radar and navigational instruments—but the *Stockholm* relied on just one officer, with three seamen assisting. One manned the crow's nest, another served as helms- man, and the third was on standby, ready to take a lookout's spot on the bridge when the officer had to leave it to be in the wheelhouse or the chartroom. The captain and chief officer did not stand regular watches, but they would be summoned in times of fog or when major course changes were needed.

At 9:00 P.M., having taken supper in his cabin, Nordenson came to the bridge for his final evening check. Some 40 minutes later, he ordered Carstens to alter course to 87 degrees, a shift of the helmsman's wheel slightly to the left. Taking into consideration the northerly current, that course would put the *Stockholm* 1 to 2 miles south of *Nantucket Light- ship* when it passed the boat.

The route charted by the captain placed the *Stockholm* directly in the path of westbound ships. The *Stockholm* was, in fact, traveling 20 miles to the north of the route recommended for European-bound lin- ers in an international agreement. The principle of separate lanes for ships heading in opposite directions dated all the way back to the 1850s, following the loss of some three hundred lives in the fogbound collision of the American steamer *Arctic* and a French ship off Newfoundland.

The modern accord on assigned lanes, called the North Atlantic Tracking Agreement, was endorsed by the U.S. Coast and Geodetic Sur- vey, but it was strictly a voluntary arrangement among certain transat- lantic shipping companies. The Swedish-American Line, and the Italian Line as well, did not follow the recommendation.

Nordenson felt he had good reason to ignore the recommended eastbound lane. Taking that more southerly route between Ambrose Light, the checkpoint outside New York Harbor, and *Nantucket Light- ship* meant additional mileage on Swedish liners' trips to northern ports. It also required that these liners cut across westbound lanes when swinging toward Canada and Scotland, something Nordenson consid- ered dangerous. Meeting ships head to head, or nearly so, was safer than meeting them in a crossing situation, he felt. In his thirty-six years with the Swedish-American Line and his more than four hundred Atlantic crossings, Nordenson had headed east on the track followed by westbound ships except during periods when ice was likely to be encountered.

Carstens's 3½-hour watch promised to be routine. When it began, the sea was smooth with an irregular swell, the air temperature about 70 degrees. The moon, full except for a sliver, shone above the ship's starboard side, only occasionally obscured by a passing cloud. The sky was overcast with a hazy horizon, the visibility 5 or 6 miles. A gentle breeze blew from the southwest.

Weather reports previously available to Carstens had shown fog east of *Nantucket Lightship,* but not to the west. The lightship had put out a Morse code message at 7:40 P.M. reporting visibility of only 25 yards, but Carstens knew nothing of this. He was familiar with the lightship's foghorn but unaware he could receive fog alerts from the boat.

When Carstens checked the radar screen during his first hour on watch, it showed not a single ship in sight. Carstens had studied radar operation in Sweden, but had received no instructions on use of the *Stockholm*'s RCA radar sets before coming aboard. He was confident nonetheless. He would tell of receiving these instructions after joining the ship, of having studied a manual issued by RCA and having been tested many times on use of the radar by other officers on the *Stockholm.*

At about 10:00 P.M., Nordenson returned to his cabin to work on papers and his personal diary. As usual, he left orders to be summoned if the *Stockholm* ran into fog or other difficult weather conditions. At any rate, he directed Carstens to call him when the *Stockholm* approached *Nantucket Lightship*—now some 40 miles away—so he could set a northerly course on the Great Circle route, heading first toward Sable Island off Nova Scotia.

Lacking loran, Carstens relied on his radio direction finder to fix his position at 10:04, honing in on beacons from Block Island and *Nantucket Lightship.* The expected northerly current had pulled the *Stockholm* 2.5 miles north of Nordenson's desired course, but Carstens decided to wait before making an adjustment.

Taking another fix at 10:30 P.M., Carstens found the *Stockholm* was 2.75 miles farther to the north than Nordenson had ordered. He told the helmsman, eighteen-year-old Sten Johansson, to turn his wheel 2 degrees to the right, bringing the course to 89 degrees, to compensate for the drift.

At 10:40, the three seamen under Carstens's supervision changed positions. Peder Larsen switched from his standby spot to take the helm from Johansson, who climbed to the crow's nest, relieving twenty-year-old Ingemar Bjorkman, who moved to standby. Larsen, a Dane who had been a seaman for eight years but had signed on with the *Stockholm* only 11 days earlier, admittedly had to be watched carefully since at times he was more interested in his surroundings than in making sure his steering conformed to the compass setting. Larsen was known to allow the ship to yaw—or move from side to side—excessively at times, perhaps by a couple of degrees.

Carstens paced the bridge, went to the wheelhouse to check on Larsen, then returned to the bridge. Still concerned over the northerly current, he decided to take a third radio direction fix to determine the effect of the 2-degree change he had made at 10:30.

He sent Bjorkman from his standby spot to a lookout position on the bridge and went to the chartroom. Taking a radio fix from the beacons of *Nantucket Lightship* ahead of him and *Pollock Rip Lightship* to the south, he determined that the *Stockholm,* still being pulled by the current, was 3 miles north of the course Nordenson had set.

Carstens returned to the wheelhouse and directed Larsen to steer an additional 2 degrees to the right—to 91 degrees—hopeful that another course change would ultimately compensate for the pull of the current to the north, or left.

Over the past 20 minutes or so, the moon had continued to shine brightly to the right of the *Stockholm,* the skies variably cloudy. The horizon was clear to starboard. Carstens could see it weakly when looking directly ahead, but it darkened to the left.

The radarscope had continued to show a sea clear of ships. But now, when Carstens checked it once more, a yellow pip appeared. Carstens would say it indicated a ship 12 miles away and just to the left of the flasher that displayed the *Stockholm*'s heading.

Carstens would list the time as 11:00 P.M.—"on the even hour," according to notes he made later—but he subsequently maintained that this notation reflected the time he made the entry, not the time when the pip had appeared. That was perhaps 10 minutes before 11, he would maintain.

The presence of a pip on a radar screen disclosed the location of another ship at a precise instant. Only by plotting—or making successive notations of another ship's distance and angle of approach—could a navigator determine, without guesswork, whether an approaching ship was changing its course and how fast it was going.

Carstens would later tell of plotting the course of this pip with a wax pencil on a device called a Bial Maneuvering Board, which was next to his radarscope. But he did not record the times when he made his two plots, despite having used a plotting instructional book stating that the times should be recorded.

Carstens, the seamen on the bridge, and crewmen in the engine room would testify to the following series of events:

When the pip showed the approaching ship was 10 miles off, Carstens asked Larsen, the helmsman, for the *Stockholm's* actual heading. Larsen reported it was 90 degrees. The pip was 1 degree to port of the 91-degree reading of the heading flasher, which reflected the course on which Carstens had put the *Stockholm*. That meant that the approaching ship was actually 2 degrees to port. Using a red grease pencil, Carstens placed an X on his plotting board showing the other ship's distance and bearing.

Carstens went out to the wings of the bridge to scan the horizon—the moon still shone—then plotted the pip again. He made another X on his Bial plotting board, giving the new distance as 6 miles off and noting that the pip was now 4 degrees to port.

Drawing a line between the two X's and a separate line denoting the actual course of the *Stockholm*, Carstens saw that the other ship was sailing at a widening angle, and he concluded that if neither that ship nor the *Stockholm* changed course, the other ship would pass to the *Stockholm's* left at a distance of between a half mile and a mile.

Nordenson had issued standing orders that no ship should be allowed to pass closer than a mile abeam of the *Stockholm*. Carstens determined that he would have to turn to the right to increase the passing distance between the ships, but he concluded he still had time to do this. He wanted to see the lights of the other ship with his own eyes before maneuvering further.

When the pip showed the oncoming ship to be 4 miles off, Carstens switched his radar from a 15-mile range to a 5-mile range. He still could not see the other ship, something that puzzled him, since a ship's lights were supposed to be visible at 5 miles, and the night was mostly clear. He thought momentarily that the other ship might be in a patch of fog, but was certain he would see it in due course. His plotting indicated that the vessel—perhaps a small navy ship—was moving at a high rate of speed. A ship in dense fog would not do that, he reasoned.

Carstens had never stood watch in charge of navigation during fog except with his captain present. But he never considered that he might be running into a fogbank, and so he saw no need to call the captain now. Nor did he feel it necessary to reduce the *Stockholm's* speed of 18.5 knots, which she had been making since leaving New York

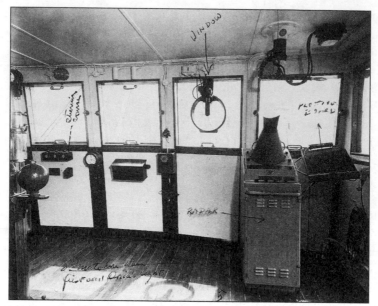

The *Stockholm*'s wheelhouse, which had been overseen by the third mate, Johan-Ernst Bogislaus August Carstens-Johannsen, in the hours before the collision. The radar set, toward right, is next to a board used to plot an oncoming ship's changing position. (Archives of Haight, Gardner, Holland & Knight)

more than 11 hours earlier—with 534 passengers and more than 200 crewmen.

When the *Andrea Doria* passed *Nantucket Lightship,* a mile to the south of the boat, at 10:20 P.M., Captain Calamai changed course from 262 degrees to 269, bringing the liner on a route almost precisely due west. He estimated he would be about one hour off his scheduled 6:00 A.M. arrival the next day at the entrance to New York Harbor.

Calamai remained on the bridge with two officers and two seamen, aided by a lookout on the bow. His foghorn sounded every 1 minute, 40 seconds. The watertight doors remained closed. And the *Doria* continued to make 21.8 knots, slightly more than 1 knot under its normal speed.

At 10:45 P.M., Curzio Franchini, the thirty-six-year-old second officer watching over the radar, picked up a pip on his screen. He placed it 17 miles off and 4 degrees to starboard.

As the minutes ticked by, Franchini watched the progress of the pip. The *Doria* had overtaken a couple of westbound ships not long before, but this vessel was headed not to America but toward the Italian liner. Calamai would later state he was surprised by the presence of an oncoming ship, that in his forty previous westbound crossings of the Atlantic in command of the *Doria* (he had missed some of its trips while on vacation), he had never spotted a Europe-bound vessel in the lane between *Nantucket Lightship* and Ambrose Light that was recommended for ships bound for the United States.

Calamai's pilot chart, issued by the U.S. Hydrographic Office, clearly showed the eastbound track as 20 miles to his south. Perhaps the radar had picked up a fishing trawler bound for Nantucket Island.

Calamai sensed no special danger, confident his radar would guide him through the fog. There could be no collision unless the other ship made a sudden movement toward him at the last moment. And so the only step he took beyond the normal fog precautions in place for the past 8 hours was to direct Franchini to intensify his radar observations.

Franchini concluded that the other ship's angle of approach was increasing to the *Doria*'s right, a clear sign that the two ships would pass in perfect safety. The *Andrea Doria* was equipped with a Marconi Locator Graph, enabling its officers to plot the progress of an oncoming ship appearing on the radarscope. But neither Calamai nor the officers on the bridge with him felt it necessary to plot.

Calamai had a decision to make. According to his radar, the other ship was approaching to his right. He could prepare for a starboard-to-starboard passage (the right side of the *Doria* running abreast of the right side of the other ship) by maintaining his heading or swinging to the left to create an even greater expanse between the two paths. Or he could swing decisively to starboard, creating a port-to-port passage.

The International Regulations for Preventing Collisions at Sea stated: "When two vessels are meeting . . . nearly head on, so as to involve a risk of collision, each shall alter her course to starboard, so that each may pass on the port side of the other. This Rule . . . does not apply to two vessels which must, if both keep on their respective courses, pass clear of each other."

The second portion of this regulation seemed to fit the situation this night, as Calamai saw it. He concluded that there was no doubt of a safe passage so long as each ship kept to its course. And so he chose the less orthodox method of passing—starboard to starboard—although he had sufficient deep water to swing toward the New England coastline and pass port to port.

Calamai walked the wings of his bridge, peering into the fogbound night, the *Andrea Doria* continuing at close to its normal speed, its foghorn bellowing. The visibility ranged from less than half a mile to three quarters of a mile as the *Doria* closed on the approaching ship, its identity still a mystery to Calamai, since neither vessel had a bridge-to-bridge radio.

For the 1,134 passengers of the *Andrea Doria,* this final evening was a time for winding down, for a farewell drink with friends recently made and perhaps a promise to meet again.

Since the *Doria* was to arrive in New York at 9:00 A.M. the next day, the partying was unlikely to outlast the stroke of midnight. But the final evening in the first-class dining room was an especially festive affair, the waiters in scarlet tuxedos with white trousers, the orchestra playing from a raised platform. The room was adorned with hanging balloons and colorful streamers, each table with a fresh floral bouquet and a complimentary bottle of champagne. Paper hats and noisemakers lent an air of New Year's Eve, the din sometimes requiring diners to shout their farewell toasts to each other. On the starboard side of the Promenade Deck, suitcases were arranged neatly in rows, to be brought down the gangplank as soon as the *Doria* arrived in New York.

Following dinner, some of the first-class passengers hoped for eleventh-hour luck. Camille Cianfarra of the *New York Times* was playing the horse-racing game—the horses represented by chesslike pieces—a spin of the wheel of fortune determining the winner. He had already won $95 at bingo and $45 in a contest challenging passengers to guess how many miles the *Doria* had covered on the previous day.

Cianfarra's stepdaughter, Linda Morgan, was hoping the family could dine with Captain Calamai, but he had to excuse himself, the fog requiring his presence on the bridge. Cianfarra had made a little joke about the fog, noting he would have to file a story for the *Times* if the ship were to be in a collision. His wife, Jane, concerned that Linda and her half sister, Joan, might be taking their father too seriously, reassured them. The captain was on watch, keeping an eye on that fog at all times, she told the girls.

At 10:30, the sisters prepared for bed in Cabin 52 on the Upper Deck, a flight above the dining room, Linda wearing yellow pajamas with a Chinese pattern, Joan in a white nightgown. Their parents stopped by to kiss them good night, but the girls were intent on carousing a bit with the extra pillows they had brought from Spain. Mr. and Mrs. Cianfarra returned to Cabin 54, immediately aft of the girls' room, and soon afterward, Linda and Joan switched off their lights and went to sleep, Linda placing her autograph book on her night table.

When the *Andrea Doria* had docked off Cannes, Thure Peterson, fifty-seven, a prominent chiropractor from Upper Montclair, New Jersey, and his wife, Martha, fifty-five, embarked on their first ocean voyage, concluding a long-anticipated European vacation. They had flown to Sweden to visit their parents' birthplaces, traveled through Denmark, and then Dr. Peterson, president of the Chiropractic Institute of New York, had lectured at a European chiropractors' meeting in Switzerland. The Petersons had planned to fly home, but Martha longed for an ocean trip, and she prevailed on her husband to change plans.

After enjoying a roast beef dinner and champagne to celebrate the final night, they returned to their cabin, No. 56, just aft of the Cianfarras. The Petersons dozed off just before eleven o'clock, Mr. Peterson sleeping, as was his custom, in the nude, Mrs. Peterson in a white pleated nightgown.

Cabin 58, aft of the Petersons' cabin, belonged to two priests, Rev. Richard Wojcik and Rev. John Dolciamore, who were returning from their studies in Rome to resume teaching duties at University of St. Mary of the Lake Mundelein Seminary outside Chicago. Father Wojcik, thirty-three years old, had spent three years at the Pontifical Institute of Sacred Music. His most valued possession was a hardbound book called *Liber Gradualis,* containing chants for Mass and Vespers. Over the past fifteen years he had made countless notations in the margins to enrich the singing. That book was now in his luggage, piled with all the other suitcases on the Promenade Deck.

The two priests were finishing dinner, expecting to turn in early, when they were greeted by Father Paul Lambert, a priest from Pennsylvania, known by now to Father Wojcik as "a Scrabble nut." The three priests had played Scrabble during the trip, and now Father Lambert urged them on for one more game. Instead of going back to their cabin, Father Wojcik and Father Dolciamore went with Father Lambert to the card room outside the Belvedere Lounge for a final test of Scrabble wits.

Donald and Jean Ruth, a couple from the Long Island village of Woodmere, were, like the two priests, ready for an early good night. They were about to go to their cabin, No. 48—two forward of the cabin occupied by Linda Morgan and Joan Cianfarra—when they, too, agreed reluctantly to one last social obligation. Another couple, Alfred and Beverly Green of New Rochelle in New York's Westchester suburbs, whom they had met aboard ship, insisted that the Ruths join them for a farewell drink in the Belvedere Lounge.

But the Greens were not as persuasive with their newfound friends the Carlins. Walter Jeffreys Carlin was an exceedingly active man at age seventy-five, chairman of the Lafayette National Bank of Brooklyn, a partner in a Wall Street law firm, and an influential figure in Brooklyn's

Democratic Party. But on this night, he was not feeling particularly energetic and neither was his sixty-four-year-old wife, Jeanette. They resisted the Greens' invitation for a drink in the lounge and headed instead to Cabin 46 for a good night's sleep.

The *San Francisco Chronicle* executive Ferdinand Thieriot; his wife, Frances; and their son Peter were intrigued by the horse-racing game that had fascinated Camille Cianfarra. They watched the spinning of the wheel of fortune, joined by the Passantes, the Denver couple with whom they shared the luxury suite 180. Soon after ten o'clock, Mr. and Mrs. Thieriot bid good night to the Passantes and headed for their bedroom in the suite while Peter went to his single cabin closer to the bow. The Passantes weren't ready to retire to their sitting-room sleeping quarters in No. 180. They went to the Belvedere Lounge for a drink.

There they would find Marion and Malcolm Boyer, who had taken luxury suite 178. Mr. Boyer, an executive with Standard Oil of New Jersey and formerly general manager of the Atomic Energy Commission, had hoped to get to bed early, but his wife was lingering for a last cup of coffee and a cigarette.

Down in the tourist class social hall, impromptu music making continued well into the evening, and the Sergio family was having a grand time.

Early that summer, Paul Sergio, a shoemaker from South Bend, Indiana, had returned with his wife, Margaret, to their native Calabria for a visit to Margaret's mother. They were coming back to America aboard the *Andrea Doria* on a particularly joyous note, orchestrating a family reunion. Paul's younger brother, Ross, a carpenter, and his teenage son, Anthony, had been living in Indiana with Paul, Margaret, and their six children during the past two years, saving money to bring Ross's wife, Maria, and their other four children—Giuseppe, thirteen; Anna Maria, ten; Domenica, seven; and Rocco, four—to America. Now Paul was accompanying Maria and the youngsters across the Atlantic. On the final night at sea, Paul and Margaret were throwing a party for the extended family.

Both branches of the Sergio family left the hall at about 10:30, and Paul dropped Maria and her children off at their cabin, No. 656, on the starboard side of C Deck. Rocco wanted to sleep in his uncle's room, but Paul told the boy he had best get to bed right away: they would see each other again early the next morning.

PART II

The Collision

CHAPTER 7

"Why Doesn't He Whistle?"

It was a few moments past eleven o'clock when the *Stockholm*'s watch finally spotted the ship it had been tracking on radar. Ingemar Bjorkman, the lookout on the bridge, hollered, "Lights to port!" Carstens would tell of spotting two white mast lights of an approaching ship and a weak red light shining on the portside tip of the ship's mast crowbar. The pip on the *Stockholm*'s radarscope showed the vessel at 1.8 to 1.9 miles distant.

Carstens would testify to the following sequence of events:

Grabbing binoculars, he went from his radarscope to his bridge's port wing for a better view of the white lights, whose position relative to each other would indicate the direction in which the oncoming ship was traveling. The forward white light was slightly to the left of the white aft light, indicating that the ship was heading a bit farther to the *Stockholm*'s port side. He estimated the angle at 20 degrees.

Concluding that the ship would pass to the *Stockholm*'s left at a spacing of about six tenths of a mile, Carstens acted to widen the margin of safety. Standing at the door of the port wing, he shouted to Larsen, the helmsman, directing him to steer to starboard 20 degrees. When the helmsman had done that, turning his wheel around several times, Carstens told him to steady it and return to center position. The two ships now would be at least a mile apart when they passed each other, Carstens figured, the minimum spacing directed by his captain.

Carstens had not been sounding a fog signal, having encountered only patches of fog. It did not occur to him that the red light shining on the other ship's port side was "weak" because that ship was emerging from fog, and that its captain would have had little chance to see the *Stockholm*. There could be other reasons for a barely discernible red light, Carstens would later say: red and green (starboard) lights on approaching ships were often dim. The light may have been weak because of dirt or salt covering it, or perhaps it was simply a weak bulb.

Nor did Carstens sound the whistle signaling a turn by the *Stockholm* when he ordered his helmsman to shift course by 20 degrees to starboard. His reasoning: if two ships are in sight of each other—as these two finally were—a signal would not be required on the high seas, but only in narrow waters, according to the nautical rules of the road, as he understood them.

Moments after Carstens saw the white lights for himself, the telephone on the wheelhouse's rear wall rang. Carstens answered it, turning his back from the oncoming ship. The caller was Sten Johansson, the seaman in the crow's nest. "Light 20 degrees to port," he announced, by now old news.

"All right," said Carstens.

Seconds later, Johansson was astonished to see the white lights change position. The forward light had crossed to the right of the rear light. This meant that the ship was turning toward the path of the *Stockholm* and would cross its bow. But the crow's-nest seaman did not phone the bridge to report the disastrous turn of events. His only job was to tell of an initial sighting, he concluded, and he had fulfilled that obligation.

Ingemar Bjorkman, on the starboard wing as lookout, also saw the lights switch, and he rushed to find Carstens.

Returning to the port wing of the bridge with his binoculars, Carstens saw the looming calamity for himself. A huge ship was heading across his bow, showing its starboard side, row upon row of portholes alight. No longer did this ship show a red port light. Now it was showing its green starboard light.

Carstens grabbed the twin levers of the engine-room telegraph and plunged them downward to Full Speed Astern, and he shouted to his helmsman, "Hard a-starboard!" Larsen turned his wheel as fast as he could.

The chief engineer, Gustaf Assargen, had left the engine room at about 8:45, read for a while in his cabin on the Sun Deck, next to Captain Nordenson's cabin, then had gone to sleep. When he heard the engine telegraph ring, he rushed to change out of his pajamas. But before he could dress, the *Stockholm* lurched, knocking him forward. He finished changing, then hurried down to the engine room.

The second engineer, Justra Svensson, making his first trip on the *Stockholm,* was standing on the maneuvering platform of the engine room when the telegraph bell sounded. Three motormen were with him, and the third engineer, Edwin Bjorkegren, was in an adjoining room.

Responding to the clang of the telegraph order directing Full Speed Astern, Svensson knew an emergency was at hand. Normally, a standby order would be given prior to a directive to reverse engines. Assisted by a motorman, Alexander Hallik, Svensson turned the starboard engine and then the port engine to the Stop position, an intermediate move before going into reverse. Then Svensson ran back to the starboard engine and turned its wheel to Full Speed Astern. He was about to reverse the port engine as well when he felt a jolt and was hurled 12 feet forward.

On the bridge of the *Andrea Doria,* the radar operator, Second Officer Curzio Franchini, had switched the range on his set from 20 miles to 8 miles when the ship approaching the Italian liner—its size and type still unknown—seemed about 7 miles away. With the scanner on a close-up setting, the image of the pip representing the approaching ship was suddenly enlarged. But it didn't seem particularly menacing. Franchini estimated that the two ships would pass starboard to starboard separated by about a mile of open sea.

But the radar reading by the *Andrea Doria* officer was wholly incompatible with the radar reading aboard the *Stockholm.* The *Doria's* conclusion that the *Stockholm* (the *Doria* didn't yet know its identity) was approaching to its right could not be reconciled with the *Stockholm's* belief that the *Doria* (its identity still unknown to the Swedish liner) was approaching to its left. One conclusion had to be wrong.

The *Doria's* helmsman, Carlo Domenchini, now asked Captain Calamai if he could go below for a cigarette. The captain granted permission, and the wheel was taken by Giulio Visciano, a forty-three-year-old seaman.

At 11:05—according to testimony Calamai would give—the *Andrea Doria's* radar showed the oncoming ship 14 degrees to starboard. The captain told the newly arrived helmsman to shift 4 degrees to the left, slightly increasing the passing distance. The *Stockholm* was evidently between 3½ and 5 miles away at this point.

Moments later, the *Doria* having changed course from 269 degrees to 265 degrees, Franchini reported that the other ship was 2 miles away with a bearing of 30 degrees to 40 degrees to the right, the separation having widened. The *Doria* continued to blow its foghorn. But Calamai and Giannini, the third officer, standing on the right wing of the bridge with him, heard no foghorn from the approaching ship.

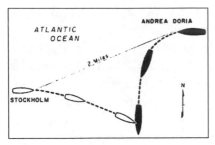 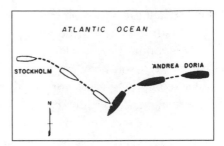

At left, the *Stockholm*'s version: The *Andrea Doria* approached to portside, then made a sweeping left turn into the Swedish liner's path. At right, the *Andrea Doria*'s version: The *Stockholm* approached to starboard, then made an abrupt right turn into the Italian liner's path. (*Marine Engineering/Log*)

"Why don't we hear him?" Giannini asked Calamai. "Why doesn't he whistle?"

Giannini went to the wheelhouse to look at the radar, saw that the approaching ship was less than 2 miles off and still at a considerable angle, picked up a pair of binoculars, and returned to the bridge. Then Giannini and Calamai each spotted a glow. The captain thought it was coming from a point perhaps 1.1 miles off, at an angle of 20 to 25 degrees. The passage, he concluded, would indeed be a safe one.

Franchini, hearing the officers talk of spotting the ship for the first time, started to leave his radar set in the wheelhouse to see for himself. Just then the phone rang. It was Salvatore Collace, the lookout on the bow. "I see lights on my right," he reported.

Taking another look with his binoculars less than a minute after he spotted the glow, Giannini saw that the relative positions of the other ship's white masthead lights indicated it was turning toward its left, away from the *Doria*. But then the unthinkable occurred: the masthead lights reversed themselves, and now Giannini could see a red glow—the light on the left side of the mast. The other ship was turning into the *Doria*'s path.

"She's bearing down on us!" he shouted. "She's coming right at us!"

Calamai had to make a decision in seconds.

"Hard a-port," he ordered.

Visciano turned the wheel as fast as he could, around and around, while Franchini ran to the automatic fog signal and yelled to Calamai to signal his sharp left.

Calamai pulled a hand whistle on the bridge, sounding two short blasts, alerting the other ship to the turn he was making.

"Captain, what about the engines?" Franchini asked. He was about to pull the engine telegraph handles, ordering that the ship be stopped. "No, let them be," Calamai responded. "We need all the speed we've got now." The captain knew the ship could turn faster if she did not slacken her speed.

Calamai hoped to outrace the other ship, moving to the left more quickly than it could turn right. But the *Doria* moved forward for perhaps half a mile before she began to respond to the helmsman's frantic maneuver.

"Is she turning?" Giannini hollered at the helmsman. "She is beginning to turn," Visciano responded, hearing the gyrocompass click as it recorded the change of heading.

But Piero Calamai lost his gamble. His sharp left turn at full speed was neither fast enough nor wide enough to avert calamity.

CHAPTER 8

"I Think We Hit an Iceberg"

Captain Calamai leaped back. The ship emerging from the fog seemed to head straight for him. But it struck the *Doria* below the bridge, the highest reaches of the collision coming four decks beneath it.

Curzio Franchini, the officer who had been watching the radar, ran to his cabin for a life jacket. Third Officer Eugenio Giannini did the same, and before returning moments later, he placed a crucifix beneath his shirt. It had been given to him by his mother when he first went to sea as a junior deckhand.

The *Stockholm*'s icebreaker bow sliced easily through the *Andrea Doria*'s starboard side, snapping girders and ripping bulkheads, the sound of metal crashing on metal echoing through the North Atlantic night, a shower of sparks dancing along the hulls of the interlocked liners. Tons of seawater flowed into the Italian ship through a huge hole in her right side, 40 feet across at the top of a penetration that mirrored the shape of the *Stockholm*'s bow.

Guido Badano, the second officer junior, had been in his bunk for a little more than half an hour, having been relieved on the bridge watch earlier in the evening by Giannini. Badano's quest for sleep had been punctuated by the intermittent sounding of the foghorn. Then an alarming sound echoed in his cabin—the two-whistle blast that signaled Calamai's sudden swing to the left. At 11:10, Badano felt a violent blow followed by the clanging of fractured metal. Then he heard Giannini shouting for his fellow officers to come to the bridge. Badano threw on his clothes, grabbed a flashlight and his life jacket, and raced to his captain's side.

Seconds before the collision, Captain Gunnar Nordenson, busy in his cabin with paperwork, had heard the engine telegraph bells—the message from the bridge to the engine room directing a reversal of engines. Nordenson grabbed his cap and ran up the stairs to the bridge. Before he reached the top, he felt the impact. But the sensation was "rather weak," he would say, and he had no idea the *Stockholm* had collided with another ship, much less suffered severe damage.

On the port wing of the *Stockholm*'s bridge, Third Mate Carstens-Johannsen barely even felt a jolt when his ship knifed into the *Andrea Doria*. Running from a stand behind the engine telegraph, which was still at the Full Speed Astern position he had just set, Carstens entered the wheelhouse and pushed an alarm button signaling crewmen to close the watertight doors.

Carstens was en route to the captain's cabin when the two men met each other at the door between the chartroom and the wheelhouse.

"What happened?" Nordenson asked.

"We collided with another ship."

Nordenson ordered Carstens to shut the watertight doors, but was told they were already closed. When Carstens recounted the events preceding the collision, Nordenson asked why he hadn't been summoned. Carstens told the captain he had no reason to do so because visibility had been good.

In his cabin below the bridge, Second Officer Lars Enestrom experienced the collision more intensely. He had gone to sleep a few moments earlier—having been reading Walter Lord's *A Night to Remember,* the recently published best-seller about the *Titanic*'s sinking—when he was awakened to a sensation that someone had lifted up his cabin. It seemed, however, to be part of a dream. His body was thrown forward, his feet hitting the edge of his berth. Drinking glasses, books, and magazines fell off the shelf above his bed, the drawers of his dresser flew out, and his desk-pad, lamp, and fruit bowl went flying. He heard the fire-alarm siren wail.

When he leaned out of one of the two large portholes he had kept open to bring in the night air, Enestrom saw a crewman wearing a life jacket at a lifeboat station. He thought the sailor looked "pale as a corpse." Next to the crewman were several elegantly dressed passengers who had evidently been on deck or in the lounges when the ship was rocked. They seemed puzzled, unable to comprehend what had happened. Craning his neck forward, Enestrom saw smoke billowing from the prow and the contours of a brilliantly lit ship that was disappearing into fog. His hands shook and he became dizzy. After sitting on his sofa to get hold of himself, he changed into his white uniform and set out for the *Stockholm*'s bridge.

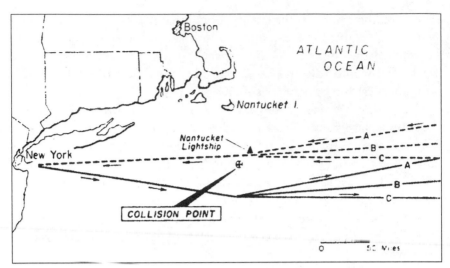

The collision occurred about 45 miles south of Nantucket Island and 19 miles west of *Nantucket Lightship*, astride the path recommended for ships heading to the United States. The *Stockholm*'s captain chose not to take the path 20 miles to the south recommended for ships heading to Europe. (*Marine Engineering/Log*)

There he encountered Carstens-Johannsen, and he would never forget the moment. "Enestrom, I think I'm going crazy," Carstens blurted out, his face muscles quivering, his entire body shaking. "Why would she turn to port?" he asked as he wandered around the bridge.

Enestrom decided he must shake Carstens out of the shock that had seemingly immobilized him. At any rate, Carstens's account of how the other ship had crossed his bow with an unfathomable left turn made little sense, since none of the other officers had been on the bridge during the seconds preceding the crash. "This is not the time to talk about that," Enestrom said sharply. "Now it's important for all of us to be efficient."

Enestrom glanced at the plotting disk next to the radar. It was blank. "Haven't you plotted the ship?" he asked Carstens.

Carstens would maintain that he had erased his wax-pencil markings from the plastic plotting board prior to the collision.

The *Stockholm*'s sharply angled bow struck first at the topmost point of the collision, along the *Andrea Doria*'s Upper Deck, where most of the first-class cabins were located. Cabins 52 and 54—where Linda Morgan; her half sister, Joan; her mother, Jane; and her stepfather, Camille Cianfarra, slept—bore the full force. But the top of the *Stockholm*'s bow spared neither the cabins to the left nor to the right of the

Cianfarra family. It smashed walls, sent furniture flying, and collapsed ceilings in at least eight cabins on this deck, penetrating perhaps 30 feet into the *Doria,* one third of its width. The fire-resistant lining that separated the *Doria*'s hull from her interior paneling began to smolder, filling corridors with smoke.

One flight below, on the Foyer Deck, the *Stockholm*'s bow demolished luxury suite 180, where Ferdinand and Frances Thieriot were sleeping. It also destroyed luxury suite 178, but it was empty despite the late hour; its occupants, Marion and Malcolm Boyer, had lingered for Mrs. Boyer's last cigarette in the Belvedere Lounge. After wrecking the *Doria*'s most spacious cabins, the *Stockholm*'s bow stopped just short of the chapel.

Perhaps twenty cabins were smashed on A Deck, holding the cabin-class passengers, and another five were destroyed on B Deck, where many of the tourist-class passengers were lodged. The cavernous garage on B Deck was ripped open, the Norseman "car of the future" never to be driven a single mile. Since the *Stockholm*'s bow was tapered at the bottom, the width of penetration lessened on C Deck, the lowest passenger deck. But its tourist-class cabins, filled mostly with Italian immigrants, were the smallest ones on the ship, the most closely crowded together. Possibly fifteen were in the path of destruction.

Below the passenger cabins, the *Stockholm* penetrated the *Doria* in the worst possible area and most vulnerable point: a starboard compartment containing half the deep fuel tanks, between bulkheads 153 and 173. The tanks—five on the starboard side and five on the port side—were mostly empty, since the *Doria* was just 10 hours from New York. Its fuel needs were now being met by the outermost of those starboard tanks. As seawater poured into the starboard tanks while the five portside tanks remained untouched, the water's weight instantly started to topple the magnificent liner.

Within a minute or two, the *Doria* was listing 18 degrees to starboard. The ship was designed so it was not supposed to list more than 7 degrees in the first moments of a collision, not more than 15 degrees in the worst possible case. She would have to list 20 degrees before water flooding any one of her eleven watertight compartments would overflow the top of a watertight bulkhead at the A Deck level, leading to progressive flooding of the other compartments and the *Doria*'s eventual sinking.

The engine rooms, consisting of three large chambers in the center of the ship, suffered catastrophic damage. The collision opened a large hole in the first room forward, the generator room, containing five diesel generators for the ship's main electrical system. Aft of it was a room with six boilers supplying hot water for passengers and crew, and steam for the turbine motors. Closest to the stern was the main engine room, containing the twin turbine engines and most of the controls for the pumps. The collision ruptured the starboard turbine motor, which began spurting oil.

The cargo hold, forward of the deep fuel tanks, was flooded as well.

With the deep fuel tanks, the generator room, and the cargo hold flooded, three compartments had been breached—one beyond the maximum tolerable limit.

At first the *Doria* and the *Stockholm* had clung to one another for perhaps fifteen seconds and drifted. Now the damage worsened as the *Stockholm* slid along the *Doria's* side, its jagged bow tearing the hull and ripping open the starboard wing tanks along the engine room.

Moments earlier in the Belvedere Lounge, the glittering late-night spot just below the bridge, Dino Massa and his orchestra were playing "Arrivederci Roma." Couples were dancing, enjoying drinks, or simply watching the sea. Sebastiano Scandurra, one of the waiters, was serving a scotch and water to passengers who were singing softly to the beat of the band.

Eugene Gladstone, a realtor, and his wife, Freda, on their way home to Toronto from a convention in Vienna, were seated with their regular dinner companions, Dr. Sol Ritter and his wife, Pearl, of New York City. The men were sipping scotch and sodas, the women enjoying tea.

Freda was in need of a soothing drink, having been on edge since the day after boarding at Gibraltar, when the Gladstones had been given a tour of the ship by a young engineer who boasted, "You could shoot this baby full of holes and she would still stay afloat." Freda had flushed. "Anything wrong?" her husband had asked. "I don't like his boldness in challenging the sea," she said. As the *Doria* made her way serenely toward New York, Freda had grown increasingly nervous. She had trouble sleeping, blaming the vibration of the air conditioning. She had even complained of the sun's glare bouncing off the waters.

The Gladstones had ordered prints of photographs taken at a cocktail party given by Captain Calamai, and as Gene glanced at his watch, noting it was past eleven o'clock, he remembered he had to go to the photo shop and pick them up.

He was walking to the door of the lounge when he was thrown off balance by a terrific jarring. He turned around, to go back to his wife, when another, more violent crash, shook the room. It sent him flying.

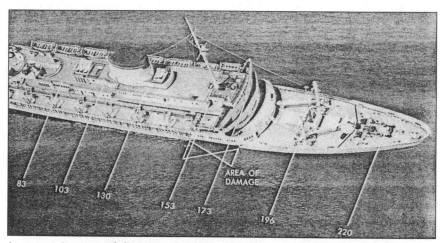

An approximation of the spot where the *Stockholm*'s bow penetrated the *Andrea Doria*'s starboard side. Numbered bulkheads—the barriers between watertight compartments—are superimposed onto a photo of the listing Italian liner. (*Marine Engineering/Log*)

He picked himself up, ran the remaining eight steps to get to Freda, then was slammed into a paneled wall.

Dancers were thrown off their feet, careening 20 to 30 feet along the floor. The bandsmen crashed against tables, propelling the people sitting at them against a wall. At one side of the lounge, people piled in a heap. The serving counter tipped over and the liquor cabinets crashed against it. Bottles and glasses broke open.

"I think we hit an iceberg," Gene Gladstone told his wife as he scrambled to his feet.

"No, we collided with another ship," she said. "Look! You can see its lights through the window."

Gene turned and saw the lights, but he couldn't believe it. "It must be another ship, Gene," his friend Sol Ritter insisted. "Look, it's going the other way. We are passing it."

Jerry Reinert, a twenty-one-year-old Brooklynite, returning home from a European tour—a gift from his widowed mother upon his graduation from Rensselaer Polytechnic Institute in Troy, New York—was chatting at a table with Isa Santana, a Manhattan woman, and acquaintances who owned an antiques shop in New Orleans. Reinert felt the boat rock, then saw the bartender, facing away from him as he reached for a bottle, slam backward against the bar and collapse.

Ruth Roman was having a drink in the lounge with her traveling companion, Janet Stewart, when she heard what seemed "like a very

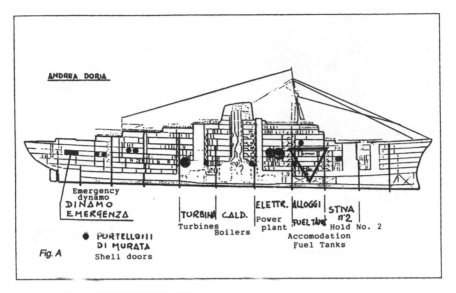

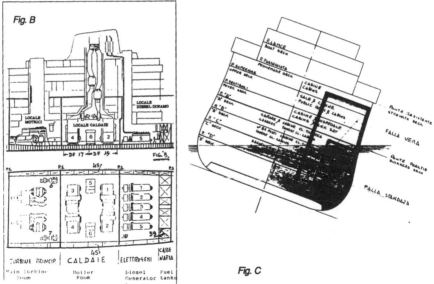

Figure A triangle approximates the shape of the *Stockholm*'s bow at the area where it penetrated the *Andrea Doria*. The bow pierced the starboard deep fuel tanks, labeled as accommodation fuel tanks. Bulkheads surrounding that compartment gave way, resulting in flooding of cargo hold No. 2 and the power plant, or generator room. Figure B shows the deep fuel tanks (the outer starboard tank, No. 39, was in use at the time of the collision) and, aft, the three chambers of the engine room—the generator room, the boiler room, and the main turbine room—all of which flooded. Figure C represents the decks penetrated by the *Stockholm*, the highest being the Upper Deck, containing first-class cabins. (Courtesy of *Andrea Doria* Working Group, Genoa, 1988)

big firecracker." Now she was betrayed by the one extravagance she acknowledged. She professed to disliking nightclubs and flashy clothes, but had a fondness for shoes. Her thirty-five pairs were mostly Indian moccasins, but on this night she was wearing high heels and a tight-fitting dress as she danced away the final hours. Those heels hardly seemed a match for the instantly listing stairs. So she threw them off as she ran to find her three-year-old son, Dickie, who was with his nurse in their cabin two flights below.

In the card room next to the lounge, the Scrabble game among Father Wojcik, Father Dolciamore, and Father Lambert was suddenly over. It seemed to Father Wojcik as if someone had sneaked up and kicked the back of his chair. The priests would put their calling to good use in the hours to come, but for now they decided to wait where they were until receiving instructions.

In the cabin-class ballroom on the Promenade Deck, one level below the Belvedere Observation Lounge, another band was playing.

Mike Stoller, the young songwriter, and his wife, Meryl, had planned to get to bed early so they could awaken in time to take movie pictures when the *Doria* passed the Statue of Liberty, hoping to capture the scene as their grandparents might have witnessed it upon arriving at Ellis Island.

But Meryl and several other young women had promised to dance with some shy Italian immigrant boys, so it would not, in fact, be an early good night for the Stollers. Mike had accompanied Meryl to the ballroom grudgingly, and while Meryl and her friends were chatting with the Italians, he grew bored. He sipped a glass of champagne, then decided to peek in the card room to see if he might join a poker game.

Just then, the ballroom shook. Mike did a little jig to keep the champagne from spilling, but Meryl's glass flew from her hands and shattered. Meryl thought she heard someone shout "iceberg," the fear in many minds with *A Night to Remember* having revived memories of the *Titanic*.

Mike had no idea what had happened. When he looked out the elliptically shaped windows of the Promenade Deck—he could see out, since the ballroom, too, was enclosed by glass—it seemed as if a huge letter opener were ripping the side of the *Doria*.

Joan Dier, a secretary from Buffalo, New York, had planned to return home later that summer on the Holland America Line, but switched to the *Doria* to attend a friend's wedding in Syracuse. She had been dancing in the cabin-class ballroom, wearing a smart orange evening dress, and her date was escorting her back to her table. She went flying, landing, fortunately, in a leather chair.

In the tourist-class lounge on the curiously named Upper Deck, which was, in fact, one level farther down, crewmen and passengers sang and danced in an impromptu show.

Kathy Kerbow, the twenty-year-old college student who had marveled at the *Doria*'s grace when it came into sight at Gibraltar, had obtained one of the last available cabins. She had a berth on the bottom deck, sharing her room with a Sicilian woman and her teenage children, none of whom spoke English. They were so fearful being at sea for the first time, they insisted the lights be kept on at night. Kathy spent most of her time with other young people, and now she was dancing with a German boy who was en route to Mexico, where his father worked in a Volkswagen plant. She heard the sound of shrieking metal. Seconds later, her dancing partner had disappeared. "Where in the world are you?" she said to herself. Then she saw a bartender slam a metal accordion door shut, safeguarding his liquor.

In the tourist-class dining room on the Foyer Deck, one level lower, a couple of hundred passengers were watching the Technicolor movie *Foxfire*, starring Jeff Chandler as a part-Apache mining engineer who wins the marriage hand of an eastern heiress played by Jane Russell.

Beatrice Bucci, a twenty-seven-year-old nurse at a hospital in Beverly, Massachusetts, returning from a visit to her brother at the Navy base in Naples, was sitting with her date. Ashtrays flew, the room filled with smoke, people screamed and ran, and she thought, "This is it," the ship is sinking, and she surely would die. Her date tried to pry her from her seat, but she was frozen in panic, holding on to the edge of her table. The man raced off without her. Deciding she would simply have to regain her senses, she began helping fellow passengers make an orderly ascent to a lounge one flight up.

Philip Ansuini, a fourteen-year-old emigrating from Perugia with his father, Domenico; his mother, Giulia; his brother, Pasquale, ten; and sister, Melania, eighteen, was puzzled rather than panicked. At the instant in *Foxfire* when a mine caved in, he heard a rumble, a vibration of sorts. Could there be a connection? How could it be possible that the cave-in was creating that sensation? Then tables and chairs began to roll.

Pat Mastrincola, a high-spirited nine-year-old from New Jersey, returning in tourist class from a visit to Italy with his mother and his eight-year-old sister, Arlene, had been having a fine time all through the trip trying to explore the *Doria*. But each time he had attempted to hop a railing and get to the bridge, or the engine room, or the lounges in first or second class, a crewman had arrived to shoo him back. He kept trying but became convinced he was running into ambushes. Somehow, all the crewmen knew when he was coming.

On this night, Pat was his rambunctious self, scampering around behind the *Foxfire* screen, the romantic Western holding nothing of interest for him. Then the projector and the screen toppled over. Pat was pinned against a wall momentarily by a runaway table, but crawled to where his mother had been seated.

"My baby, my baby," she cried out.

"I'm all right, Mom," Pat assured her.

"Not you," his mother said. "Your sister. She just went down to the cabin."

Pat raced down to B Deck to find her.

CHAPTER 9

"Don't Worry, There's Nothing Wrong"

For all the music, dancing, and tinkling of glasses, the *Andrea Doria*'s ballrooms and lounges were hardly packed with revelers during the final hour of the final full day at sea. With the *Doria* scheduled to pass the Statue of Liberty sometime after 8:00 A.M. Thursday, early wakeups were in order, and so most passengers had returned to their cabins, were preparing for bed, or already had gone to sleep.

The actress Betsy Drake had called it a night, planning to enjoy a book. She had spent time during the trip with Camille and Jane Cianfarra—Mrs. Cianfarra had interviewed her in Spain for a magazine article while Cary Grant was making *The Pride and the Passion*—but was not particularly enamored of shipboard social life and had passed up the last night's entertainment in the Belvedere Observation Lounge.

Anguished though she had been by Grant's romancing of Sophia Loren on the movie set, Drake had experienced anxiety over his well-being. "I had a terrible premonition that something was going to happen when I boarded the *Andrea Doria,* but I thought it was going to be something that happened to Cary," she recalled long afterward. "When that first lurch of the ship came, I thought, 'Thank God, it's happened to me.' I think if anything had happened to Cary, I might have killed myself."

Drake's cabin on the Boat Deck shook. Unhurt, she put her fashionable Ben Zimmerman suit back on, donned a life jacket, and headed for her muster station. What she did not have were the jewels given her by Grant—reportedly valued at almost $250,000—and her semiautobiographical novel. They were locked in a ship's safe for removal the next morning.

After enjoying their roast beef dinner, Thure and Martha Peterson returned to Cabin 56 on the Upper Deck at 10:30 P.M.

When the couple had boarded the *Doria,* Mrs. Peterson, five feet, three inches, had found that she couldn't see out their cabin's porthole. So her husband, more than six feet tall and weighing more than two hundred pounds, took the outer bed. Mrs. Peterson settled for the bed against the elevator shaft.

Getting into bed in her white pleated nightgown, she started to read a book she had bought in Denmark, but by eleven o'clock she had dozed off. Thure Peterson had nothing to read. He, too, was soon asleep. Moments later, he experienced a vague notion of something dark piercing the wall of his cabin, and he sensed a thud, then the noise of plates ripping all around him. He was barely awake now, but felt he was moving through the air, and then he blacked out.

The three priests who had been playing Scrabble in the card room off the Belvedere Lounge returned to their cabins to get their life preservers.

When Father Richard Wojcik and Father John Dolciamore reached the corridor outside their cabin, No. 58, they came upon an eerie scene. All was silent, not a person in sight. Father Wojcik opened the cabin door, flicked on the light, and was startled to see his bed, beneath the porthole, sliced in two and covered by debris. The priests grabbed their life jackets and then Father Wojcik turned off the light and locked the door. He hoped to come back and salvage what he could.

In their brief return to the cabins, the priests had failed to notice a figure lying in the wreckage of Father Wojcik's bed. It was Thure Peterson, who had been hurled from the adjoining cabin.

Peterson regained consciousness soon after the priests left and found himself in absolute darkness.

"Marty, Marty, are you all right?" he called to his wife.

He heard a faint response: "My legs. They're caught."

"Don't move," Peterson said. "Help will be coming."

And then he heard Martha say: "There seems to be someone here with me."

Finding his hands free, Peterson pushed away pieces of furniture, torn mattresses, and plasterboard. He was bleeding from the head, his feet were bloodied from slivers of broken glass, his chest and stomach muscles ached, but the burly chiropractor got to his feet. He did not see his wife, and there was something odd about the cabin—the layout seemed to be reversed. Stumbling toward the spot where he thought he heard his wife's voice, he found only a wall. He groped for the door, but noticed that the clothes closet was not where it was supposed to be. Then he realized he was no longer in his cabin. He entered the corridor, finding it dimly lit—emergency power had kicked in—then looked at the cabin door that closed behind him. It was No. 58.

The door to his own cabin, No. 56, was locked, but the bottom panel was torn, and he managed to crawl through it. When he got inside, his hand touched a face. It was cold, the life having evidently passed from it. And then, to his right, behind a mound of debris, he heard two voices—his wife's and that of another woman.

Peterson returned to Cabin 58, hoping he could find a route from it to free the women, who were trapped in a trianglelike space. The wall of the elevator shaft that separated the hallways leading to Cabins 56 and 58 formed one side. A pile of wreckage that defined the gaping hole left by the collision formed the second. What was left of the partition between the two cabins formed the third. And the cabin was tilting. At any moment, Peterson thought, the women might slide into the ocean.

Peterson was able to pull up the bottom part of the partially demolished partition between the two cabins—it rose 18 inches from the floor—and crawled through it. He found his wife lying on her back, arched around the corner of the elevator shaft, her legs immobilized by wreckage. Beside her was the body of a man, the person whose face Peterson had brushed moments earlier. It was Camille Cianfarra, the *New York Times* correspondent, who had been hurled into Cabin 56 from his bed in Cabin 54 at the same time Thure Peterson had been thrown from Cabin 56 to Cabin 58. Cianfarra's wife, Jane, had been catapulted into Cabin 56 with him and was trapped above Mrs. Peterson, her body in a crouch, her legs twisted.

Mrs. Cianfarra could not see her husband's body and had no idea what had become of her daughters. Linda Morgan and Joan Cianfarra had been swept from their beds in Cabin 52, but Peterson had not ventured into that cabin and so could supply no news on the girls, hopeful or otherwise.

Promising to get help, Peterson crawled through the partition back to Cabin 58. He was about to reenter the corridor when he realized he was naked, having gone to sleep in the nude. He tore a piece of beige and maroon curtain from the cabin's closet, wrapped it around his middle, and climbed to the Promenade Deck one level above.

Walter Carlin, the seventy-five-year-old Brooklyn banker and lawyer, and his sixty-four-year-old wife, Jeanette, were preparing for bed in Cabin 46, having declined the invitation from Alfred and Beverly Green for a drink in the Belvedere Lounge. Walter Carlin was brushing his teeth in the washroom near the end of a long corridor leading from the sleeping quarters, while Jeanette was reading. The collision knocked him off his feet. When he got back up, then made his way into the sleeping area, he saw a large hole. He did not see his wife.

Donald and Jean Ruth of Long Island would have been in their cabin aft of the Carlins had they not accepted the Greens' invitation for a drink. When Donald Ruth came down from the Belvedere Lounge to grab life jackets for himself and his wife, he found the cabin in shambles.

The Philadelphia mayor, Richardson Dilworth, and his wife, Ann, had gone to sleep at about ten o'clock in Cabin 80, nearer the stern. They awoke to a jolt, and then Dilworth heard a scraping sound. The ship shuddered "like a wounded animal," he would say.

"I think there's been an explosion," the mayor told his wife. "No," she said. "That was just like the way they described what happened to the *Titanic*."

The hole opened by the *Stockholm*'s bow extended only to a point some 60 feet forward of the Dilworths' cabin, so they were merely shaken. Having planned to be up at 6:00 A.M. for a good breakfast, since the mayor wanted to be back at his desk by afternoon, they had hung their clothes at the head of the bed, planning to dress quickly. That they did—seven hours ahead of schedule.

When they opened their cabin door, they encountered dense smoke. They rushed through it and made their way to a higher deck.

Ruth Roman, tossing away her high heels, raced down from the Belvedere Observation Lounge toward the cabin where her son was sleeping with his nanny. A sailor grabbed her, thinking she had panicked and lost all control. She tore loose from him, then ripped her sheath dress up the back so she could move more freely on the listing stairs. She found Dickie and the nanny, Grace Els, then grabbed life preservers and took them to an open deck.

Roman had once played a scene in the movie *Three Secrets* in which she was cast as a mother waiting for a son stranded on a mountaintop. This time she had rescued her boy—at least for the moment.

Nora Kovach had gone to the purser's office at eleven o'clock to pick up photographs of the dinner at the captain's table that she and her husband, Istvan Rabovsky, had attended the night before. She returned to their cabin on the port side of the Upper Deck, the ballet dancers having given up the more expensive cabin that later went to Thure and Martha Peterson.

They were about to go to sleep when they heard a loud noise. They tried to open their door but found it stuck. Istvan kicked it ajar, only to find the hallway filled with smoke. He grabbed Nora's hand, and they ran up a staircase. Moments later, Istvan realized they had left their passports behind. In the Communist world they had fled three years earlier, failing to produce identity papers when the police asked for them meant serious trouble. Istvan told Nora he was going back for the passports, but she begged him not to risk it. "Everyone will understand your papers were lost on a sinking ship," she pleaded. But back he went, battling to stay on his feet. He held his arms against the walls of the listing stairs and then pressed his hands against the sides of the narrow corridor on their deck. He found the passports on a table and rushed back to rejoin Nora.

Angela Grillo, a twenty-nine-year-old Brooklyn woman, and her three-year-old son, Anthony, were returning from a visit to the boy's paternal grandparents in Catania, Sicily, followed by stops at Rome, the Vatican, Sorrento, and Naples. They had planned an August return aboard the *Cristoforo Colombo,* but after four months abroad, Mrs. Grillo was eager to be back with her husband, Carmelo, who worked for the Italian Line, helping oversee arrivals in New York.

Although passengers had been told to place their luggage on the starboard side of the Promenade Deck Wednesday afternoon, Mrs. Grillo's husband had advised her to keep her bags in her cabin. He would use his position with the line to speed the luggage through.

Mrs. Grillo and her son had been asleep in Cabin 147 on the port side of the Upper Deck. Now she regretted the decision to keep her luggage. The bags, together with furniture sent rolling by the jolt, had blocked the cabin door. She struggled for 20 minutes, finally got the door open, and then made it with the boy to the Boat Deck, two levels higher. There she was relieved to see her dining room companions, Rigoletto and Anna DiMeo, an elderly couple from Pescara, Italy. The DiMeos assured Mrs. Grillo they would help her look after Anthony.

On the Foyer Deck, where the specialty shops blended with the deluxe suites and a few single first-class cabins, thirteen-year-old Peter Thieriot stirred from sleep, vaguely aware that something was amiss. But he heard nothing. He looked out the porthole of his cabin and noticed that the level of the sea seemed to have risen. But that didn't make much sense, and he went back to bed. Had he peered into the corridor, his night's sleep would have ended. The collision had shattered the ceiling and smashed the plate-glass window of the gift shop.

After dozing for a while, Peter found himself falling out of bed. He turned on his light and was puzzled to see his cabin tilting, the ceiling split. He finally looked into the hallway and came upon a bizarre sight—a mannequin had fallen through the window of the dress shop and lay stretched out beside him.

Still failing to grasp what had happened, Peter dressed and set out to find his parents in Cabin 180, some 50 feet toward the stern. He picked his way through the rubble, but a bulge in the corridor's starboard wall blocked his path.

Thomas Kelly and Raymond Goedert, young priests returning to Chicago from their studies in Rome, were preparing for bed in cabin class on A Deck. Father Kelly had just gotten into his pajamas when he experienced a thud, almost as if the ship had hit a pier, and he noticed how the engines were no longer vibrating, as if a heart had stopped beating.

Father Kelly slipped his clerical suit over his pajamas, forgetting his collar, and put on his shoes but neglected to don his socks. He placed his passport in the inner pocket of his jacket but left behind a chalice, a cherished gift from his family. Father Goedert fled the cabin in trousers and a T-shirt.

In the corridor, all was commotion—people running back and forth in their nightclothes, unsure which way to turn. The priests dashed up a flight of stairs, then encountered a steward who told them, "Don't worry, there's nothing wrong."

In Cabin 236 on A Deck, Alba Wells, a twenty-nine-year-old Italian war bride who had settled with her husband and three children in a Birmingham, Alabama, suburb, was returning from a trip to Europe with the youngsters. Her three-year-old daughter, Rose Marie, had been sleeping. Her other daughter, Shirley, eight, and her son, Henry, nine, were watching *Foxfire*. Mrs. Wells had experienced terror long before. In 1945 she suffered a broken right arm and a nerve injury that temporarily blinded her in an Allied bombing of her home in Livorno and had been hospitalized for four months.

Now it was her younger daughter who was most immediately in peril. The collision had pinned Rose Marie's left hand between her upper bunk, torn from its mooring, and the cabin wall. Mrs. Wells ran into the corridor, shouting for help, then rushed back inside and pulled on the iron bed but could not free the child.

Her dining room steward, concerned when he had not spotted the family in these first moments, arrived to see whether anyone might have been trapped. He joined Mrs. Wells in tugging at the bed, then left to find a crowbar, but not before telling the mother that if all else failed, her daughter's hand might have to be amputated.

By then, Shirley had returned to the cabin, but Henry was still missing.

The door to Cabin 230 became jammed, trapping three women—Margaret Carola and two sisters, Christina Covina and Amelia Iazzetta. The fourth bed had been booked by Margaret Carola's mother, Rosa, but she was suffering from cancer and had been assigned a bed in the ship's hospital.

Mrs. Iazzetta's seventy-two-year-old husband, Benvenuto, rushed to the cabin and pounded on the door as smoke filled the corridor. A steward pleaded with him to join other passengers fleeing the deck, but he insisted he could not leave until he got the women out. The steward tried to force the door open, to no avail. When water began to flow through the corridor and the smoke became thicker, he persuaded Iazzetta to flee with him, promising that help would soon arrive.

In the adjacent cabin forward, four women traveling singly were also trapped. The cabin beyond that was occupied by two Italian nuns, Sister Theresa Del Gaudio, of Salerno, and Sister Marie Grechi, of Cremona, who had been among the founders of the Xaverian Missionary Sisters of Mary, established in Italy 10 years earlier. They were coming to America to study nursing techniques at St. Vincent's Hospital in Worcester, Massachusetts. The nuns had gone to bed early at the suggestion of the *Doria*'s chaplain, Monsignor Sebastian Natta, so they could attend 5:30 A.M. Mass. Now their cabin had been destroyed, and no one could get inside.

In a nearby cabin, Sister Angelita Myerscough, thirty-five, a one-time farm girl from Ruma, Illinois, who had joined the Adorers of the Blood of Christ at age sixteen, also had gone to bed early, aided by a sleeping pill. Returning from two years of Italian language study, she was eager to arise early enough to attend Mass, have breakfast, and see the Statue of Liberty.

When the ships collided, it seemed to Sister Angelita as if a huge crate had hit the outside wall of her cabin. But she was groggy from the sleeping pill and started to fall back asleep. Her cabinmate, a young

Italian woman she knew only as Giovanna, shook her awake, made sure she donned her life jacket, and insisted on remaining in the cabin until Sister Angelita left it, fearing the sleeping pill would prove more potent than the adrenaline of the moment.

Sister Angelita indeed fled the cabin, and she had the presence of mind to don her habit's red sash, the symbol of her order. "If I die, I want that on," she said to herself.

David Hollyer and his wife, Louise, in Cabin 374 on the starboard side of A Deck, were returning to their permanent home in Worcester, Massachusetts, after an extended stay in Europe, most recently in Munich, Germany, where David had worked as an engineer for Radio Free Europe.

David threw on a pair of pants over his pajamas, while Louise grabbed her husband's suit jacket and carried it with her as they scrambled to their muster station, the cabin-class ballroom on the Promenade Deck. The ballroom's windows were broken, and hand instruments littered a floor strewn with glass shards. A piano was rolling, one of its legs having fallen off.

Louise, wearing only a shorty nightdress and still carrying her husband's jacket, was approached by a woman in an evening gown who had been dancing when the collision occurred and was perhaps slightly drunk and in shock, having no comprehension of a looming disaster.

"This is disgusting," the woman said, reproaching Louise. "What a way to dress."

But David and Louise were each sporting something this woman lacked—a life vest. "Lady, don't look now, but you don't have a life jacket," David responded. "It's going to be a long swim if you don't find one pretty quick."

There wouldn't be much more bickering at that rendezvous point. None of the ship's officers showed up, so the passengers who had assembled, waiting for instructions, soon wandered off.

Mike Stoller headed down from the cabin-class ballroom in search of life jackets for himself, his wife, Meryl, and a woman who had asked that he find hers as well. He was only able to get to his own cabin and grab two life jackets, which he would give to the women. On his way back, the songwriter passed a woman sitting on the floor, saying the rosary, and a man carrying twin infants. As he started up the stairs, a panicked family tried to take the life jackets away. "They're not for me," he explained, going into a stance like a football player about to spring out of the line and plowing through.

Charles Annino, his wife, Lillian, an Italian war bride, and their children, George, ten, and Sandra, four, were returning to his native Illinois, the Anninos having spent nine years in Italy, where Charles worked for the U.S. Embassy and the U.S. Information Service. Finished with their comic books, the children were in two lower bunks, the parents in two uppers, when they heard what Charles would describe as a "big bang." Then it seemed as if someone were dragging chains at the bottom of the boat.

George fell out of bed and said with a sob, "Daddy, save me, I'm afraid," but Sandra remained asleep. Then Mrs. Annino began to scream, awakening her daughter, who started to cry. The Anninos grabbed life jackets and fled their cabin.

Elisabeth Hanson, thirty-eight, and six months pregnant, was asleep with her children, Andy, twelve, Don, ten, and Ardith, seven, in Cabin 280 on the starboard side of A Deck, a few rooms back from where the *Stockholm*'s bow hit, when they were awakened by what felt like a rowboat bumping against a dock.

Mrs. Hanson, her husband, Alfred, and the children had spent the previous year in Torino, Italy, where Alfred, a nuclear physicist at the University of Illinois, had been studying on a Fulbright fellowship. After putting his family aboard the *Andrea Doria* at Genoa, he had returned to Torino to finish up some business, then flew to New York to pick up the family car, stored on Long Island. He planned to meet his wife and children at the dock, then drive them back to Urbana.

When the ships collided, Andy, seeing the flash of lights, slammed the porthole cover of their cabin. His mother, having no idea what had happened but alarmed by the tilting of the cabin floor, yanked life jackets out of four metal lockers and threw the jackets on the floor. They slid toward the cabin's outer wall, and so did she.

A steward in the hallway shouted, "Ladies and gentlemen, come out of your cabins and go up on deck!" Mrs. Hanson placed life jackets over her children's nightclothes and they climbed three flights.

The *Andrea Doria*'s chief physician, Dr. Bruno Tortori-Donati, and his assistant, Dr. Lorenzo Giannini, were in the purser's office off the first-class foyer when they felt the jolt and saw thick white smoke. Suspecting an engine-room explosion, the doctors headed for the hospital on A Deck, where they marshaled five nurses to await casualties.

Dr. Tortori-Donati's first task was a visit with two American women in his care. Mary Onder, sixty-five, had fractured her thighbone while traveling to Italy aboard the *Cristoforo Colombo* the previous April.

The injury had not been set properly at a hospital in Genoa, and now she was returning home. The other patient, Rosa Carola, seventy-one, had been carried aboard the *Doria* on a stretcher at Naples, suffering from cancer of the larynx, a heart condition, and fluid in the lungs.

Dr. Tortori-Donati assured the women he wouldn't abandon them and then checked the men's ward, where a cabin boy named Gaetano Balzano was being treated for an abscessed tooth and a fever. But he was nowhere to be found, evidently having traded his hospital bed for a safer spot higher on the ship.

The doctor climbed toward the bridge for a report from Captain Calamai, only to be interrupted repeatedly by passengers demanding news of what had befallen the *Doria*. He never reached the bridge. Hearing an announcement directing passengers to go to their muster stations, the doctor headed back down to the hospital. He now knew the *Doria* was in danger of sinking.

Two male nurses lifted Mrs. Onder's bed, assisted by the woman's husband, who had arrived to check on her. Dr. Tortori-Donati and the chief women's nurse, Antonia Coretti, carried Mrs. Carola from the ward. Although sedated, she cried out for her daughter, Margaret Carola, who at that moment was trapped with two other women in their A Deck cabin.

Mrs. Onder and Mrs. Carola were carried up the tilted stairs at an excruciatingly slow pace. The ordeal sent Mrs. Carola into cardiac failure, but she rallied when Dr. Tortori-Donati administered injections to relieve a fluid buildup. The women finally arrived on the Promenade Deck, three flights up from the hospital, and were left in the care of nurses to await a lifeboat. The trek had taken a full hour.

In tourist class, the lowest levels, the water was rising, cabins were crushed, and fuel oil flowed.

An hour or so before the collision, Leonardo Paladino, the tailor from Bari, had enjoyed a beer with a friend, then sat down to watch *Foxfire*. His wife, Giovanna, and their three young daughters had gone to bed. But Leonardo grew uneasy, worrying that one of his children might be tossed out of bed by the boat's normal rocking, so he returned to the family's cabin in the middle of the movie. He was taking off his shirt and pants, loosening his belt, preparing to change into pajamas, when the boat shook. The Paladinos placed life jackets on the three children and fled with them to a higher deck.

Rose Adragna of Pittsburgh struggled up the listing stairs with her two-year-old daughter, Olivia, after escaping her cabin so quickly that she had neglected to take the girl's bottle. The baby kept crying for her milk, but the mother knew she could not go down again. Giuseppe Riniacco, an Italian immigrant, grabbed diapers and a bottle for his daughter, Maria, and held her in one arm, the diapers in his other arm, as they went up the stairs.

Nine-year-old Pat Mastrincola, having been sent by his mother from the *Foxfire* showing to fetch his eight-year-old sister, Arlene, from the family's cabin, found that his explorations of the ship during the past week had paid off. At first the boy was disoriented by smoke, but then he noticed a Red Cross imprinted on a glass first-aid cabinet. He realized this was the spot where he should turn, that he would find his cabin at the end of the corridor. And so he did, sister Arlene safe inside.

Antonio Ponzi, fourteen, coming to America with his twenty-year-old sister, Marcella, shared Cabin 664 on C Deck with an Italian man in his twenties named Antonio Lombardi.

"Do you want me to shut the light off?" the teenager asked. "Yeah," said his roommate. Seconds later they heard a bang, then saw water rushing under their cabin door.

The two Antonios tried to get out, but the door wouldn't budge. Then a portion of the ceiling collapsed. Ponzi was just 5 feet tall and "thin as a toothpick," as he described himself. The older Antonio supplied the brawn to free them, wielding the fallen ceiling plank as a battering ram to punch the door open. The Antonios escaped through a rapidly flooding hallway, passengers screaming all around them.

The De Girolamo family from Ischia occupied a pair of cabins on B Deck; the father, Francesco, and his four sons, ages three to seventeen, in Cabin 450, and the mother, Anna, and her teenage daughter in Cabin 478. Francesco and his oldest son, Antonio, were still awake, the other three boys having gone to sleep.

"Holy virgin, we've hit the rocks," the father cried out.

"Dad, what rocks?" Antonio said. "We're in the middle of the ocean."

Antonio ran to get his mother and sister, who joined the rest of the family, and they all went up the stairs, leaving life jackets behind in their haste.

Frank Russo, at age sixteen, had left his parents behind in his village of Caraffa, in Italy's Calabria region, but he wasn't quite alone aboard the *Doria,* and he had a promise of a job in America.

Frank was an American citizen, his parents having been born in New Jersey, then taken to Italy by their families when they were babies. He was accompanied on the *Doria* by family friends, Giuseppe Guzzi, sixty-five, and his wife, Antoinette, fifty-six, who were returning to Easton, Pennsylvania, where they owned an open-air market. The Guzzis were bringing Frank with them as a favor to his parents following a seven-month visit to their native Italy. They had loaned the Russos money for Frank's passage in tourist class and said he could work at their market.

The Guzzis could have afforded a first-class cabin, but to give Frank a sense of security, they took a cabin on C Deck, a few rooms from the teenager, who had been assigned a young Italian man as his roommate.

Suffering from seasickness, Frank had gone to bed after dinner Wednesday evening, and his roommate also turned in early.

Sometime after eight o'clock, Giuseppe Guzzi came to Frank's cabin and woke him.

"Come upstairs, there's a party," he said.

"I don't feel so good," Frank told him.

Mr. Guzzi relented. "Tomorrow, in Easton, we'll celebrate," he said.

When the crash came, Frank was thrown from his upper bunk and hit his head on a sink. As he scrambled out the door with his roommate, they were met by a wave of water, and by the time Frank reached a stairway, the torrent had risen above his waist. Presuming the Guzzis had gone to their party in an upper-level dining room, he headed up the stairs without first searching for them.

Paul and Margaret Sergio, returning to Indiana, had a cabin on the port side of C Deck. Margaret's sister, Maria, and her four children were on the starboard side. When the ships collided, Paul and Margaret fled into the hallway in their pajamas. They fought past panicked passengers streaming toward a stairway, trying to reach Maria and her children, but a steward blocked their way.

Paul and Margaret were told there was no one left on the starboard side of the ship. "Everyone has gone up," the steward said. They went up the stairs, too, leaving behind their life jackets and a letter that Margaret had written to her parents back in Italy. It told of a wonderful trip.

CHAPTER 10

"Need Immediate Assistance"

After the *Stockholm* broke away from the *Andrea Doria,* the Italian liner hoisted two red lights to the mast behind the wheelhouse and sounded a two-blast signal, indicating to any ships in the vicinity that she was drifting out of control. Captain Calamai yanked on the telegraph to the engine room and ordered the ship stopped.

Curzio Franchini and Guido Badano, the second officers, took a loran fix in the chartroom to determine the *Doria*'s exact position while Calamai wrote out a distress message for radio operator Carlo Bussi. They passed the coordinates to Cadet John Conte, who rushed them to the radio room. It was now about 11:20, some 10 minutes after the crash. Operating on 500 kilocycles—the frequency assigned for a distress message—Bussi tapped out three dots, three dashes, then three dots, for SOS, using the *Doria*'s call sign ICEH. And he turned on the automatic radio alarm, which transmitted 12 dashes, each 4 seconds in length and separated from each other by a one-second interval, for a total of 60 seconds. The alarm triggered bells in the cabins of radio operators on ships not maintaining a 24-hour watch for the 500-kilocycle distress messages, alerting the operators to go to their transmitters and await a distress call.

The *Doria*'s message read:

SOS de ICEH
SOS here at 0320 GMT
LAT. 40.30N 69.53W
NEED IMMEDIATE ASSISTANCE

The men in the engine rooms worked frantically to restore the liner's balance. They began pumping out seawater that had entered the pierced starboard fuel tanks, but water continued to flow in. Soon the pumps and valves that might have been used to relieve the flooding were underwater and could not be reached.

The generator room—providing electrical power—as well as the boiler room and main engine room began to flood. Seawater continued to enter them through the holes punched by the *Stockholm*'s bow, and water and oil drained down from the high decks, seeping through their ceiling gratings.

At least the smoke in the passenger corridors died down. The sparks spawned by the friction of the collision presumably had started small fires, but these were confined to the spaces between the *Doria*'s skin and the cabin walls.

Captain Calamai ordered tarpaulins uncovered from the eight metal lifeboats hanging along the port side and the eight on the starboard side of the Boat Deck.

When the winch brakes were released, the davits were supposed to attain the launching position, and the sixteen boats were to slide down to the Promenade Deck, one level below, where the passengers would board them. But this plan went awry.

These lifeboats could be launched properly as long as the ship was not listing more than 15 degrees. But the list to starboard had reached 18 degrees almost immediately and was worsening. As a result, the davit arms holding the lifeboats on the port side—the ship's high side, away from the point of impact—were facing skyward instead of toward the water, immobilizing these eight boats. Staff Captain Osvaldo Magagnini, First Officer Carlo Kirn, and a host of seamen pushed the boats, straining mightily, driving their shoulders forward, but the boats would not budge. Soon they gave up.

Only the eight lifeboats on the starboard side could be launched, but these could hold just 1,008 people. The *Doria* was carrying 1,706. It had departed Genoa with more than enough lifeboat capacity, but now its plight was like that of the *Titanic,* which had left Southampton with lifeboats for only half its passengers.

While most of the *Doria*'s passengers were gathering on the high side of the upper decks, evidently the safest point for the moment, crewmen worked to bring the starboard boats down to the Promenade Deck.

The mounds of luggage piled on the starboard side of that deck during the afternoon were obstacles to taking passengers off. But there was a far greater problem.

The first two starboard boats—No. 1, with a capacity of fifty-eight, and No. 3, which could hold seventy (the right-side boats bore odd numbers)—were jammed in their davits and could not immediately be lowered. The other six boats—Nos. 5 to 15—did slide down to the Promenade Deck. But when the crewmen succeeded in that maneuver, they saw that the ship's list had left these boats hanging too far from the rail for the passengers to reach them. The sailors tried to haul the boats back with ropes, but they wouldn't move. These lifeboats would have to be lowered to the water before the passengers could board them.

Boats Nos. 1 and 3 were eventually pushed free of their jammed davits. The No. 3 boat was, in fact, secured to the Promenade Deck, but it would be the only one of the eight starboard boats to be boarded from that level.

Captain Calamai directed Guido Badano, the second officer junior, to make an announcement over the loudspeaker, first in Italian and then in English, telling passengers to go to their muster stations. Calamai decided not to sound the alarm for abandoning ship—six or seven short blasts followed by a long one. He feared that would cause a panic, particularly if the passengers learned that half the lifeboats were useless.

The captain still had a slight hope of saving the *Doria*. If she could limp to shallow water 20 to 30 miles away, she could be beached and later towed by a tug. But when Calamai embarked on this plan, he found that the *Doria*'s starboard engine wasn't operating. The port engine did start up but soon began to rumble, and the *Doria* wobbled. Calamai gave up, unwilling to endanger the safety of his passengers any further. The arrival of rescue ships was now their only chance to be saved.

On the *Stockholm*'s bridge, Captain Nordenson and his senior officers watched from the port wing as an ocean liner drifted away. None of them yet knew the identity of this ship that had emerged from the fog, but Nordenson thought the stern resembled that of the *Kungsholm*, which he once commanded. That liner had become the *Italia,* owned by the Home Lines. As the *Doria* receded from view, its lights grew hazy. It was retreating into the fog from which it had appeared.

The *Stockholm*'s chief officer, Herbert Kallback; the second officer, Lars Enestrom; and the second officer junior, Sven-Erik Abenius, could see that the *Stockholm* was leaning slightly, but noticeably. (The ship was down 3½ degrees at the bow and was listing 4 degrees to starboard.) "Are we taking in water?" Enestrom wondered. "Are we starting to sink?"

Nordenson went to the radar screen, remaining calm amid the turmoil. Enestrom asked the captain if he had any orders for him. Nordenson did not respond, continuing instead to peer at the echo on the radar screen—the retreating *Doria*—watching it move slowly to starboard. Enestrom went to one of the bridge wings, hoping to see the other ship, but he could not spot her.

Nordenson finally took his eyes off the radar. He had ordered the engine room to begin pumping operations, and now he directed Enestrom to find out whether the collision bulkhead—the first line of defense behind the bow—was intact. The captain needed to know whether seawater had rushed into the cargo room behind that bulkhead.

Carstens took a radio bearing to fix the *Stockholm*'s position but doubted it was accurate since he received a small shock when he touched his equipment, presumably indicating a malfunction.

The *Stockholm* had been ripped for 75 feet from her raked prow back along her deck line. The damage extended for about 55 feet along the waterline and approximately 40 feet underwater along her keel. More than 300 tons of steel had been ripped away, the once-graceful bow now a mass of wreckage.

On his way to the prow at the captain's orders, Enestrom noted it was still foggy, but he saw that the moon had started to shine through the gloom, shimmering on the sea. Calm swells slowly pushed the *Stockholm* up and down. He saw passengers in small groups, some walking around aimlessly, others smoking cigarettes. Crewmen were beginning to gather at the lifeboat stations, seeking to calm what few passengers were about and adjusting their life jackets.

Joined by Abenius, Enestrom came upon a scene of utter destruction at the bow. A large portion of the long forebody had disappeared, and what remained of the deck resembled the bellows of an accordion. In the light coming from the poles of the mast, iron plates looked like crinkled pieces of paper. The remnants of cabin furnishings lay in a heap. At the top of the jumble was a broken capstan with all of its drive gears and motors exposed. The ship's bell was waving like a flagpole next to it.

Enestrom and Abenius heard a voice shouting, "Help me, help me, I can't see!" They rushed to the port side of the No. 1 hatch, where they found a young crewman named Karl Elis Osterberg, his face covered with blood, trying to pull himself free from a fellow sailor seeking to help him. "Where's the doctor?" Enestrom asked. "They'll soon be here with a stretcher," said the sailor, trying to comfort the injured man.

"Thank God, you want to help," Osterberg murmured, tears running down his cheeks.

Enestrom now rushed down the hallway that led to the interior prow. When he opened the doors, a thick wall of smoke bellowed toward

The *Stockholm* emerged from the collision with its bow a mass of wreckage. (U.S. Coast Guard)

him, and he could hardly see. Holding a handkerchief in front of his nose, he ran down the stairs. When he reached A Deck—the lowest deck on which crew cabins were located—he heard voices issuing orders. Moving as far forward as he could, he saw the deck steward and night watchman pulling out beds, chairs, and blankets. The crewmen were working furiously, in an effort to cut away cabin doors, knowing the heavy capstan lying loose above them could come crashing down at any moment.

At least twelve cabins, each with two berths, had been crushed. But there was no way of telling how many crewmen had been inside when the ships collided. Water was rushing into the hallway, fire hoses already stretched along its length. A repairman worked with a blowtorch, trying to remove metal plates blocking cabin doors. Chief Officer Kallback held a light as he dug out rubbish from the fourth cabin back on the starboard side.

"I see an arm over there!" someone shouted, and Kallback stiffened.

"This will be the second body I have to pull out," the *Stockholm*'s second-ranking officer told Enestrom. And then Kallback cursed in frustration. From the light of Kallback's lamp, Enestrom could see a hand sticking out from overturned beds and crushed metal.

Soon Enestrom was in water up to his knees, and he realized that he needed to open a large provisioning door on A Deck—situated above the water level—to let the water run out. After getting authority from the captain, Enestrom and Abenius loosened all the nuts on the door, which opened inward. The water pressure made the door difficult to open, but with the help of other crewmen, the door gave way. The water rushed out, the starboard tilt began to lessen, and the ship assumed a more upright stance. Then the crewmen carefully shut the door.

Enestrom went to the bridge to give Nordenson a report on conditions. The captain asked him if he thought the bulkhead between the first and the second compartments would hold. "Absolutely," Enestrom said.

The *Stockholm* was built to a safety standard less demanding than that of the *Doria,* since the Swedish ship's keel had been laid prior to the 1948 Conference on Safety of Life at Sea, which mandated that a ship be able to stay afloat even if two watertight compartments were flooded. The *Stockholm,* which had nine watertight compartments (to eleven on the *Doria*), could not be assured of remaining buoyant if more than one watertight compartment were pierced.

Stewards were ordered to knock on the doors of all the cabins and tell the passengers to don life jackets and report to the public areas. The mandatory evacuation drill had not yet been held; it had been scheduled for the next day, the first full one at sea.

The passenger cabins were undamaged, the lights still on, the slight list hardly noticeable. Many passengers slept through the collision. But seawater that had rushed into the crumpled bow area and fresh water from ruptured pipes flowed into some of the passenger corridors, at points 2 feet high.

Ernest Wallman, a sixty-six-year-old locomotive engineer from Minnesota, and his wife, Esther, heading for a vacation in Sweden, had just stretched out on their bed. So far, life on an ocean liner had been everything the trainman had envisioned. "I never had it so good," he told his wife. Just then they were thrown to the floor. Mrs. Wallman told her husband they must flee quickly, the ship was sinking. But he was hardly alarmed, announcing they would not leave their cabin until he found his false teeth.

In the first-class dining room, the headwaiter, Caspard Larsen, was aghast. The buffet table had lurched, sending the smorgasbord tumbling to the floor.

Carol Johnson, in her upper-deck cabin with her five-week-old daughter, Karin, felt only a rocking sensation when the ships collided seconds after she heard the strains of "Arrivederci Roma."

"We've just hit a ship," she blurted out to Karin, who was highly unlikely to respond but represented the only outlet for her astonishment.

"What's going to happen if we have to jump into the water?" Carol wondered. She did not know where the life jackets were stored, and even if she found them, how could she cradle Karin while abandoning ship?

An agitated steward knocked on her cabin door, told of the collision she had, in fact, just witnessed, and ordered her to don a life jacket.

In crew cabin 4M, Carol's husband, Bill, was practicing the Swedish he had spoken in his Brooklyn home as the child of immigrants, while his cabinmate, Alf Johansson, a tall, muscular thirty-year-old seaman from Göteborg, was trying to improve upon his fairly decent English. Johansson planned to be married upon the *Stockholm*'s return to Sweden, and he was, Bill Johnson thought, a young man "full of life." The two had known each other for just a couple of hours, but already Bill thought he would be invited to the wedding.

Bill Johnson was excited at the prospect of seeing his parents' homeland. But Johansson was explaining to his newfound American friend and coworker how all was not perfect in Sweden. And the Swede was puzzled as to why Johnson, a minister, was continuing his studies in religion when there were so many other things he might do with his life.

All this made for lively conversation as they chatted, albeit a bit haltingly, each in the other's language, the American seated in the small cabin, the Swede lying in an upper bunk.

One moment, Bill Johnson was explaining why he studied religion. In the next moment, he blacked out. When he regained consciousness, he was lying in the rubble of what had been a ceiling and walls. The cabin's bed and the furniture and suitcases were strewn around him, the door jammed, men in the corridor trying to force it open. Johnson thought he heard someone say "iceberg," but he could not fix in his dazed mind whether that happened before or after he was knocked out—or, indeed, if he had heard this at all.

After a few moments, the door was pried open and Johnson was helped out, bleeding slightly from a bump on the head. He saw nothing of Alf Johansson, who had already been carried out with a fractured skull and two broken legs.

Farther back in the crew quarters, Sig Oscarsson, a waiter in his sixth year with the Swedish-American Line—he had started on the *Gripsholm*—shared a cabin with Lars-Goran Olson, a steward.

At times Oscarsson's duties entailed more than waiting on tables. Occasionally a passenger had to be calmed. On Oscarsson's previous crossing aboard the *Stockholm,* a woman at one of his tables told of having been on the *Titanic* as a young girl. She eventually married and raised a family in the United States, and now she was en route to visit family members in her homeland of Finland. It was her first trip aboard an ocean liner since surviving the *Titanic,* and she was very nervous. Her children had prevailed upon her to make the crossing, and now Oscarsson provided reassurance as well. One was hardly likely to experience the sinking of an ocean liner twice in a single lifetime, he pointed out.

Just before the *Stockholm* collided with the *Doria,* Olson left the crewmen's cabin to take a shower, leaving Oscarsson asleep. When Olson returned, he shook Oscarsson awake. "Put on a life belt and pants, we hit something."

"What are you talking about?" the waiter asked. "I didn't feel anything."

"Just do what I tell you; let's get on deck."

Their cabin had not been damaged, but if Oscarsson had needed convincing, that evidence came seconds later when the lights went out in the crew area, water sloshed on the floors, and they heard screams from the forward section. Olson would remember it was "a panicky first quarter of an hour. Nobody knew what had happened."

Casualties were confined to the crewmen in the cabins behind the bow. Some of these quarters were empty, since many crew members were working overtime in the kitchen. But Alf Johansson and a few fellow crewmen caught the full impact of the collision.

Karl Elis Osterberg, the mess boy whom Enestrom had come upon, suffered a fractured skull, and his roommate, Sven Ahlm, also was injured. Carl Jonasson and Sune Steen were swept from their cabins and disappeared. After burning a hole through the wall of cabin 5A, engineers found Wilhelm Gustavsson unconscious, with a broken leg and one eye hanging from its socket. Lars Falk, a twenty-year-old pantry boy, was discovered in another cabin with a crushed skull and a broken neck.

The collision smashed the chain locker in front of the first bulkhead, causing the two 700-foot-long anchor chains to unwind. A nineteen-year-old kitchen boy named Evert Svensson was caught up in the chains and carried to the ocean floor 225 feet below. Then the chains became entangled in something on the bottom, immobilizing the *Stockholm.*

Kallback and his search party had reached only as far as the bulkhead 50 feet behind the bow, the first barrier against flooding the ship in the event of a head-on collision.

The No. 1 cargo hold, 80 feet behind the bow, had been ripped open, probably from the impact's concussion. Seawater rose 11 feet

Bill Johnson, a harrowing
moment soon to come; his wife,
Carol, and their five-week-old
daughter, Karin, upon boarding
the *Stockholm*. (Courtesy of
William and Carol Johnson)

high in this hold, reaching to B Deck. If the water rose another level
higher it would lap over the top of the bulkhead at the bottom of A
Deck. The ship would progressively flood, and it could sink.

Nordenson ordered the engine room to pump out the water in this
hold, but little progress was made at first. The ship was soon down at
the bow by another 7 inches, the water in the cargo hold reaching the
13-foot level. But there was an encouraging note: The second watertight bulkhead, 130 feet from the bow, was undamaged. The No. 2
cargo hold, behind it, remained dry.

In the radio shack, Sven-Erik Johansson, the third radio operator, had
been alone on the evening shift, tapping out a routine message to Göteborg. Johansson was thrown to the floor by the first jolt of the collision. He got back in the chair and began a new message, telling why the
first one had been interrupted. "Sorry, We Have Collided," he reported—
the briefest of explanations, a hair-raising and perhaps barely believ-
able message for the radioman receiving it. Then a second jolt sent
Johansson flying again, and his back struck the sharp corner of a drawer
that had shaken loose from a desk. He was in no shape to continue.

The second radio operator, Ake Reinholdsson, was sleeping on a sofa in his cabin, awaiting the start of his midnight shift, when his feet slid and he hit a radiator. It seemed to him as if the *Stockholm* had slammed into a huge rubber ball. He felt the ship shaking and sensed a wavelike motion, and he thought it was being pulled to starboard. Soon after that, Reinholdsson felt another jolt and thought the *Stockholm* was being pulled with even more force to the right. Then the entire ship shuddered.

Reinholdsson had been a crewman on the Swedish-American Line for 8 years, the past year and a half on the *Stockholm*. He knew that a ship didn't come to a sudden stop without a calamitous explanation.

Convinced there had been a collision, he dressed quickly and took the fastest route to his radio shack several decks above—the elevator. Later, he would realize that this wasn't very wise, since the ship might have lost power, leaving the elevator trapped between floors, but there hadn't been time for logic.

The first radio operator, Bengt Mellgren, passed up the elevator, sprinting across the Sun Deck, a longer but safer route to the radio room.

As he made his way to his post—it took perhaps 10 minutes from the time he had been jolted awake—Reinholdsson remembered what his teacher at the Swedish Navy Radio School had counseled: "When you are working as radio officers, you will be completely alone, and the burden will be on you if the ship requires contact with the outside world. If an accident occurs, you don't have time to read in books what to do."

Reinholdsson took over from the radio operator who had twice been bounced from his chair since Mellgren, the chief operator, had not yet arrived. At 11:22, the bridge directed Reinholdsson to learn the identity of the other ship. One minute later, Reinholdsson transmitted the *Stockholm*'s call sign, SEJT, three times, followed by the international emergency signal that alerted radio operators to an imminent distress message.

The first response to that alarm came from a ship-to-shore radio station at Chatham, Massachusetts: "Okay, *Stockholm*, we are listening for you now."

Reinholdsson transmitted his first message of a long night: "Just collided with another ship—ship in collision please indicate."

At that moment, an SOS broke in. The *Andrea Doria* was calling for help.

PART III

The Rescue

CHAPTER 11

"This Is No Drill"

At the East Moriches Coast Guard station on Long Island, Radioman First Class Robroy Todd was looking forward to the end of his five-o'clock-to-midnight shift. The thirty-one-year-old petty officer first class, a Navy radar man aboard the USS *Maryland* during World War II and a Coast Guardsman for the previous eight years, had spent a routine evening at the listening post, leaving him plenty of time to ponder more personal matters: this was his third wedding anniversary.

Since Todd had been on call during the morning and afternoon, requiring that he remain at his home in the adjoining village of Moriches, the celebration would wait. Todd and his wife, Mildred, had settled for an anniversary dinner the next evening at the home of Mildred's parents in Central Islip.

Even that prospect grew distant indeed when Todd's radio came alive at 11:25 P.M. with a pair of Morse code distress messages arriving almost simultaneously. Todd transcribed the one signed SEJT first, since that transmission was stronger. His watch supervisor, Radioman Chief Jim Sharpe, checked the book of international call signs. SEJT signified the ocean liner *Stockholm*. The signoff for the other message—ICEH—denoted the *Andrea Doria*.

Todd acknowledged the calls, tapping out RRR for Roger, Roger, Roger, and signing off NMY for his call station. Then he activated the teletype to Coast Guard search and rescue facilities and radio stations along the East and Gulf Coasts.

At the eleventh-floor offices of an old textile loft building at 80 Lafayette Street in Lower Manhattan, Lieutenant Harold W. Parker Jr. had been preoccupied with something far afield from his official duties. His chronic headaches, the consequence of too many cigarettes, had returned.

Parker was the search and rescue coordinator this night for the 3rd Coast Guard District, stretching from Delaware Bay to Rhode Island.

Over the past few hours he had plenty of time to think about those headaches because there had been nothing to search for and no one to rescue. Since Parker had arrived from his Staten Island home at 7:00 P.M. for his overnight shift, there hadn't been so much as a fishing boat overdue.

Parker had resigned himself to a humdrum night in the long room, which also served as headquarters for Admiral Cy Perkins, the Coast Guard's commander of the Eastern Area, in charge of all units east of the Mississippi River.

A native of Alaska, Parker was a Coast Guard brat—the son of a lieutenant commander—and a graduate of the Coast Guard Academy, Class of 1950. After a variety of seagoing assignments, he had been stationed at the rescue center for the past 14 months.

He supervised six enlisted men, two of them chief petty officers, who kept track of ships of all sizes in the Atlantic Ocean on a huge wall chart. Using long sticks, they placed 3-inch magnetic replicas of ships on the charts and put the vessels' names or call letters underneath. These represented the ships' positions when they had last called in, a report to the Coast Guard on latitude and longitude required every 24 hours. Most of the time the Coast Guard had no need to contact an oceangoing ship, but the chart had its dramatic flourishes. It looked like something out of the World War II newsreels showing Wrens plotting the positions of the approaching Luftwaffe during the Battle of Britain.

These charts also listed the major Coast Guard cutters in the eastern half of the United States and their ready status. Each of the nation's nine Coast Guard districts was required to have one cutter on A, or Alpha status, prepared to respond instantly to an emergency, and one on B, or Bravo Zero, in port or at anchor but ready to proceed with a full crew in 20 minutes. Then came the B2 cutters, required to respond within 2 hours of an alert, and finally cutters with lesser readiness status.

The teletype machines running along the center of Parker's office clattered intermittently with routine messages. But just before 11:30 P.M., four bells sounded, followed by a pause and then another four bells—a message of highest priority. It was from Radioman Todd at East Moriches.

The Coast Guard lieutenant had no immediate indication that the *Andrea Doria* was in danger of sinking. That would come only as more messages arrived, reporting the *Doria*'s increasing list and providing what the Coast Guard called an SOB—a Souls on Board tally, listing the presumed number of passengers and crew on a stricken ship. But

Parker went into action immediately, directing that all available Coast Guard cutters be sent to the scene.

The collision had occurred just inside the jurisdiction of Admiral Roy Raney's 1st Coast Guard District, with headquarters in Boston, but this was going to be a major rescue effort, so it would be overseen by Admiral Perkins's Eastern Area Command, out of Manhattan.

Parker also directed Coast Guard stations to activate an all-ships broadcast on the long-range 500-kilocycle Morse code, directing ships anywhere near the collision scene to let the Coast Guard know where they were and what they could do to aid the rescue effort. Parker and his petty officers knew that while their wall charts with those little magnetic ship markers might impress a civilian, they were sorely limited. The positions listed for ships were often hours old, and some vessels simply didn't bother to call in every day.

Coast Guardsmen on eleven cutters were beginning to scramble, the engines firing up, the lifeboats uncovered.

The cutter *Campbell*, a hunter of German U-boats in World War II; the cutter *Yakutat;* and the sailing ship *Eagle* were off Cape Cod, carrying Coast Guard Academy cadets, along with their regular crews, on training exercises from Panama to Newfoundland.

Dick Worton, a second-class bosun's mate on the *Yakutat*, responsible for watch-standing and maintenance, had been asleep in the crew quarters above the propeller, lulled by the familiar rhythm of the engines. But he was awakened by their revving, a sense that the cutter was vibrating, and the rush of turbulent water splashing against the hull. Worton put on his uniform and hustled to the bridge. He learned that the captain had ordered the cutter to get moving.

Moments later, an alarm sounded signaling an emergency at sea. Every day at noon, the alarm whistle would be activated, followed by a loudspeaker announcement to all cabins: "This is a test—disregard, disregard." This time the crewmen were told: "This is no drill."

The *Yakutat*, a 311-footer carrying about 160 men, was a Navy patrol boat in World War II but had been converted into a Coast Guard weather boat. It would go out for as much as 21 days at a time to any of eight weather stations in the North Atlantic—each a grid of 110 miles by 110 miles—and provide storm warnings to ships. The cutter could make 18 or 19 knots in clear weather, and it had four lifeboats, two motorized and two with oars. It set out at top speed for the collision site, the entire crew awakened and preparing the lifeboats.

The buoy-tender *Hornbeam*, also of World War II vintage, was in port at Woods Hole, Massachusetts, on Bravo 6 status, not expected to be ready for an emergency in less than 6 hours. But the message arriving from the Coast Guard headquarters at Boston, monitored by Ensign Robert Boggs of Pasadena, California, the twenty-six-year-old acting executive officer and the duty officer this night, offered no such luxury. The *Hornbeam* was told that a ship might be sinking with at least a thousand people aboard. It was to get under way as soon as possible.

Most of the crewmen were making the nightly bar rounds in town or were at home, if they didn't live on the cutter. Boggs sent a few men familiar with the Woods Hole bar scene to find their mates, and he directed the quartermaster, who manned the gangway, to place phone calls to the others at their homes.

Boggs desperately needed Elmer Lee, the warrant bosun, who could organize a possible towing of the *Doria*. The Cape Cod telephone operator cranked the phone at Lee's home, but no one answered. Boggs insisted she keep trying. Finally Lee came to the phone, then rushed to his cutter.

Two freshly painted oar-propelled lifeboats, with a capacity of fifteen persons apiece, had been drying out on the *Hornbeam*'s dock. They were hauled onto the cutter, joining the two motorized lifeboats, each holding twenty to twenty-five persons. The *Hornbeam*'s 900-foot hawser, or towing rope, was also on the dock, still wet from a minor towing operation for a disabled boat. It was dragged aboard, and to make room for possible survivors, the cutter's buoys (the largest one weighing 20 tons) were lifted off with a crane. With some twenty-five of forty-three enlisted men and all four officers aboard, the *Hornbeam*'s skipper, Lieutenant Roger Erdmann, ordered departure for the collision scene.

The cutter *Evergreen* was en route from Newfoundland to Woods Hole, having concluded its annual work with the international ice patrol, an outgrowth of the *Titanic* sinking. The *Evergreen* sought out icebergs in North Atlantic shipping lanes, then provided warnings to ships approaching them. The chore was essentially routine, except for a moment of high sentimentality. When the *Evergreen* had passed over the spot where the *Titanic* went down, it dropped a wreath.

Having been at sea through the late winter, spring, and summer, Yeoman Frank Brown of Plymouth, Massachusetts, an oceanographic research specialist attached to the *Evergreen,* was suffering from "channel fever." He was so eager to be ashore again that he had trouble sleeping, and would spend the late-night hours shining his shoes or gabbing with fellow crewmen. Shortly before midnight, he knew that no sleep would come this night. Word arrived from the bridge: an ocean liner had been hit, it may be sinking. The *Evergreen*'s skipper, Lieutenant Commander L. F. Lovell, diverted to the collision site, but his top speed was only about 12 knots.

At the pier in New London, Connecticut, the 255-foot cutter *Owasco* was tied up with only one third of its crew aboard.

The *Owasco*'s skipper, Lieutenant Charles Masters Jr., was spending the night at the Groton home of his executive officer, Neale Westfall, sleeping on a living-room Hide-A-Bed. Masters didn't want to be disturbed and had taken the phone next to the bed off the hook. Knowing where the captain was, the officer of the deck called the home. Upon getting repeated busy signals, he asked the Groton police to go there. They banged on the door and awakened the captain.

The *Owasco* was a true oceangoing vessel. It could be at sea 40 days at a stretch, sending large weather balloons aloft to check for fronts approaching from the east, and it was large enough to pick up a goodly number of survivors.

The cutter was using water supplies and electricity from shore. It needed boilermen to adjust valves to get the steam switched on, to shift from shore power to ship power. The boiler tenders hadn't all returned from shore leave, so the crew improvised. John H. Casten Jr., a machinist's mate from Kansas, volunteered to become a boilerman as well.

The 125-foot cutter *Legare,* vintage 1927, was in New Bedford, Massachusetts, designated for getting under way within 2 hours of receiving a call.

Although assigned to search-and-rescue operations, the *Legare* had experienced little excitement over the past months. The cutter's typical assignment: find a fisherman—usually an immigrant from Portugal's Cape Verde Islands—who had claimed to have run out of fuel, and tow him back to New Bedford. The way Ensign David Corey of Jamesville, North Carolina, one of the *Legare*'s junior officers, saw it, many of these fishermen, subsisting on boxes of crackers and cans of beans, would simply stay at sea for a week, catch all the fish they could hold, then allow themselves to run out of fuel and get a free ride back home courtesy of the Coast Guard.

On this night, Max Ferrill, the *Legare*'s radioman, was watching a late movie on television at the apartment where he lived with his wife and four children. At 1:00 A.M., the phone rang.

"Get your butt down here," the officer of the deck told him. "We have two ocean liners collided. We're leaving as soon as we get a crew."

Ferrill dressed, jumped into his car, and drove to the dock. Soon after he got there, the skipper, Lieutenant Philip G. Ledoux, arrived from a party he had attended with other Coast Guard officers. Ledoux was a mustang—an enlisted man promoted to officer—having once been a bosun's mate. Ferrill, who had served previously on three other cutters, thought his skipper was the best ship handler he had ever seen. It was said he could find a disabled fishing trawler 200 miles offshore in 12-foot seas with no trouble, then tow it back with ease.

Ledoux seemed in a jovial mood when he arrived at the cutter, the effects of the partying not quite having worn off. Ferrill went to his radio shack, fired up his equipment, and at about 1:50 A.M., the *Legare* set off at 11 knots, perhaps fourteen of its twenty crewmen having made it back from shore leave.

While the cutter moved through fog, Ledoux came to the radio room a dozen times to remind Ferrill he couldn't fall asleep. That was the last thing Ferrill had in mind, and he finally grew exasperated. "Keep the Old Man out of here," he told the executive officer. "I'm going to lock the door, and he'll kick it down."

As the *Legare* continued to the collision scene, the fog lifted, the sea was calm. It seemed to Ensign Corey "you could reach up and pluck a star."

The Coast Guard had hoped to dispatch light planes to search for survivors, supplemented by helicopters to evacuate the grievously injured, but the Salem Air Station in Massachusetts was socked in by the fog at midnight. Its aircraft would have to wait.

At Brooklyn's Floyd Bennett Field, converted to Coast Guard use after serving as New York City's first commercial airport, an alarm pierced the night at about one o'clock.

Paul Grimes, a twenty-year-old aviation machinist's mate from Bowling Green, Florida, stirred from sleep. Back on June 19, Grimes had witnessed a horrific sight. He was aboard a Coast Guard plane escorting a Venezuelan airliner that had experienced engine trouble off the New Jersey coast. While the Super Constellation was dumping fuel before attempting a return to New York's Idlewild International Airport, it burst into flames and disintegrated. All seventy-four aboard were killed in what was then the highest death toll involving a commercial airliner. That casualty total was eclipsed only 11 days later, when 128 people died in the collision of a United Airlines plane and a Trans World Airlines plane at 21,000 feet over the Grand Canyon.

Now Grimes was summoned for a collision at sea. He could only watch when that Venezuelan plane went down. This time he was embarking on a mission in which he could actually do some good, or so he hoped. He would fly over the *Andrea Doria* aboard a twin-engine

PBM, a World War II–vintage bomber built by the Martin Company, once employed to attack German submarines but now a search-and-rescue craft. The plane, carrying a crew of six, would be dropping parachute flares to illuminate the collision scene for ships seeking survivors.

As the cutters made their way to the collision site, Lieutenant Parker, back at search-and-rescue headquarters in Lower Manhattan, encountered a situation hardly envisioned in his Coast Guard Academy training. A horde of reporters and cameramen descended on his office, and the television crews took over, stringing cables out the windows to generator trucks on Lafayette Street for "live" updates. Parker put up with that for a while, but when one newsman ripped a report out of a teletype machine before anybody from the Coast Guard could see it, his patience was at an end. He ordered the reporters to retreat into a hallway to await briefings, placing everything off-limits except for the public affairs office, where they could phone their editors.

Two petty officers were dispatched to guard access to the teletype machines. They had been manning those wall charts with the little magnetic ships. Now, they hoped, the vessels represented by those toylike figures were on their way to avert a disastrous loss of life.

CHAPTER 12

"How Many Lifeboats?"

Some 15.5 miles southeast of that patch of the North Atlantic where the *Andrea Doria* and the *Stockholm* faced each other in ruin, the United Fruit Company's 400-foot freighter *Cape Ann* was bound for New York from Bremerhaven, Germany.

S. Charles Failla, the lone radioman in the crew of forty-five, was reading in bed, having shut down his radio shack an hour and a half earlier. At 11:25 P.M., the automatic alarm signaling distress at sea sounded in his quarters. He ran to his shack, picked up the first messages from the *Stockholm* and the *Doria*, and hurried to notify Captain Joseph A. Boyd.

Boyd, a forty-nine-year-old native of County Down, Ireland, had been on his bridge for 12 hours in a dense fog, and now the visibility was virtually nil. It was grueling work, but Boyd was a veteran of a quarter century at sea. And he had been in far more perilous circumstances. While he was on North Atlantic convoy duty in June 1942, his ship barely escaped an attack by a German submarine.

Receiving copies of the distress calls from his radioman, Boyd told his third mate, Robert Preston, to take over the radar watch, then fixed his position and the location of the *Doria* given in her SOS. He ordered the engines set to full speed—the *Cape Ann* would go from 14 knots to a maximum 17—and at 11:53 P.M. he sounded the alarm bell ordering the crew to lifeboat stations.

Failla radioed the *Doria* that the *Cape Ann* was on its way and received a pointed reply: "How many lifeboats?"

The *Cape Ann* answered: "Two."

The *Doria* was not pleased. "Danger immediate," it replied. "Need boats to evacuate a thousand passengers and five hundred crew. We need boats."

Nineteen miles east of the *Doria,* the distress calls were picked up by a ship assigned to the U.S. Military Sea Transportation Service. Bound for New York, the vessel had a mostly Navy crew of more than two hundred but bore the name of an Army war hero.

On April 22, 1945, Private First Class William H. Thomas of the 38th Infantry Division and a native of Wynne, Arkansas, was leading a squad attacking Japanese troops hidden in hill positions in the Zambales Mountains on the Philippine island of Luzon. Private Thomas was hit by a grenade that blew off both his legs below the knees. Refusing medical aid, he kept firing his rifle until it was shot out of his hands, and then he hurled his last two grenades, killing three enemy soldiers. Later that day, he died of his wounds.

For assuring the capture of the enemy position, Private Thomas was presented posthumously with the Medal of Honor, the nation's highest award for valor. He was honored further with the christening of a hospital ship in his name. That ship was converted to a transport, and in mid-July 1956, the *Private William H. Thomas* had left Leghorn, Italy, carrying soldiers and their dependents back to the States.

Two of the *Thomas's* three radiomen—Harry Rea, who was newly signed on, and James Serrano, the third operator—were chatting when the distress calls came in.

Rea had recently worked at the Mackay ship-to-shore station in Southampton, Long Island, handling Morse code messages to and from ocean line passengers, but then decided to go back to sea. He wanted to join a merchant ship, but when he learned one day that the *Thomas* was about to leave the Brooklyn Army Terminal for Italy and Spain and was in need of another radio operator, he took the job.

Knowing all the ocean liner call signs from his work for Mackay, Rea recognized the distress message sign-offs—SEJT and ICEH—and realized at once that a disaster loomed.

"Geez, that's the *Stockholm* and the *Andrea Doria,*" Rea told Serrano. "You get one and I'll get the other."

As soon as the two operators finished copying the messages, Rea took them to the chartroom, handing them to Joseph Shea, the *Thomas's* civilian Merchant Marine captain, and his chief officer. He reported that the *Stockholm* and the *Andrea Doria* had collided.

The officers charted the *Thomas's* position—7 miles south of *Nantucket Lightship*—and then the captain noticed that the messages had call signs but no names.

"That doesn't say *Andrea Doria* on it," Shea pointed out.

"That's the call signs—I know them," Rea replied.

"Well, have it confirmed," Shea said. "Go get your call book."

But the chief officer told the captain: "You're only nineteen miles from them. If you don't turn the ship and go toward them for a rescue, you're gonna be in loads of trouble."

Shea ordered the ship to speed to the *Doria,* and everyone promptly forgot about confirming the call signs.

Ernie Melby, a Navy electrician, was asleep with three cabinmates when the chief bosun's mate of the *Thomas,* going through the ship to awaken the entire crew, flicked on their lights and told them to be on the aft starboard deck in 10 minutes.

The following exchange ensued:

"Okay, you guys, get up, everyone's supposed to get on deck."

"What the hell for? Get out of here, you're drunk."

"I'm serious. There's a passenger liner that's sinking."

"Oh, bull. Are you crazy?"

Melby asked why the captain didn't get on the public-address system to inform the crew if a disaster were indeed at hand.

"The Old Man doesn't want five hundred passengers and soldiers up on deck getting in our way," the bosun's mate explained, referring to the Army men and their dependents whom the *Thomas* was taking home.

The arguing went on for a few minutes, but the crewmen were persuaded to get dressed, albeit with a vow that if a joke were being played on them, retribution would follow.

The *Thomas* headed off into the fog at maximum speed—at least 21 knots—the crew feeling the vibration of the engines pressed to their limit.

The *Private William H. Thomas* wasn't the only ship named for a World War II hero that was steaming in the seas near Nantucket this night.

On May 7, 1942, Lieutenant Edward Henry Allen of Pekin, North Dakota, was shot down by Japanese aircraft while flying his Navy scout plane from the aircraft carrier *Lexington* during the Battle of the Coral Sea. He was posthumously awarded the Navy Cross, the service's highest award for valor except for the Medal of Honor. In October 1943, a 306-foot destroyer escort was christened in his honor at the Boston Navy Yard.

The *Edward H. Allen* was preparing for action in the Pacific when World War II ended. She was decommissioned soon afterward, then returned to the Navy in 1951 as a training ship.

When the *Stockholm* and the *Andrea Doria* collided, the *Allen* was 75 miles southeast of *Nantucket Lightship*, returning from Canadian waters with two hundred reservists near the end of a two-week cruise. She was heading to Newport, Rhode Island, for gunnery practice, accompanied by the destroyer escort *Heyliger* and its reservists, then would go on to New York and send its crew back to civilian life.

Although the *Allen* had only one radioman, it lacked an automatic alarm system that would alert the radio operator to a distress call while in his sleeping quarters. Late Wednesday night, the *Allen*'s skipper, Lieutenant Commander Boyd H. Hempen, a reservist himself from Illinois farm country, was using sonarmen to fill in at the radio room. They were listening to the 500-kilocycle emergency frequency while the regular radioman slept.

When the sonar specialists picked up the distress calls, they notified Hempen, who summoned the radioman to monitor further reports and then directed the *Heyliger* to head with him to the scene. Hempen sent messages as well to Admiral M. E. Miles, commander of the Third Naval District in New York, and to the commander of destroyers, Atlantic Fleet, at Newport, Rhode Island, advising of a change in mission. Gunnery practice was hereby canceled.

Some 45 miles northeast of the *Doria*, the Tidewater Oil Company tanker *Robert E. Hopkins* was off Cape Cod, its captain, René Blanc, a study in concentration under the hood of his radar screen. En route to Corpus Christi, Texas, from Fall River, Massachusetts, after delivering fuel oil, the 425-foot tanker, with a crew of forty, was making its way slowly through fog-shrouded waters thick with fishing boats. A lapse of concentration by Captain Blanc for just a moment could mean a collision.

The *Hopkins*'s radioman had become ill before the trip, his place taken by a twenty-eight-year-old Merchant Marine operator named Ray Maurstad, whose seagoing days went back to Liberty ship duty in the World War II invasion of Okinawa. Maurstad, joining the Hopkins for just one trip while on vacation from his regular ship, the cargo/passenger vessel *African Dawn*, was doing double duty this night. He was the purser as well as the radio operator.

Maurstad was typing away in the radio room, trying to finish the payroll, when an SOS sounded on the transmitter, followed almost immediately by an XXX, indicating an urgent message was to follow. The tones were different, so Maurstad knew these were coming from two different ships.

Maurstad copied the *Doria*'s SOS and the *Stockholm*'s report that it had collided with another ship, and responded with the *Hopkins*'s call sign, telling the liners to stand by for further messages. When he went to the bridge, he found "Frenchy" Blanc still peering at his radar under the hood.

"Captain, I have SOS messages," Maurstad told him.

"Sparks, I'm busy," Blanc replied, using the universal nickname for radio operators.

"It's right in front of us," Maurstad persisted.

Now he had caught Blanc's attention. The captain took the messages to the chartroom and calculated the time it would take to arrive at the *Doria*—perhaps three hours. "Sparks," he said, "tell them we're on our way."

Forty-four miles to the east of the collision scene, Captain Raoul De Beaudéan was scanning his dual radar screens in the chartroom of the venerable ocean liner *Ile de France*, preoccupied with the densest fog he had ever encountered.

A fifty-three-year-old nobleman—a baron of a family titled in the days of Charlemagne—De Beaudéan cut a formidable figure, tall and erect and at times sporting a monocle, though that was more for the amusement of his passengers than a display of self-importance. A native of Nice, now living with his wife and children at Tours in the Loire Valley, De Beaudéan had formerly been second in command of the *Liberté*, the old German liner *Europa*, given to France as war reparations in 1950. Now he held the preeminent position in the French Line as captain of the ship once known as "the Boulevard of the Atlantic," the liner favored by the American bohemians and intellectuals captivated by the Paris of the 1920s.

When the *Ile* made her maiden voyage in springtime 1927, she was, at 793 feet, the largest passenger ship launched since World War I. In an era of ballyhoo, she was hailed by the French Line for her main dining room "twenty feet wider than the Church of the Madeleine."

The *Ile* never vied for the Blue Riband, signifying a record speed for the North Atlantic crossing, and she was never the biggest liner of the pre–World War II years. Her allure rested on the comfort of her accommodations and her exquisite cuisine. She was the *Andrea Doria* of her time.

During World War II, the *Ile de France* came under British control as a troopship, carrying hundreds of thousands of Allied soldiers. When the war ended, she was the sole survivor of the great French liners. The *Paris* burned and capsized at Le Havre in 1939, and the *Nor-*

mandie caught fire while being transformed into a troopship at a Manhattan pier in 1942.

The *Ile*'s hull, still in good condition, served as the foundation for a wholly remodeled liner. She was outfitted at the St. Nazaire yards with a modern silhouette (two funnels replacing the old three) and redecorated in a late version of Art Deco, incorporating furnishings from the *Normandie*.

On July 21, 1949, the *Ile* sailed from Le Havre on her maiden postwar voyage to New York. Over the next decade the French came to call her the "St. Bernard of the Atlantic," for she would respond to SOS calls ten times. In September 1953 her crew saved the lives of twenty-four seamen on the sinking British freighter *Greenville,* caught in a storm as it neared Liverpool.

Now, on this final Wednesday of July 1956, the *Ile* had departed for Plymouth, England, and Le Havre at 11:30 in the morning from her berth off West Forty-eighth Street, precisely the moment the *Stockholm* left her dock a half mile to the north.

The *Ile* was 150 miles into the Atlantic when darkness arrived at about eight o'clock. De Beaudéan had a light meal, then read in his cabin as his ship approached the notoriously foggy waters off Nantucket. At 10:00 P.M. the watch officer phoned to report "we are in fog."

De Beaudéan went up to the bridge, where precautions had automatically been taken. The engines were on standby for a possible change in speed, and the foghorn was sounding.

As the *Ile* passed 6 miles south of *Nantucket Lightship* at about 10:15 P.M., De Beaudéan entered his dimly lit chartroom. He noticed that the barometer was not especially active, a portent of unchanging weather through the night. He moved next to a wing of his bridge, glanced up, and was stunned to discover that his two funnels had disappeared from view. The fog also had obliterated the illumination on the aft deck. On the unlit forward deck, the mast had been swallowed up in the gloom. De Beaudéan was accustomed to fog, but he had never experienced the density he encountered this night. He thought of the treacherous London fogs that left pedestrians hopelessly lost.

The captain fetched a cup of tea, taking it to his "fog" seat, a high-legged chair whose deformed, well-worn stuffing absorbed the dampness of the night, transmitting it to his backside. It was like being seated on the grass on a cool autumn evening, he thought, and he pondered having the chair reupholstered. He remembered a captain who once rigged up a one-legged chair, figuring that if he fell asleep during fog watch it would topple over and awaken him with a bang. But that innovation had not taken hold.

Moments later, the officer at the port radar called out "an echo." A large white pip—its size suggesting an ocean liner—had appeared at a spot on the range finder. The progress of the pip over the next minutes represented a ship going in the opposite direction, probably headed toward *Nantucket Lightship*. By eleven o'clock the echo had disappeared at the bottom of the screen.

The captain and the men with him on watch resigned themselves to a long night on the bridge. De Beaudéan planned to ask for more tea before long. It would help fight off the hours of boredom that surely awaited him as he peered into his radar sets.

That tedium—and De Beaudéan's concentration on his radar—was broken at about 11:30 with the approach of the chief radio operator, Pierre Allanet, who reported, "Captain, a message." For a moment, De Beaudéan thought it was the usual order to deliver flowers, champagne, or money to a passenger, though he could hardly fathom why such a request would be passed on to him. But the radioman was not seeking aid in routing well wishes. The captain could see through the shadowy lamplight that the operator was highly agitated.

"There's been a collision," Allanet reported.

He handed De Beaudéan a pink sheet containing the distress message from the *Stockholm*, "Just collided with another ship." An SOS had been received from the *Andrea Doria* as well, and other messages were coming in.

De Beaudéan realized that the pip he had spotted on his radar screen as he passed *Nantucket Lightship* had been the *Doria*.

At 11:44 P.M. the captain sent a message to the *Doria* providing his coordinates and asking, "Do you need assistance?"

Seven minutes later, the *Doria* sent its second SOS, and five minutes after that, the *Ile* radioed: "Captain *Andrea Doria*. Am going to assist you. Will arrive 0545 G.M.T. [1:45 A.M., Eastern time]. Are you sinking? What assistance do you need?"

The *Doria* responded: "Master *Ile de France*. Need immediate assistance."

De Beaudéan glanced out the window of his chartroom and could see nothing. The fog was still all-consuming. After waiting five minutes, he telephoned the radio room, hoping for an additional response from the *Doria*.

"The *Doria* no longer answers," the radio operator told him. "We are listening to the reports to keep you informed."

De Beaudéan was unsure what the *Doria* really wanted. Did she need a tug? A comforting presence alongside? A modern ocean liner was not likely to sink. And he had to consider the safety of his own ship and the 1,767 passengers and crew, who could be imperiled by speeding through fog to a rescue operation perhaps crowded with other vessels. A delay in his schedule would, moreover, present an expensive proposition for the French Line. The *Ile*'s passengers and crew consumed $4,300 worth of food every day, and the liner devoured a ton of fuel per mile.

But De Beaudéan could not ignore the *Doria*'s plea. If, upon arriving at the collision site, the *Ile* found that its aid had not been needed, the necessary explanations would be made to his bosses. And so De Beaudéan ordered the helmsman to swing around.

A flurry of messages soon made it clear to De Beaudéan that the *Doria* was listing and could not launch all her lifeboats. And she was transmitting with emergency battery power, an indication that seawater had flooded her engine room. De Beaudéan learned that the *Stockholm*'s bow was crushed, her forward hold flooded, her captain not daring to launch his own lifeboats to aid the *Doria* until being sure he could keep his own liner afloat.

De Beaudéan had joined the French Line in 1923, served in the French Navy during World War II, then resumed his career as a senior officer aboard French liners. Now, in a career at sea stretching back three decades, he was about to meet a supreme test.

His order went out: "Prepare to launch eleven lifeboats."

And so, within a half hour of the first distress calls, at least six ships—the freighter *Cape Ann*, the military transport *Thomas*, the Navy destroyer escorts *Allen* and *Heyliger*, the tanker *Hopkins*, and the liner *Ile de France*—had changed course, speeding to avert what loomed as one of history's worst peacetime disasters at sea.

CHAPTER 13

"We Are Bending Too Much"

In the crushed bow of the *Stockholm*, a teenage girl lay half buried in timbers and girders. The last thing the girl could remember, her parents had bid good night to her and her younger sister with a kiss, then returned to their adjoining first-class cabin on the *Andrea Doria*. In no hurry to go to sleep, the sisters had remarked about how comfortable they would be with extra pillows they had brought along from their home in Spain. Finally they had gone to sleep, the older girl's autograph book on a nightstand beside her.

Now the girl was awake and in pain.

She heard what seemed to be crashing and banging. Her left arm felt as if it were on her stomach and she had no control of the arm, could not move it. Just how she had injured that arm, and what was causing all that noise, she had no idea. And then she heard someone crying. She thought it was her mother.

Born in Mexico and raised in Spain, the girl called out in Spanish, "*¿Donde esta mama?*"

In an almost unfathomable happenstance, the only Spanish-speaking member of the *Stockholm*'s crew, a thirty-six-year-old cleaning man named Bernabe Polanco Garcia, was nearby. He wondered who else could be speaking Spanish on this ship. And how was it that a girl's voice was coming from an area where only crewmen were allowed?

Early Wednesday evening, while his bunkmate went above to get some air, Garcia—married to a Swedish woman and fluent in that language—had been reading Johan Strindberg's novel *The Red Room*, a satire of nineteenth-century Swedish life. He had just dozed off when he heard faint sounds that seemed to be coming from another ship. Feeling the pull of reversing engines, he went up to the deck and came upon a mass of wreckage in the bow area. And he gazed at a fantastic image—another ocean liner in the mist. Then he heard sobbing.

Following the sound of the cries, Garcia climbed over the wreckage and found a girl in blood-stained yellow pajamas with a Chinese design, only her head and arms showing. He worked to free her and then, having heard her call for her mother, asked the girl in Spanish: "Was she here? I am a man from Cadiz."

The girl told the seaman her mother had been with her. What has happened?

Garcia picked the girl up and began to carry her to the ship's hospital. The *Stockholm*'s chief purser, Curt Dawe, en route to the bridge, stopped them and asked the girl who she was.

She told him she was Linda Cianfarra, the name she used at school.

Dawe checked his manifest and could not find a *Stockholm* passenger by that name.

Then the girl gave the name on her passport—Linda Morgan.

Dawe checked again, but his puzzlement only grew, for he could not spot that name either.

"Isn't this the *Andrea Doria*?" the girl asked.

"No, it isn't."

The purser now knew what had happened. The girl had somehow been thrown onto his liner from the ship the *Stockholm* had struck.

Garcia turned Linda over to another seaman and then, remembering how she was calling for her mother, returned to the bow, hoping the woman would be there. Fifty feet from where Garcia found Linda Morgan, he saw a woman lying still. But she was beyond shattered wood and steel and he could not reach her.

A while later, an officer in the purser's department named Valdemar Trasbo also saw the woman. She was sitting upright, her back to the bow. Trasbo managed to get to her and tried to pull her by her arm, but was shocked to see it come loose from her body. Then he attempted to pull her toward him by her long-flowing reddish-brown hair. A lock came off in his hand. Horrified, he crawled away. It was not Linda's mother, but sixty-four-year-old Jeanette Carlin, the woman who had been swept from her cabin while she was reading in bed a few feet from her husband, Walter, who had been brushing his teeth.

Linda was the first patient to reach the *Stockholm*'s hospital. Yvonne Magnusson, one of the liner's two nurses, had rushed to her post, awakened by a jolt but having no idea what had happened. That the *Stockholm* had collided with another ship in the middle of the

ocean had not occurred to her. Now the nurse administered 0.25 percent morphine sulfate to dull Linda's pain as she awaited the liner's
physician, Dr. Ake Nissling. For Nurse Magnusson, this was the beginning of 30 hours of uninterrupted labors.

The autograph book Linda had left on her nightstand was soon
found in the mangled bow where Dr. Nissling was tending to injured
crewmen before arriving at the ship's hospital.

Garcia was convinced that Linda's family had died on the *Andrea
Doria,* and he later went to Captain Nordenson for advice on how he
could adopt her.

Before the captain could trouble himself with the American laws on
adoption, he had a more pressing concern—keeping the *Stockholm* from
a second collision. After separating from the *Stockholm,* the *Doria* had
emerged from the fog once more and was drifting toward the Swedish
liner's smashed bow. Nordenson ordered Full Speed Astern and shouted
to the helmsman, Peder Larsen, for a hard starboard turn. But the
Stockholm didn't move. The anchor chains that had unraveled, taking
seaman Evert Svensson with them, were still tangled on debris along
the ocean floor, something Nordenson was not yet aware of.

The *Doria* continued to drift, but there would not be another collision. The Italian liner floated by the *Stockholm*'s bow less than a third
of a mile apart from her.

More good fortune would ensue for the *Stockholm.* Stewards and
pursers finished checking the *Stockholm*'s passenger cabins and found
no one seriously injured. Several doctors who were traveling as passengers—including Dr. Horace Pettit, who had seen the *Doria*'s lights in
the instant before the collision—had volunteered to aid the ship's hospital personnel in tending to the Swedish seamen and *Doria* survivors
who were hurt.

Bill Johnson, having come within inches of losing his life when his
crewmen's cabin was crushed, left his grievously injured cabinmate and
rushed to his wife and daughter. He found them just fine, still in their
cabin. Carol bundled the baby in a blanket, donned a life jacket, and
took her to an area where passengers were beginning to gather. Bill
went, too, but his family reunion was short-lived. His supervisor
approached him and announced: "You—lifeboat."

Johnson was in no way an able seaman, had in fact never gone to
sea before, but he was being ordered to board a lifeboat and head for
the *Doria* in the vanguard of a massive rescue effort.

On the Italian liner, the generator room was abandoned at
12:30 A.M., the seawater waist high and the list at 27 degrees. The elec-

trical load was transferred to an emergency generator on A Deck and to the two turbine-operated dynamos of 1,000 kilowatts each in the main engine room.

With electrical power having steadily been lost—the dynamos in the generator room turned off as the rising water reached the electrical parts—the *Doria*'s radio transmitter and receivers were switched to emergency battery power. The remaining electrical power helped maintain the ship's lights.

In an effort to correct the steadily increasing list to starboard, the engineers emptied the double-bottom starboard tanks 15 and 17 that had been filled with seawater as ballast. They transferred oil from the starboard outboard tank below the generator room to the wing tanks on the opposite side. But it was a losing battle.

At 12:14 A.M. the *Doria* radioed the *Stockholm*: "You are one mile from us. Please, if possible, come immediately to pick up our passengers."

The traditions of the sea compelled Nordenson to dispatch his lifeboats, but he thought it odd that the *Doria* had not loaded her own boats. He was, moreover, reluctant to give up even a few lifeboats on the chance that something he hadn't envisioned could endanger his ship. At 12:20 the *Stockholm* radioed back: "Here badly damaged. The whole bow crushed. No. 1 hold filled. Have to stay in our present position. If you can lower your boats, we can pick you up."

A minute later, the *Doria* responded: "You have to row to us."

Prolonging the dispute, the *Stockholm* replied a minute after that: "Lower your lifeboats. We can pick you up."

Thirteen minutes later, Captain Calamai told the *Stockholm* why he wasn't dispatching his own boats. "We are bending [listing] too much. Impossible to put boats over side. Please send lifeboats immediately."

After receiving assurances from his engineers and from Second Officer Lars Enestrom that the *Stockholm* was in no danger, Nordenson agreed to the *Doria*'s plea. He told Calamai he would send lifeboats in 40 minutes, then ordered that all three of his motorized boats be lowered together with four boats propelled by levers. Nordenson held back his other four hand-propelled boats in case the *Stockholm* should run into unexpected trouble.

Taking a microphone in hand, Nordenson spoke over the public-address system. "I am sorry to have to inform you that we have collided with the Italian ship the *Andrea Doria*," he said, speaking in English. "While the *Stockholm* has suffered some serious damage, we are out of all danger. We will soon be manning some of our lifeboats. These are not for ourselves. It is to try and save passengers and crew on the *Andrea Doria*. She is listing seriously and is in need of our assistance."

Although the *Doria* could not launch its eight portside—or high-side—lifeboats because of the list, it did dispatch the eight boats on its starboard—or low—side, though all but one would be boarded on the water rather than at the Promenade Deck.

Three *Doria* lifeboats arrived at the *Stockholm* at about 12:45 A.M. Each boat could carry 146 persons, but these boats were less than half full. And when the *Stockholm* crewmen shined a spotlight, they were stunned. Almost all of the first survivors were men. And few of them wore the orange life jackets issued to passengers. Most of the people in these boats were wearing gray life jackets. They were stewards, waiters, kitchen help, and chambermaids, protected by the life preservers issued to the *Andrea Doria*'s crew.

CHAPTER 14

"Let's Pray to St. Ann"

The officers of the *Stockholm* became lifeboat commanders.

Shortly after 1 A.M., the Swedish liner dispatched three motorized lifeboats to the *Doria*—No. 7, commanded by Second Officer Lars Enestrom; No. 8, under Junior Second Officer Sven-Erik Abenius; and No. 1, taken out by Johan-Ernst Bogislaus August Carstens-Johannsen, who was hoping to atone for any blunders he might have committed in those final moments before the collision.

Enestrom was accompanied by a motorman assigned to monitor the engine and five crewmen who were prepared to dive into the water to pick up survivors who had fallen or leaped from the *Doria*. The fog was thinning, the moon was shining, and the sea was calm with mild swells as lifeboat No. 7 made its top speed of some 8 knots. The trip took about 15 minutes, the *Doria* having drifted to a point about 2 miles from the *Stockholm*.

Enestrom's lifeboat—the first to arrive from the *Stockholm*—glided toward the *Doria*'s aft section, where ropes and a large, wide cargo net hung from the lowest deck, passengers crowded above them calling for help. Enestrom's crewmen grasped the lower part of the netting, keeping it flush against the *Doria*'s hull, and Enestrom shouted in English for the people to hurry. Passengers started to come down, but some were kicked off the netting and driven into the water by others above them frantic to be first into the lifeboat. The lifeboat crew fished out the weaker passengers, and then Enestrom saw a man aiming a large suitcase at his lifeboat. "No, no," the Swedish officer shouted, gunning the engine into reverse. The man hurled the suitcase anyway, but it splashed into the sea.

As the lifeboat began filling up, Enestrom could see that most of its occupants were *Doria* crew members, some still wearing the white coats of waiters or stewards. When the boat was nearly full, he spotted a woman holding a child over the railing. He held up his palm, signaling the woman to wait, and backed up. Then he motioned for the woman to throw the child into the sea. It came down feet first and was plucked from the water. The mother then climbed down the net and got into the boat.

Abenius arrived in lifeboat No. 8 and took the place of Enestrom's boat, which returned to the *Stockholm* and unloaded its passengers onto A Deck. Enestrom's motorized lifeboat towed a lever-propelled lifeboat on his second trip to the *Doria*. When he was halfway to the liner, he saw a couple of empty motorized lifeboats that were drifting. He believed they were taken out by a few crewmen from the *Doria* who got onto the *Stockholm* and then abandoned them.

When Enestrom's lifeboat pulled up to the *Doria* a second time, he saw a woman about to throw a child down. He ordered his crewmen to grasp four corners of a blanket and hoist it, then signaled the woman to drop the child. It landed in the middle of the net and seemed entertained by the little adventure, almost ready to do it again. Four more children were flung into the blanket while passengers came down the netting and climbed into the motorized boat, and the lifeboat it had towed. A man of distinguished appearance sat down next to Enestrom, let out a sigh of relief, and proudly displayed a full bottle of whiskey. Enestrom was eager to ask for a sip but resisted the temptation.

Then Enestrom spotted a couple leaning against the *Doria*'s rail, just above a ladder. He steered toward the ladder and called to the man and woman in English to enter his boat. But the man pointed to his wife and shook his head, indicating she was afraid to come down.

Carstens left for the *Doria* in his motorized lifeboat just after the last of the *Stockholm*'s four hand-powered lifeboats departed. When he arrived at the Italian liner, a woman, hanging onto a swinging rope, smashed into his shoulder and knocked him toward the edge of his lifeboat. The woman swung past him and landed in the water but was fished out. Carstens plucked a girl from the water and gave her his jacket. Then the boat was borne up on a wave beneath the overhanging stern, and its tiller smashed against the *Doria* and fell into the sea. The boat pushed off with forty survivors, an emergency oar wielded by two crewmen having been fitted into the empty tiller spot as a makeshift steering mechanism. That lifeboat would see no further action this night.

But the rescue operation was merely beginning.

On the Boat Deck of the *Andrea Doria,* Elisabeth Hanson was mustering her courage. Six months pregnant, and her husband having flown ahead to New York, she had only herself to rely upon in saving her three young children. She placed life jackets on them in their cabin, then they climbed to an upper deck. But in her haste, she had neglected to fasten the belt on her daughter Ardith's life vest. A woman without a life jacket had spotted the oversight and secured the belt, forgetting for the moment her own precarious situation.

Stranded with her children and having just read Walter Lord's *A Night to Remember*, Mrs. Hanson had every reason to panic. But the account of the *Titanic*'s sinking seemed oddly to give her comfort—she felt that she would know what to do to save herself and the youngsters. And she was at home on the water. She had been swimming and jumping off high diving boards since she was eight years old and often had been aboard rowboats and canoes, bringing a familiarity with life jackets.

Nonetheless, she needed help. She approached two young men, and in a matter-of-fact manner engaged them in conversation, suggesting that someday they might write a best-seller about their experiences. Then she asked if they could help her look after her children. They responded coolly, as if to say, "Well, lady, if we happen to find ourselves next to one of them in the water . . ."

By then, Mrs. Hanson was feeling the movement of the child in her belly. She tried to repress her anxiety, lest it lead to premature labor. The only words she had heard over the loudspeaker were *"Stati calmi"* (Stay calm).

Spotting a lifeboat close to the *Doria*, Mrs. Hanson took her children down to the Promenade Deck, hoping they could descend to the boat from there. She went ahead of them on the listing stairs, fearing that if they preceded her, she might fall on top of them if she stumbled.

She got to the railing on the Promenade Deck's starboard side by sliding on her rear from the port side, forsaking the ropes rigged by the *Doria*'s crew from the high side to the low side. She thought they might not be sturdy enough to hold a woman in an advanced state of pregnancy. Her daughter, Ardith, slid as well, but her two boys made their way to the rail by holding on to the ropes.

Ropes were hanging from the rail, enabling passengers to slide down to that lifeboat below. But Mrs. Hanson didn't notice them. At any rate, in view of her pregnancy, she was not a likely candidate to slide down, and that route might have been a tough chore for her children as well.

A rope ladder was dangling from a higher deck, closer to the bow. No one was using it, but Italian immigrants alongside Mrs. Hanson shouted *"padrone, padrone"* (landlord, or, in effect, a rich person). They believed the higher ladder was a privilege reserved for those in first class.

It was well past 1:00 A.M. when Mrs. Hanson decided how her family would get to the lifeboat: she would fling the three children into the water and jump in afterward.

She dropped twelve-year-old Andy first, since he was a good swimmer and could test that strategy for the rest of the family. He was quickly fished into the lifeboat and grinned up in triumph. Mrs. Hanson was ready to drop her son Donald and daughter next, but noticed that the lifeboat had drifted directly beneath the rail. No longer was there open water to cushion the youngsters' plunge. She didn't know whether the crewmen manning the boat were from the *Andrea Doria* or a rescue ship, and she didn't speak or understand Italian, but she motioned for them to back off. *"Via, via,"* she shouted, hoping that meant "Away, away."

The sailors were from the *Stockholm*, but they did pull away a bit, and she dropped seven-year-old Ardith. Just as her daughter hit the water, a *Doria* crewman plunging from the deck above landed atop the girl. But she was unhurt and she stayed afloat, thanks to the woman who had tied the life jacket Mrs. Hanson had forgotten to fasten.

A young man in the lifeboat, wearing only shorts, leaped into the water and grabbed Ardith, who was floundering, unable to swim. Mrs. Hanson then dropped the third child, ten-year-old Donnie. As he swam toward the lifeboat, a feeling of dread came over the mother—now she was separated from all her children. With her knees drawn up to protect her belly, she jumped into the sea, then was pulled into the lifeboat sideways to avoid stress on her stomach.

Mrs. Hanson sat between Donnie and Ardith, hugging them tightly. Andrew huddled alongside a nun in her habit.

Now a harrowing moment unfolded in Mrs. Hanson's lifeboat.

Tullio Di Sandro, a thirty-five-year-old electronics technician from northern Italy, emigrating with his wife, Filomena, and their four-year-old daughter, Norma, had carried the child, in her nightclothes, from their third-class cabin. They were huddled at the starboard rail, 15 feet above the water. The father was about to jump into the sea with the child, but he feared she would swallow too much water to survive, so he shouted for the sailors in the lifeboat to catch the little girl. But in his panic, he tossed the child before the crew could spread a blanket. Norma's head struck the lifeboat's rail, knocking her unconscious.

A sailor tried to revive the girl by dabbing her face with seawater, but she did not stir. The crewman wrapped her in a blanket and took her to a sheltered part of the boat. Preoccupied with her three children, Elisabeth Hanson had not seen Norma's plunge. But she heard a thud, turned, and saw the sailor carrying the child, her limbs dangling. As they passed in front of her, Mrs. Hanson covered her children's eyes. She did not want to look too closely either, but she did glimpse up and see the stricken faces of a man and a woman—evidently the child's parents. Unaccountably, they were making no attempt to follow the girl into the lifeboat.

Soon after the lifeboat got under way for the *Stockholm,* Mrs. Hanson spotted a small man—an Italian immigrant she had seen with his family during the trip—sitting near her. He was staring straight ahead, his face grim. Mrs. Hanson soon realized why he was not lifting his eyes. In looking back at the *Doria,* she saw his wife and daughter clamoring at him from the rail. He had saved himself but left them behind.

Dickie Roman, the three-year-old son of Ruth Roman, had been having a fine time amid the turmoil. Miss Roman had taken the boy and his nanny, Grace Els, from their cabin to an open deck, found a deflated party balloon, blew it up, and told Dickie he was going on a picnic. Then the actress erected a barricade of sorts with life preservers and blankets, fastening them around Dickie and the nursemaid so they would not roll down the deck, out of control. She lay beside them, put her arms over her head, and thought, "I may have to swim with Dickie. I'll need all my strength."

She tried not to show her anxiety, then found her nerves unraveling when a steward leaped into the sea to rescue a woman who had fallen from the listing deck. But she gained reassurance from the selflessness of others. She saw a waiter heating milk and distributing it to the mothers of small children, and a ship's musician moving among the passengers, trying to calm them.

At about 2:00 A.M., Miss Roman took hold of her son and slid with him and the nanny from the high to the low side of their deck. A cadet sailor named Giuliano Pirelli strapped the child to him and took him down a rope ladder into a *Stockholm* lifeboat. Miss Roman started down the ladder after him as Isa Santana, a passenger from Manhattan in the lifeboat with her six-year-old daughter, Annabel, pleaded with the crew to wait. But the boat left without the actress. As it pulled away, Dickie waved to his mother with one hand, held the balloon in his other hand, and shouted "Picnic! Picnic!" Dickie would be bundled up by a woman from Colorado named Ruby MacKenzie, and he grew quiet as the survivors headed to the *Stockholm.*

Miss Roman remained on the ladder for 10 minutes, hoping the lifeboat would return and pick her up. When it didn't, she went back to the deck, and she descended later into another lifeboat with her traveling companion, Janet Stewart, and the nursemaid. Miss Roman looked back and saw the huge hole in the *Doria*'s starboard side. "Must be a pretty good boat to stand up to that," she thought.

David and Louise Hollyer, returning to Worcester, Massachusetts, after David's stint with Radio Free Europe in Munich, were among hundreds remaining on the high side of the Promenade Deck, unaware that lifeboats were being launched on the low side. A few people played pinochle, the Hollyers noticed, hoping to keep themselves from imagining the worst.

Others could not cope. The Hollyers saw one man who was already drunk go to a bar, get a bottle of scotch, and crawl back to his spot over broken glass. Another passenger grabbed the bottle and threw it overboard, practically driving the man to tears.

On the Boat Deck, one level above the Hollyers, the effort to free the portside lifeboats had brought only a nasty moment for Louise when a wrench dropped by a sailor struck her head. But the wrench deflected off her curlers—she hadn't had a chance to remove them upon fleeing their cabin—leaving her with only a cut on the side of her forehead.

When several hours had passed with no lifeboats in sight, the Hollyers made a pact: If necessary, they would hold hands and leap to their deaths together.

Ultimately they joined passengers moving toward the *Doria*'s low end, then discovered that lifeboats from the *Doria* and the *Stockholm* had been loading passengers there. Louise insisted that her husband go down a rope ladder ahead of her. She feared that if she descended first, the crewmen might tell David at the last moment that he couldn't depart until all the women and children had left the ship.

Their ladder reached only to a point eight feet above the water, so they would have to jump into the sea, then swim to a lifeboat. David had torn up a leg when a man used him as a springboard in a panicky leap moments earlier upon seeing another lifeboat heading off, but he made it down the ladder, then dropped into the water. Louise started down, only to freeze when she saw a flicker of white flashing near the hull.

"There's sharks down there!" she shouted to David.

"You've got to come in, there's no choice," her husband told her. "The ship is about to turn over."

A passenger higher on the ladder stepped on Louise's hands, trying to kick them free so she would drop off and give those behind her a chance to escape. Finally, she leaped into the ocean—and saw no sharks.

David, already in the lifeboat, joined with a seaman in hoisting Louise over its six-foot-high side. But she was slick with the oil that had spilled onto the *Doria*'s decks, slipped, and landed face down in the bilge. One of the sailors offered her an orange, a gesture he hoped might ease her agony. Covered with bilge water, she was simply intent on getting off the bottom of the boat. But she appreciated the gesture. The seaman looked to be about sixteen years old and, she thought, he was awfully cute.

In the hour it took the lever-propelled lifeboat to get to the *Stockholm,* Louise became nauseated. "Dave, I lost my seasick pills," she told her husband. Overhearing that, a priest sitting alongside the disheveled and scantily clad Louise remarked, "Madam, looking at you I'd say you lost everything."

When the Hollyers arrived at the *Stockholm,* they were met by their waiter, who had been on one of the first *Doria* lifeboats to depart. "I've been here for hours. What kept you?" the waiter quipped. "I got all my tips, but they were a little wet."

The Hollyers had tipped the waiter the night before. Now, Louise thought, they were sorely in need of a loan from him, since they had nothing.

The *Stockholm* received one young woman who was utterly traumatized.

Theresa Buccelli, twenty-two years old, was coming from Italy to join adoptive parents—her mother's brother and his wife—who were waiting in New York to take her to their home in Cleveland. The youngest of seven children from the village of Tracco, near Rome, Theresa had lived a sheltered life. Her father died when she was three years old, and she had grown up protected by her brothers and sisters in a deeply religious family. She considered entering a convent, but instead devoted herself to her elderly mother. When she reached seventeen, arrangements were made to have her adopted in America with the hope that she would return one day, well educated and perhaps wealthy. But the plans lingered, and she became engaged to a young man in her village.

The adoption procedures finally were completed, the engagement put off, and Theresa was looking forward to a new life in America. But she parted from her family with little in possessions except for gifts from her mother—a small amount of gold, a religious statuette, and beautifully crafted jewelry.

Asleep on C Deck, the *Doria*'s lowest level, Theresa had been awakened by screams in the corridor. Reciting the rosary, she made it up to the Boat Deck. A slender, sensitive girl, away from home for the first time, utterly alone on a stricken ship, knowing no English, she was overwhelmed by her plight and her confusion. Instead of waiting for a lifeboat, she returned to her cabin—on the level most imperiled—and hid there, awaiting the end.

A sailor hunting for stray and injured passengers glanced into Theresa's cabin and found her shivering in a corner. He led her back to the Boat Deck, won her confidence, and persuaded her to climb down a rope ladder into a lifeboat. She was taken to the *Stockholm*, having suffered only a slight injury to her left hip. Her gold and her jewelry were still in her cabin.

Pastor Ernest LaFont, the missionary with the Church of God, led his wife, Grace, and eleven-year-old son, Leland, to the Promenade Deck from the tourist-class dining room, two levels below, where they had been watching *Foxfire*. The LaFont family gathered with a group of students. They all said a prayer and vowed to remain together no matter what happened. When a dining room steward whom LaFont recognized came by, the missionary asked, "Hey, what's going to happen?" The steward threw up his hands and continued on.

Then LaFont spotted Henry Wells, whose mother was still in the family's cabin, trying to free three-year-old Rose Marie, pinned between her bed and a wall. "Where's your mother?" LaFont asked. "I don't know," said the boy, who had also been watching *Foxfire*. The LaFonts would take Henry with them to the *Stockholm*.

Fathers Thomas Kelly and Raymond Goedert, the priests from Chicago, had become separated after fleeing their cabin.

When Father Kelly arrived at his muster station on the enclosed Promenade Deck, he saw that many passengers had no life jackets, so the priest and a few others set out to find some in the cabins two decks below. After careening from wall to wall on the tilting staircase, they entered cabins whose doors had been left open. They found that almost all the lockers above the closets contained a life jacket or two left by passengers who had been elsewhere when the collision occurred or had fled in such haste that they neglected to take them. Father Kelly and the others in the salvage party each took half a dozen life vests and returned with them to the Promenade Deck. Then they all descended twice more for additional life jackets, knowing they might be overwhelmed by a rush of water at any moment.

Father Kelly remained on the Promenade Deck for a couple of hours, the loudspeaker crackling with intermittent and broken communiqués in Italian. He understood the language but could not fathom anything he heard. The voices seemed to be panicked, speaking in half sentences. He spotted a few crewmen scurrying about, but they evidently had no idea what they were supposed to do.

Three members of the crew came by and began singing in an attempt to bolster morale. The *Titanic*'s band may have played on until the end, but the passengers with Father Kelly were in no mood for music. They told the makeshift little choir to keep quiet.

Daniel Rosenblatt, a psychologist at McLean Hospital in Belmont, Massachusetts, working toward a doctorate at Harvard, encountered a similar response when he offered a musical interlude to ease the tension. Spotting a woman in a mink coat, he began singing Adelaide's refrain to Nathan Detroit from *Guys and Dolls*. But Rosenblatt had managed only a few bars of "Take Back Your Mink" when another passenger chastised him for his frivolity.

While waiting for instructions he would never receive, Father Kelly entered a lounge running the length of the ship. Furniture had careened across a dance floor, cymbals and drums had fallen over, and, most ominous, he smelled fuel oil.

The priest saw a steward who, while tying the furniture down, was smoking a cigarette.

"Do you think that's a good idea?" Father Kelly asked, expecting an explosion any moment.

"It's fine," the steward replied.

It occurred to Father Kelly that it was now Thursday, July 26, the day on the Catholic saints' calendar known as the Feast of St. Ann, honoring the mother of the Blessed Virgin Mary, a great favorite of Italians.

"Let's pray to St. Ann," he suggested, hoping to comfort the Italian immigrants all around him.

Fellow passengers came to Father Kelly for confession, some having never before approached a priest for prayer.

"I'm not Catholic, Father, but can you do something?" the priest was asked by more than one person.

"Are you sorry for your sins?"

An affirmative reply brought absolution.

Father Kelly gave general absolution as well, having determined that all those stranded with him were in a crisis that warranted it. He thought of the World War II soldiers who received general absolution from their chaplains in the hours before they invaded a beachhead.

Father Kelly felt comfortable around water, having worked as a lifeguard instructor. But as the night wore on, his anxiety grew. He noted how heavy curtains, closed during the trip when the sunshine streaming into the enclosed Promenade Deck became bothersome, had begun to drift out from the wall. The angle gradually increased, one more indication that the *Doria*'s list was worsening.

About 90 minutes after the collision, he opened a sliding window, looked down, and saw the keel coming out of the water. He realized it would take a remarkable leap to clear it if he had to jump into the sea or a lifeboat.

Until that point, the priest had cast aside thoughts of death. Now came a "moment of truth." He accepted the possibility that his life was ending.

"If I'm going to go down, I want to do something worthwhile," he resolved.

Seeing that passengers still on the high side were to be evacuated at last, he decided that if it were the last thing he ever did, he would help these people.

It was almost impossible to walk on the high side because of the list and the deck chairs littering the area. The *Doria* reminded Father Kelly of a crazy house in an amusement park, where the only way to maintain balance was to run.

But now he had a mission. The priest took off his shoes, hoping his bare feet would provide better traction, and he helped run women and children along the rail on the port side and get them to a small incline near the stern that they could climb with the aid of ropes that had been strung. Once the passengers managed that, they held on to a banister and walked in a half circle to the starboard side.

A host of passengers—women and children first—were taken into lifeboats. Later, when it came Father Kelly's turn, he was still carrying his shoes as he descended on a Jacob's ladder. It was designed to be stabilized against the side of the ship, but the ladder was flapping, since no one was holding it at the bottom. As the priest struggled to descend, his feet were at times above his head. Finally, the ladder was steadied by someone in a lifeboat and he got into it, still clutching his shoes.

A powerboat came alongside Father Kelly's lifeboat, which was propelled by levers, and threw the boat a line, preparing to tow it. But the boat's engine failed. The sailors on the lifeboat threw the line back and got under way. It would be slow going with those levers, but the crew was in no mood to wait for the powerboat to get its engine working again. The *Doria* seemed about to topple onto the lifeboat at any moment.

As the lifeboat moved away, Father Kelly thought, "How lucky I am, we're saved." But the euphoria soon disappeared. Another ship, evidently a Danish freighter, approached to the port side. On its mast, the freighter bore the customary pair of white lights. When both lights were spotted by another vessel, that meant a ship was approaching at an angle. But if the two lights were in alignment, meaning that only one source of light could be seen, the ship was heading straight on.

The passengers and crew in Father Kelly's lifeboat saw only one light on the freighter. A collision was looming. The lifeboat had no lights of its own, so it seemed the freighter had not spotted it.

Several of the lifeboat passengers lit matches, and then one of the sailors in the boat struck a whole book of matches. It flared and then died. But the crewmen on the bridge of the freighter had seen the flashes of light and stopped short of the lifeboat. They lowered their landing ramp, waved to the survivors, and invited them to climb aboard. But the freighter was an unappealing savior, rusted and greasy. The prospect of getting to the *Stockholm* was far more inviting, so the lifeboat continued on.

When Father Kelly arrived at the Swedish liner, he noticed that many of the *Doria*'s stewards were already there, standing in line for pillows and blankets.

A Swedish sailor saluted the priest and said, "Good evening, sir, we're the ones who sank you."

Father Raymond Goedert, Father Kelly's roommate, had said the rosary with passengers as they awaited rescue, and as he intoned the Hail Mary—"pray for us sinners, now and at the hour of our death"— he thought: "What a short life." His twenty-ninth birthday was that October.

Father Goedert remained on the high side for a couple of hours, then discovered that he would indeed be saved. He made it to the low side and descended to a lifeboat on a ladder, leaping the final few feet into the craft just as it was about to pull away. When he looked up, he saw the high-side lifeboats on the *Doria* hanging uselessly on their davits, the angle impossible for launching. "Boy, these engineers," he said to himself.

The priest found an empty seat in a lifeboat that required the passengers to push and pull levers. He settled for that gladly, but what happened next gave him pause.

"I'm sure glad to see you guys," he remarked to a crewman. "We're grateful you saved us. What ship are you from?"

"The *Stockholm*."

"Oh, that's fine," Father Goedert said. "By the way—what's the name of the ship that hit us?"

"The *Stockholm*."

The priest contemplated jumping overboard.

Joe Griffith, a sixteen-year-old from Oklahoma, had been traveling alone, en route home to finish high school after spending a year and a half with his father, who was working for a Dutch oil company in Catania, Sicily. Griffith and his cabinmate, a young man from Swarthmore, Pennsylvania, named Martin Franck, fled their cabin on B Deck. Griffith grabbed his life jacket, but he was wearing only his pajama bottoms, having just come out of a shower. When he arrived on an upper deck, he joined with several other passengers in breaking open a locker that contained additional life vests, hoping to give these to passengers who had arrived topside without any. But when the men got the locker open, a half-dozen crew members—kitchen help, stewards, or engine-room personnel, it seemed to Griffith—were among the first to grab the vests, in some cases after a struggle with passengers.

Griffith spent a couple of hours hanging on to the rail on the high side, then slid across the deck on his butt and boarded a lifeboat for the *Stockholm*.

Frank Russo, the teenager heading to America with his future employers and family friends the Guzzis, scrambled up the stairs from C Deck, just ahead of the rising water. He was comforted by the belief that Giuseppe and Antoinette Guzzi were upstairs at the party they had invited him to. When he arrived on an upper deck, Russo gave his life jacket to a woman from Massachusetts who had been at his dinner table. He found another one, then set out to look for the Guzzis. When he couldn't find them, he assumed they had already been rescued. So he busied himself with helping elderly passengers and children descend into lifeboats before he was taken to the *Stockholm*.

Lifeboats reaching the Swedish liner stopped in front of a large, square cargo opening. Two crewmen stood there, each taking an arm to help a passenger across the gap.

When one of Elisabeth Hanson's youngsters crossed into the *Stockholm*, the mother called out, "Don't drop my child between the boats," then felt foolish about the outburst. When it was her turn, Mrs. Hanson patted her stomach to indicate the seamen should be gentle in view of her pregnancy.

Arriving passengers deposited their life jackets in a corner next to the opening. The Hansons added theirs, but Donnie would return and pick up a child-sized life vest as a souvenir.

The Hansons were taken to a coffee shop. Next to them, sitting around a large, round table, were *Andrea Doria* crewmen who had left the ship before the Hanson family had been rescued. One of them said the *Doria* would certainly sink.

"*Quando?*" asked Mrs. Hanson.

"*Mezzogiorno*" (By noon), the crewman replied.

A stewardess gave her cabin to the Hansons. There Donnie and Andrew wrapped themselves in blankets on the floor. Mrs. Hanson and her daughter, Ardith, crowded onto the single bunk. Their ordeal over, they were asleep in minutes.

CHAPTER 15

"We Won't Leave You"

Thure Peterson, battered from the blow that had sent him reeling into the next cabin, summoned all his strength to climb one flight of stairs to the Promenade Deck, where he hoped to get help in freeing his wife and Jane Cianfarra from the wreckage half burying them.

Responding to Peterson's pleas for assistance, a twenty-five-year-old seminarian named Raymond Waite, returning to St. Charles Borromeo Seminary in Philadelphia after six weeks in Rome, accompanied the chiropractor back to the wrecked cabins.

Peterson and Waite raised the partition between Cabins 58 and 56 and crawled into No. 56 but made little progress in dislodging the debris. Waite set off to find the ship's chaplain, Monsignor Sebastian Natta, for the administration of last rites to Camille Cianfarra while Peterson looked for someone else to help him pull away the boards and mattress pieces. Again he climbed the sloping stairs.

Two levels below the Peterson cabin, Giovanni Rovelli, a thinly built, forty-eight-year-old cabin-class waiter from Genoa, had gone to bed early in his six-man room on A Deck, an old watch suspended from a chain on a pipe above him reading 10:50 when he doused his light. Twenty minutes later, Rovelli awakened from a jolt that sent the watch spinning. A steward ran into the cabin and grabbed a life jacket, shouting, "We're going down."

Although he had no idea what had happened, Rovelli dressed quickly. Seeing smoke in the corridor and believing that a boiler had exploded, he hurried to a fire station. It was there that he learned from a fellow crewman that the *Andrea Doria* had been struck by another ship.

When Thure Peterson reached the Promenade Deck a second time, he encountered Rovelli, who was with the first-class headwaiter, Pietro Nanni. If other crewmen were confused, if kitchen workers were intent on abandoning ship ahead of passengers, these two men saw their duty clearly. They were distributing life jackets and showing passengers how to slide down the sloping deck to the low side, where they could descend into lifeboats.

The two waiters agreed to go with Peterson to the pair of wrecked cabins and help him rescue the women. Peterson and Rovelli crawled into Cabin 56, but there was no room amid the wreckage for Nanni, so he headed off to help others. They turned on a flashlight to gain a sense of the women's injuries. Martha Peterson had no feeling in the lower half of her body, her back and legs evidently broken. Jane Cianfarra was bloodied by head injuries, one leg probably broken, but appeared to be in less desperate straits.

Peterson set out to find a doctor, leaving Rovelli to comfort the women. The waiter was a family man—he lived in Genoa with his wife, Pina, and seven-year-old son, Gianni—but his thoughts were not for his safety, nor for his family if he were to go down with the ship. He would do all he could to free Mrs. Peterson and Mrs. Cianfarra.

Rovelli removed some of the planking atop the women, but needed a jack for the heavier debris. Shortly after midnight, he went in search of one, promising to be back. "I won't leave you," he assured the women.

Returning to the Promenade Deck, where he hoped to find a jack in a paint locker, Rovelli slipped and cut his leg on a stanchion. He threw his shoes over the side, realizing he could get better traction barefoot. But for all his trouble, the locker held no jack. He returned to the women with only his bare hands to clear the debris.

Thure Peterson attempted to obtain morphine for his wife and Mrs. Cianfarra, but the two ship's doctors he approached on the Promenade Deck were too busy for him. He climbed three levels higher to seek help from Captain Calamai. Putting aside his overwhelming burdens for a moment, Calamai heard Peterson's plea for experienced crewmen to dig the women out, and he assured the chiropractor he would help him.

Peterson began the trek back down the stairs, now at an angle almost impossible to negotiate, and returned to Cabin 56 at 12:30 A.M.

Rovelli was still there, having removed much of the debris covering the women. He had stuffed the torn wood into the gaping hole of the tilted cabin floor, all the while finding it almost impossible to keep his balance.

The two men freed Mrs. Cianfarra's right leg, but her left leg remained entangled in bedsprings. Now Raymond Waite, the seminarian, appeared once more. Peterson, still clad in nothing but that torn curtain around his waist, had asked Waite to find some clothes for him. He had

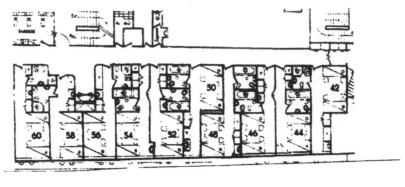

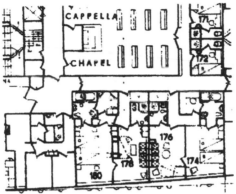

At top, a section of the *Andrea Doria*'s Upper Deck smashed by the *Stockholm*'s bow. Linda Morgan and Joan Cianfarra were in Cabin 52, Camille and Jane Cianfarra were in Cabin 54, and Thure and Martha Peterson were in Cabin 56. Fathers Richard Wojcik and John Dolciamore had Cabin 58, but were playing Scrabble on a higher deck when the collision occurred. On the Foyer Deck, one level below, Ferdinand and Frances Thieriot were in Cabin 180, which also was demolished.

accomplished that mission, producing a pair of black pants belonging to his cabinmate, Father Paul Lambert, the priest from Pennsylvania who had been enjoying a Scrabble game with two fellow priests when the ships collided. Lambert weighed about 300 pounds, his pants a size 48, absurdly large for even a hefty man like Peterson. But the chiropractor was grateful for anything he could get and put the pants on in Cabin 58, using a strip of the cabin curtain as his belt.

Peterson tried to encourage his wife to hang on. "Help is coming, Marty," he told her. "The captain has said so."

"Darling, how will they ever get me out of here?" she despaired. "Why don't you save Mrs. Cianfarra and yourselves."

"Take it easy, we won't leave you, we'll get you out," Rovelli assured her.

One of the ship's doctors whom Peterson had approached arrived belatedly with a hypodermic needle containing morphine. Peterson took it, crawled under the partition into Cabin 56, and injected his wife and then Mrs. Cianfarra in their left arms.

Peterson and Rovelli resumed trying to free Mrs. Cianfarra's pinned leg, but it was no use. They needed wire cutters, scissors, and pliers to cut the mattresses and bedsprings and a jack to lift the heavier debris.

Peterson made his third trek up the stairs—his second to the bridge— in search of wire cutters he expected to find in the radio shack. He finally gained a small victory: there were indeed two pairs of cutters in drawers that had slid open. Rovelli went below and found a large carving knife in a kitchen. He also obtained a bone saw and a pair of scissors from a nurse.

Returning to the cabin, the two men worked in shifts, one holding the mattress imprisoning the women while the other handled the tools. Peterson finally severed the last bedspring, and the men removed a heavy length of ragged paneling, drawing it across Mrs. Cianfarra's left instep, a painful maneuver. An hour and 50 minutes after she had been trapped, Jane Cianfarra was freed.

Mrs. Cianfarra's right arm was hanging limply, so Rovelli put her left arm over his shoulder, carried her piggyback to the partition between Cabins 56 and 58, then eased her under it. Peterson and Rovelli put her on a blanket they spread in the hallway of No. 58. Assisted by three male passengers and another crewman, they carried Mrs. Cianfarra on the blanket up the sixteen steps to the Promenade Deck. One of the men accidentally grabbed Mrs. Cianfarra's injured right shoulder when the blanket slipped, and she screamed. It was the first time she had cried out.

Peterson returned to his wife, who told him that even if she were freed, she would be a cripple. She pleaded with him once more to save himself, and again he promised to get her out.

Rovelli now was running along the Promenade Deck, gesturing to the sailors in lifeboats that he needed a jack. One sailor sent a semaphore signal with a flashlight, relaying the plea.

Peterson set out on his third trip to see Captain Calamai but could not find him. On his way back down, he found two doctors helping passengers into lifeboats and obtained additional morphine, but only after experiencing a moment's rage when one of the doctors said he was saving the morphine for more seriously injured people.

Peterson injected his wife again, and once more she told him to leave the ship while he still had time. Soon Peterson was off on his fourth trip to the bridge, and this time he found Calamai. He asked for a disaster crew, but was given a lone officer with a fire ax. The officer's attempts to break through debris with the ax succeeded only in showering Mrs. Peterson with additional wreckage, and he quickly departed.

Peterson found his way back to the Promenade Deck and met up with Rovelli. As the two men stood there, waiting for a jack to arrive, a sailor in a lifeboat called out, "Are you the fellow who was looking for a jack?"

The jack had been found in a locker on the military transport *Private William H. Thomas,* stored in an alcove holding damage-control equipment. It had been brought to the *Doria* on a lifeboat by an engineering officer from Buffalo, New York, named Nichols, better known to his fellow crewmen as Beep Beep for the sounds made by the Roadrunner, whose cartoons he enjoyed.

Peterson and Rovelli hauled the 150-pound jack and its 6-foot-long handle onto the *Doria* with a line extended from the lifeboat. It took them at least 15 exhausting minutes to drag the jack to the doorway of Cabin 58. Rovelli wondered how much time remained before the ship would sink. Peterson made his fifth trip to the bridge and put that question to Calamai. There was no immediate danger, the captain said.

Peterson returned to the cabin and struggled with Rovelli to jack up the last of the debris. But then they heard Martha Peterson murmur: "Oh, darling, I think I'm going."

Rovelli's hand happened to brush Mrs. Peterson's face. He found it cold. Blood trickled from her mouth.

"Doctor, I think your wife's dead," he said.

Thure Peterson listened in vain for a heartbeat. He held his wife's left wrist, searching for a pulse. There was none.

"Marty's dead," he said.

"Why couldn't it have been me?" said Rovelli. "I'm nobody."

It was 4:10 A.M.—exactly five hours since the *Andrea Doria* and the *Stockholm* had collided.

Peterson kissed his wife on the lips, removed a pearl ring from her left hand, and slipped it over the little finger of his left hand. The chiropractor and the waiter went up to the Promenade Deck, slid down a rope, and headed to sea in the next-to-last lifeboat to leave the *Doria.*

CHAPTER 16

"Lady, You're Lucky to Be Alive"

Shortly after 12:30 A.M., Captain Joseph Boyd slowed the engines of the *Cape Ann* and eased the freighter to within a quarter mile of the *Andrea Doria*. The United Fruit Company ship, 15.5 miles away when her radiomen picked up the distress calls, was the first rescue vessel to arrive.

Boyd ordered an officer and seven men into each of his two lifeboats. At 12:45 A.M. the No. 2 lifeboat, commanded by Chief Officer Roy Field, hit the water, and 10 minutes later, the No. 1 boat, under Second Officer John Jensen, was launched.

The *Cape Ann*'s two gangways were lowered, ropes and ladders were hung over the sides to await passengers, and then Boyd drew to within an eighth of a mile of the *Doria*. Seeing the liner listing, Boyd was sure a thousand people would drown, perhaps within minutes. Hearing shouts for help, he said a prayer for the passengers and then waited. Through his binoculars, Boyd saw an infant in a blanket lowered into one of his lifeboats, and then he glimpsed a woman leaping 35 feet into the boat. First Officer Field later told the captain that she had fractured both legs.

At 2:00 A.M. the No. 2 boat returned with forty survivors, among them a child rescued from the sea by Hugh Allen, a *Cape Ann* crewman who fished the youngster out after it had fallen from a survivor's grasp. A half hour later, an *Andrea Doria* lifeboat came alongside the *Cape Ann* and put fifty people aboard, and at 2:45, the *Cape Ann*'s No. 1 lifeboat brought forty more.

With many survivors having suffered fractures, the *Cape Ann* put out an urgent call for medical assistance. Captain Boyd turned over his drugs and medical instruments to two doctors who were among the survivors.

Perhaps the most anguished passengers to reach the *Cape Ann* were Elena and Clelia Iacobacci, emigrating from Italy with two other sisters, Lorenzena and Annunziata, the four having divided $1,000 from the sale of a house they shared.

The collision had thrown Elena and Annunziata from their upper berths, Elena striking the floor of their cabin headfirst and tumbling over and over.

The four sisters rushed to an upper deck and clung to a rope rigged along a rail on the high side. Then the rope broke and they all tumbled to the low side. Elena wound up near a swimming pool, injuring her shoulder and spine. She managed to arise, then crawled toward the starboard rail. Lorenzena crashed into the railing, leaving her barely able to stand.

The sisters were panic-stricken, convinced they would all go down with the ship. But they were persuaded to try shimmying down a rope to a lifeboat. Clelia grabbed a 2-inch-wide rope with one hand, but as she tried to grasp it with the other hand, she slipped the entire length, burning her hands severely, then fell into the lifeboat, injuring her back and hips. After Elena entered that boat, passengers still on the deck began tossing pieces of luggage onto it. A suitcase hit Elena on the head. She looked up, shouting, "Don't do it," but seconds later, another passenger threw something that hit her in the left eye.

Annunziata had been screaming without letup on the deck. When it came time for her to slide down the rope, she was frozen with fear, so crewmen had to carry her down. Her panic grew wilder when she lost sight of Elena and Clelia, whose lifeboat had already left for the *Cape Ann*. Lorenzena would be rescued by the *Private William H. Thomas*, and Annunziata would go to another ship.

Charles Annino, his wife, Lillian, and their two children, having scrambled past frantic passengers while rushing through smoke-filled corridors, arrived on the high side of an upper deck without life jackets. They huddled together, wrapped in blankets stored for passengers on chilly evenings. Charles had hurriedly slipped on a pair of pants and his shoes, but Lillian was clad only in a slip and house slippers, ten-year-old George and four-year-old Sandra in pajamas. The father held his daughter in his arms, clinging to a rail, unable to stand on a deck coated with mist from the fog, leaking oil, broken glass, and the vomit of seasick passengers.

The Anninos and a few others who had gathered with them found their mouths going dry, perhaps an effect of shock. "What I'd give for a

Joseph Boyd, captain of the freighter *Cape Ann,* the first rescue ship to arrive at the collision site. (Richard Faber Collection)

cigarette or a drink of water," someone said. A few people with cigarettes passed them around.

When the fog began to lift at about 1:00 A.M., Charles Annino kept his eyes on the ship's antenna, which was aligned with the now-visible moon. If the antenna moved away, that would be a sign the ship was listing more severely, Annino concluded, and he would face the prospect of leaping into the water with his family, hoping a lifeboat came in sight. There were moments when the antenna seemed to be swaying, but then it would line up again with the moon. Annino finally decided the antenna was moving simply because the ship was rolling.

Not a single officer had come by with instructions or encouragement, but the Anninos witnessed a heartening act by a middle-aged man, perhaps a waiter, who appeared with bottles of brandy or cognac. When he came upon someone who seemed injured or in shock, he knelt and gave that person a sip. With the deck almost impossible to walk on, the man kept slipping, and he careened into deck chairs. Then he fell one more time and let out a howl. He tried to arise, but stumbled once again. He got hold of the railing and slowly lifted himself on one foot. But he said his right ankle was paining him, that he could not put weight on it. He hobbled toward the stern, not to be seen again.

After a couple of hours, Lillian Annino ventured toward the stern herself, looked down, and noticed that passengers were getting into lifeboats from the low side. As the Anninos made their way toward the starboard side, they were engulfed in chaos. Holding his daughter in his arms, Annino slipped and slid on his rear end. His son fell and rolled toward the rail, seemingly about to go overboard. The boy injured his back but managed to stay on the deck. Lillian Annino fell and hurt her hip.

The Anninos finally reached a line of passengers waiting to descend to an *Andrea Doria* lifeboat. Just then a man shoved Annino and his daughter aside and rushed down a ladder ahead of them. The Anninos soon followed into that lifeboat, which went to the *Cape Ann.* When he came aboard the freighter, Annino publicly confronted the cowardly fellow survivor. But that man was not in the least embarrassed.

Like the Anninos, Mike and Meryl Stoller had spent almost 3 hours on the *Doria*'s high side. Their view of lifeboats loading on the low side had been blocked by the ship's superstructure, and the passengers who had gathered with them feared that an attempt to get to that side would only add to the starboard weight, causing the list to grow more severe.

Mike Stoller had turned at one point to a man who was evidently an engineer. "Maybe the ship will right itself," Stoller remarked. The man simply shook his head no. Once, Meryl began to panic. Mike gave her a light slap on the face that calmed her.

Meryl thought back to the collision of two planes over the Grand Canyon a few weeks earlier that killed 128 people in what was then the world's worst commercial air disaster. She wished she had been aboard one of those airliners—at least she would have died quickly.

Mike and Meryl eventually made their way to the low side. As they were preparing to go down a rope ladder, a man in the lifeboat below yelled, "Leave them," demanding that the boat get moving. Meryl, exceedingly frightened and unable to swim, was to head down the ladder ahead of Mike, but she froze. "Keep moving or I'm going to step on your hand," Mike told her, and he meant it. She made it down the ladder, and then Mike followed.

The Stollers were in the same lifeboat as the Anninos, a craft that seemed as precarious, in its own way, as the *Doria*. The rudder was broken, and the crewman trying to steer it was an elevator operator on the *Doria*. But Mike Stoller didn't mind. At least he was about to get away alive. "I'm ready to row to New York," he said to himself.

When the lifeboat arrived at the *Cape Ann,* the defective steering almost caused it to smack into the freighter's bow. And when the lifeboat managed to go around the bow, the survivors were splashed with water being discharged by a *Cape Ann* pump. Drenched and shivering, they climbed a few metal steps to safety.

As he stepped onto the *Cape Ann,* it seemed to Mike Stoller that he had been holding his breath ever since his champagne glass jiggled when the *Doria* suddenly jolted. He let the air out of his chest, and then he began to cry.

The man who had been yelling "Leave them" as the Stollers were about to descend into his lifeboat tended later to injured passengers on the *Cape Ann.* The Stollers discovered he was a doctor.

At about 1:20 A.M., the military transport *Private William H. Thomas* arrived. Captain Joseph Shea stopped about a mile from the *Doria,* fearing that if he came closer he might run over survivors swimming toward rescue craft.

About 40 minutes after the *Cape Ann* had launched its lifeboats, the *Thomas* sent out two motorized boats with four crewmen apiece, each boat able to take on thirty-six survivors. The *Thomas* also had lifeboats with oars, but held them back, since speed was paramount.

The *Thomas* was no stranger to rescues in the North Atlantic. Back in February 1955, a Navy physician aboard the ship, Dr. Ira Eliasoph, crossed in a lifeboat to the battered Costa Rican freighter *Darnel* in heavy seas and treated four crewmen for injuries suffered in a boiler explosion. He brought one of them to the *Thomas's* hospital, probably saving that man's life. The National Safety Council had presented Eliasoph, the lifeboat crewmen, and Captain Shea with an award for that rescue.

One of the *Thomas's* radio operators, James Serrano, carried a transmitter as he headed to the *Doria* aboard lifeboat No. 1, ready to relay word on the situation aboard the liner. Serrano saw an obese woman in nightclothes trying to descend on a rope. "Let go, I've got you!" he shouted. When she did as instructed, the woman fell onto Serrano and broke his shoulder. He was so shaken that he never transmitted his promised message to the *Thomas.*

All this was presumably a lot more than Serrano had bargained for when he joined the *Thomas.* He was working as a radio operator so he could gain enough civil service points for a postmaster's job in Albany, New York.

The lifeboats returning to the *Thomas* held many *Doria* crewmen—stewards and waiters—like the first *Doria* boats going to the *Stockholm.* These people and many of the Italian immigrants among the survivors were emotional wrecks, the *Thomas* crewman Ernie Melby thought. He watched as they kissed the deck of the *Thomas* and made the sign of the cross, in some cases slowing the efforts to bring the survivors behind them onto the transport. Gentle urging by the *Thomas*'s crew kept the line moving.

But some of the first-class passengers rescued by the *Thomas* were hardly panicked, as Melby saw it. They seemed to have considered themselves caught up in a magnificent adventure.

Melby noticed a tall, beautiful woman in a white evening gown, extraordinarily elegant. Then he gazed down. The woman was coated with oil and water up to her knees. But she was smiling.

"That woman has a lot of class," he thought.

The survivors were taken to the *Thomas*'s spacious dining room, given blankets and clothes, and were fed.

One woman had a question for radio operator Harry Rea: "Is that ship gonna sink?"

"It's supposed to be unsinkable."

"If it sinks, what'll happen to my Cadillac and fur coat?"

"Lady, you're lucky to be alive," interjected George Callas, the *Thomas*'s chief radio operator.

After the *Thomas* took on the last of the survivors to reach it, Ernie Melby had a task to complete. Beep Beep, the engineering officer Nichols, had asked for a favor when he set out for the *Doria* with a jack to lift the debris off Martha Peterson: "If we get back, how about finding a good, stiff drink?"

"I'll do my best," Melby had said.

Nichols expected his lifeboat to go right under the gaping hole in the *Doria*'s starboard side, placing its crew in peril of being sucked in. Even grimmer was the prospect of the *Doria*'s capsizing just as Nichols was handing over the jack.

When Nichols's lifeboat arrived back at the *Thomas*, Melby made good on his promise. Alcohol was barred from military ships, but smuggling was hardly unknown, and the *Thomas* was no exception. The weary lifeboat crewmen retired to one of the larger cabins to soothe their nerves.

CHAPTER 17

"Light Up Everything, Quickly"

It was almost 2:00 A.M.—nearly 3 hours since the *Stockholm*'s bow had slashed into the *Doria*—and nearly a thousand people still awaited rescue.

The *Doria*'s eight starboard lifeboats had been hauling passengers and desperate crewmen through the fog for more than an hour now. The Swedish liner had picked up several hundred survivors with its own lifeboats. And the freighter *Cape Ann* and the military transport *Private William H. Thomas* had rescued dozens. Yet passengers remained stranded on the *Doria*'s Promenade and Boat Decks, most of them on the high side, blocked by the liner's configuration from glimpsing the low side, where hundreds of others had descended into lifeboats.

For some passengers, the search for family members outweighed thoughts of their own salvation.

Peter Thieriot, the thirteen-year-old son of the *San Francisco Chronicle* executive Ferdinand Thieriot, was blocked by wreckage from reaching his parents' suite on the Foyer Deck. So he climbed two flights to the Promenade Deck. He was hoping that stewards or other passengers might have seen them. But no one had. Then the boy returned to his single cabin in the hope his parents might be there, looking for him. They were not.

Belatedly donning a life jacket, Peter tried different routes to reach the suite, which was down the hallway from his forward-area cabin, but each time he was halted by debris. He climbed once more, this time to the Boat Deck, where the useless portside lifeboats remained on davits pointed toward the sky. He spotted Morris Kiel, a New Orleans antiques dealer who had befriended him during the trip. Kiel had not seen the boy's parents but hit upon a way to lift his spirits.

"How about some Ping-Pong?" he suggested.

Peter politely declined.

Paul Sergio, the shoemaker from South Bend, Indiana, and his wife, Margaret, unable to reach the cabin occupied by Margaret's sister, Maria, and her four children, climbed from the third-class C Deck to the Promenade Deck.

Maria and the youngsters were nowhere to be found, so Paul started back down. But a crewman stopped him and shined his flashlight into the darkness below. Paul Sergio saw nothing but water where cabins had been. Maria and the children almost certainly had perished.

But he would not tell his wife just yet. When he returned to Margaret, he reported that the crewmen would not let him go to the forward muster stations but had assured him that Maria and the children were there, waiting for lifeboats.

Doria crewmen freed three-year-old Rose Marie Wells, whose hand had been pinned between her bed and a wall. Her mother, Alba, took the child and her eight-year-old sister, Shirley, to the stern area of the Promenade Deck, having left their life jackets at their C Deck cabin in the frenzy of the moment. But the third child, nine-year-old Henry, was still missing. Then Mrs. Wells received hopeful news: a steward told her that Henry had evidently left in an earlier lifeboat, and he implored her to depart with the girls.

Betsy Drake had gone to the high side of the ship, feeling perfectly calm. She took off her shoes, the traction on the slippery floors easier to handle without them, and placed them in her pocketbook. Then she hung the pocketbook on a clothing peg and waited for help.

The Hungarian ballet stars Istvan Rabovsky and Nora Kovach, anticipating assistance from a ship's officer, found no one to aid them. The offer they did receive was hardly welcomed. An Italian priest approached the dancers and a cluster of passengers with them to announce that the *Doria* surely would sink, they all would die, and now was the time to receive absolution for their sins. Nora was frightened terribly by the priest's proclamation of doom, but Istvan shrugged it off. In Communist countries, he remembered, nobody paid much attention to priests.

Others provided a counterweight for the alarmists.

Richardson Dilworth, the Philadelphia mayor and a dinner partner of Istvan and Nora during the trip, puffed on a pipe and cracked a few jokes, offering a calming presence. A young American doctor assured Istvan, Nora, and the passengers with them that no one would die—there would be lifeboats for everybody. How the doctor knew this wasn't clear, but the optimism helped.

Istvan Rabovsky now thought of a logistics mistake he would rue if he got off the *Doria* alive. He managed to retrieve passports when he returned to his cabin after fleeing topside with his wife in the first minutes after the collision. Now he wished he could retrieve a certain suitcase he had allowed the stewards to take that afternoon.

In a ballet he appeared in with Nora Kovach at Genoa, he wore a pair of red boots. Upon boarding the *Doria*, Rabovsky stuffed their pay for that ballet, $2,500 in cash, into those boots for safekeeping. He had seen his Hungarian peasant grandfather hide money in his boots when he trudged long distances to market, a safeguard against theft. It seemed natural to do the same at sea. But now Rabovsky's red boots, and the cash in them, were beyond reach in the pile of luggage stacked on the starboard side of the Promenade Deck.

When the ships collided, Richardson Dilworth had pulled open the door of Cabin 80 on the Upper Deck. After making their way through a smoky corridor along wet linoleum that seemed to the mayor like a toboggan slope, the Dilworths went to a high deck and clung to the portside railing for perhaps 2 hours. The mayor may have tried a few jokes to calm Nora Kovach, but there were other tactics when needed. Upon seeing a woman becoming hysterical, Dilworth slapped her across the face to bring her under control.

The Dilworths had a hard time of it later, when the passengers on the high side began moving toward the low side. While some followed a semicircle along the rail and others held on to ropes strung along a corridor from the high to the low side, the Dilworths, like many passengers, decided to slide down to the port side. As they slid together, the mayor tried to grab his wife's shoulder, hoping he could brake her landing. But he caught her foot instead. Ann Dilworth careened away from him and crashed into a glass door, suffering a severely blackened right eye.

Amid the anxiety, at least one passenger made repeated trips between an open deck and her cabin. A single trip back—to retrieve passports—had been enough for Istvan Rabovsky. But Joan Dier, the secretary from Buffalo, New York, who had been watching *Foxfire* when the ships collided, undertook three round trips. The first time, she went back for her flat-soled shoes and a life preserver. The second time, she scooped up her address book. Traveling alone, she looked after strangers, comforting some of the old people and praying with others. And then she returned to her cabin a third time, stuffing her passport, lipstick, and fourteen rolls of film into a straw bag.

Not everyone retained their photographs of a lovely summer in Europe destined for family scrapbooks. Bernie Aidinoff and his wife, Cissie, having been married the previous Memorial Day, were returning on the *Doria* from a six-week wedding trip before Aidinoff, a Harvard Law School graduate, was to begin work at the Manhattan law firm Sullivan & Cromwell. When the collision occurred, Bernie, who was in the bathroom, was knocked against their cabin wall. The Aidinoffs grabbed their passports and vaccination certificates before fleeing their cabin, but left behind ten to fifteen rolls of film, the entire record of their wedding trip.

The Aidinoffs sat on the floor on the ship's high side, waiting for instructions. There they met Ernest Grigg, an American diplomat who had been serving in the Middle East, and his wife, Margaret. Neither the Aidinoffs nor the Griggs thought the ship would sink, but they also did not know it had been in a collision. Bernie thought there was a problem in the engine room. They passed the time discussing Mideast politics. After a half hour, Grigg's wife told him to go back to their cabin and put a bathrobe on over his pajamas. And so the political talks briefly adjourned.

As the time passed with no help in sight, Cissie Aidinoff became increasingly uneasy. "Don't worry," Bernie reassured her. "The ship cannot sink."

Nerves were on edge all along the decks. Pat Mastrincola, at age nine, noticed how each time the *Doria* made a creaking sound or something broke loose and slid, flashes of panic showed on the faces of the adults around him.

While the priests and nuns ministered to spiritual and emotional needs, passengers extended small kindnesses to one another. Antonio Ponzi, the fourteen-year-old Italian immigrant who had narrowly escaped the water rushing into his C Deck cabin, was shivering as he waited for a lifeboat. Another passenger, whom he would remember only as a tall American, gave the boy his overcoat.

Helen Gebhardt had been sitting in a lower bunk, holding an alarm clock, trying to decide how far in advance of the 7:00 A.M. breakfast seating she should set it. Her husband, Neil, had looked at his wristwatch and remarked it was exactly 11:10. Then a jolt sent the alarm clock flying out of Helen's hands.

Since their cabin was near amidships, it was undamaged, and Neil thought nothing much of the rocking. For lack of a better explanation, he suggested to Helen that the cargo might have shifted. Then the Gebhardts heard a woman screaming. When they opened their cabin door and saw how the ship was tilting, they were certain there had been a collision.

They seemed to think of everything. They placed life jackets over their nightclothes, put on their shoes, and even donned topcoats they had not placed in the luggage piled on the Promenade Deck. Helen took her handbag and Neil remembered his wallet as they fled their cabin.

They climbed four flights to the Promenade Deck, and when they emerged on the starboard side were dismayed to find considerable damage even this high on the ship. The glass windows forming the outer walls on the low side of the deck had been shattered, and the heavy steel framework in which the glass was set had been jammed inward 18 inches along the deck's entire length. The baggage that had been neatly arranged a few hours earlier was strewn about.

The Gebhardts made their way to the high side of the deck and stood at one of the large open windows. When the *Doria* let out a blast of its foghorn—which it continued to do intermittently—they listened for a distant answering horn indicating help was on the way. But no answer came. When Neil looked at the illuminated ship's clock and saw it was 1:10 A.M., they still had heard nothing.

Helen asked Neil how they would be transferred to another ship when help arrived. Neil said that the rescue ship would probably pull up alongside and they would cross to it on a gangplank. They both knew that would be impossible, but the thought was enticing enough.

A group of passengers nearby began singing "It's a Long Way to Tipperary." But that bright note had its counterpoint when the Gebhardts glimpsed an elderly couple sitting in a trough between a cabin wall and the side of the deck. The woman evoked a funereal image except for one minor fashion note: She was wearing a black dress and a black coat, but her black hat was trimmed with brightly colored flowers. She sobbed with no letup.

When the parade of passengers to the low side finally got under way—a long line of people holding on to the rail and moving in a semicircle in the section around the stern—Neil Gebhardt had his worst moment.

By now he had discarded his shoes, but the angle had become so steep that even with bare feet, he had little support from the planking on the deck. When Neil took one hand from the rail, thinking he would move it around Helen's arm to give her extra support, his feet flew out from under him, jerking his other hand loose, and he slid, out of control, feet first across the deck. Lying on his back, he could see he was headed toward a swimming pool whose water had spilled onto the deck. He crashed into the wall of the pool and the supports for the diving board and broke three ribs even though his chest was padded by a thick life jacket and his topcoat. His sunburned shins were scraped raw.

But he arose, crawled to the edge of the deck, and resumed his place with Helen in the line headed toward the spot where they hoped to descend into a lifeboat.

For one resourceful crewman, the slippery, sloping deck was no insurmountable obstacle. A swimming-pool attendant known only as Giovanni displayed amazing agility. Wearing rubber-soled running shoes and shouting *"Bambini! Bambini!"* to alert parents to his mission, he mounted a single-handed rescue service for babies, carrying them to the lifeboat debarkation points.

Passengers did what they could to keep fright from turning to mass panic. Father Richard Wojcik, one of the priests returning from Rome to the Chicago area, noticed how when a passenger let out with a brief scream, giving in to the tension, others would tell the person to keep quiet.

Some people came up to the priest for confession, some said the rosary. But even a simple gesture, without religious overtones, could be comforting. Spotting one woman shaking with fright, the priest asked her if she would feel comfortable if they held hands. "Oh, yes," she said. A little later, when she left the area, she nodded in a gesture of thanks.

But a few passengers sought to take advantage of others. Father Wojcik overheard a girl, wearing a swimsuit with a frock over it, advising her mother, "Tell them you're sick so you can get off first." The mother said nothing, her face blank with a visage of sheer terror.

In the first hour or so, Father Wojcik expected the *Doria* to sink, and he envisioned dying at age thirty-three. He thought about how his music and language studies in Rome at the Pontifical Institute of Sacred Music had represented the three hardest years of his life. "What a waste," he said to himself. "You knock yourself out and it's all for nothing."

Father Wojcik was, however, superbly equipped to handle the slippery deck. Unlike many passengers, he did not go barefoot. When he had left for Rome, he decided to buy a substantial pair of shoes. He figured that the strongest available shoes were rubber-soled. Now, with footwear like those worn by the swimming-pool attendant dashing along the deck with those babies, he kept his footing, a happy contrast to the passengers in leather-soled shoes that were of no use on a waxlike deck.

Mary Marsich had become separated from her roommate and Cleveland neighbor Frances Aljinovic when they fled their cabin after seeing the *Stockholm*'s lights seconds before the collision. Marsich's muscles were cramping in the cool air topside, and she was sure she would go down with the *Doria*. She saw Italian passengers carrying pictures of the Blessed Virgin Mary, but she had nothing in hand for her own spiritual support. She composed her last will and testament in her mind and thought of what a blow her death would be to her parents.

But the passengers experiencing the greatest agony were those who had been sleeping in the third-class, lower decks where water rushed through the shattered corridors and leaking oil coated the hallways.

Robert Young, the official with the American Bureau of Shipping, saw members of a panicked Italian family come topside so heavily coated with oil that no one could provide a helping hand. Their bodies were so slick, it was impossible to hold on to them. And such was their hysteria that an Italian stewardess who tried to soothe them could not understand anything they said.

As the list grew more severe, it was no longer possible to stand on the high side of the Promenade Deck or even sit down, except at the space between the rail and the bottom of a longitudinal bulkhead that was some 18 feet inboard from the side of the ship and extended almost the full length of the deck. That space had been taken by women, children, and the elderly. The others in that area were lying on the deck, holding on to the railing.

Young could hear orders over the bridge's intercom in Italian and understood enough to know they were instructions to the crew. There was little conversation among Young, his wife, his son, and his daughter. But Young was thinking ahead. All four family members were good swimmers, and they were wearing life jackets. If no rescue ship arrived soon, he thought they all could slide to the low side (he had no idea lifeboats had already loaded on that side) and then plunge into the water when the list had become so severe that the leap would be only a couple of feet. Perhaps they would not hit the ocean with much force, and it would be warm enough to allow them to stay alive and float until help came.

By pulling himself up—in effect, chinning—Young could peer over the railing and watch the list increasing. More and more of the portside hull plating came out of the water. Eventually Young saw the emergence of the port bilge keel, an antirolling device extending for two thirds the length of the decks. As a man with wide knowledge of ships, he knew then that the *Andrea Doria* could not survive.

What Young did not know was that the emotional tide of the night was about to turn.

Raoul De Beaudéan, the captain of the *Ile de France,* had been praying silently for the fog to lift as he approached the collision scene. He considered radioing the rescue ships already there to ask about visibility in the area but decided he had used the airways enough. And then, at about 1:35 A.M., one of his officers saw the expected echoes on the radar screen—straight ahead, 12 miles away. Four pips, representing four ships, were glowing. De Beaudéan imagined what the search would be like if the fog remained dense—a careful approach to the nearest pip, then slow movement from one pip to the next, trying to identify the one that represented the *Andrea Doria.*

Then came a shout. "It's lifting. The fog is lifting, Captain. We can see the lights."

De Beaudéan moved to the bridge. He had expected to be groping blindly, but now he saw a cluster of lights some 6 miles off. The fog was indeed thinning, a breeze arriving from the south and sweeping it away.

The *Ile* turned on its searchlights, and soon afterward the captain ordered: "Announce the distance."

"Two and a half miles."

"Half speed," De Beaudéan directed, remembering that the *Ile* was still speeding at 22 knots.

The captain moved the *Ile* slightly right to get a better view of what he believed was a rescue ship. Its navigation lights were shining and it flashed its searchlights at the *Ile,* momentarily blinding the men on the liner's bridge. It was the *Cape Ann.*

De Beaudéan ordered the *Ile* to move forward slowly, trying to get as close as he could to lighten the task of the men who would be rowing to the *Doria.* When the *Ile* reached a point a mile and a half away, her engines stopped. The liner glided forward on her momentum, and then De Beaudéan ordered, "Reverse all engines slowly."

The crew now heard a confusing din—cries for help from the *Doria*'s deck.

De Beaudéan stopped the *Ile* 400 yards away, its bulk serving as a windbreak to keep the open water between the ships calm.

And then the captain issued an order that stirred the spirits of hundreds who had been stranded for 2½ hours, watching helplessly as their beautiful ship tilted and tilted, closer and closer to the end. It was an order that produced an image to be marked indelibly on the consciousness of all who glimpsed it for the rest of their lives.

"Light up our name, the funnels, the decks. Light up everything, quickly."

Switches clicked, and the block letters *ILE DE FRANCE*—aligned between her two red and black funnels—blazed through a North Atlantic night that only moments earlier had shed an impenetrable and deadly fog.

And then from the captain, a second order: "Launch the lifeboats."

The crewmen worked the winches that sent eleven boats—five from one side of the *Ile*'s hull and six from the other side—splashing into the sea. The sailors took their spots at the oar locks, and they began to row.

On the deck of the *Andrea Doria,* David Hollyer found the French liner's legend in lights mesmerizing, the playing of floodlights on bobbing lifeboats worthy of a Hollywood spectacular. "This is like a Cecil B. DeMille production," he thought.

To Istvan Rabovsky, the *Ile*'s lights "were like a Christmas tree."

Istvan's wife and ballet partner became transfixed by the lights from the heavens, the stars and the moon having appeared with the lifting of the fog. Nora Kovach concluded: "This is nature's miracle."

Jerry Reinert was seized with "incredible joy" when the *Ile* announced herself in a glow.

"It was almost as if the sky lit up," he would remember. "It meant, hey, we're gonna live."

CHAPTER 18

"You Have to Have Courage"

For Peter Thieriot, for Margaret Sergio, for Alba Wells, the searching could go on no longer. Peter's father and mother, Mrs. Sergio's sister and four nieces and nephews, Mrs. Wells's son, had yet to be found. But the *Ile de France* had miraculously appeared, and now it was launching eleven lifeboats. The French liner represented the last hopes for rescue of those still aboard the *Andrea Doria*. Perhaps there might be another miracle—a family reunion on the *Ile* or at the piers in New York when the *Stockholm*, the *Cape Ann*, and the *Private William H. Thomas* arrived, bearing the missing family members.

Peter Thieriot, unable to find his parents on his first two trips up from his cabin on the rubble-strewn Foyer Deck, climbed the stairs a third time. He met Max and Theresa Passante, who had taken the sitting-room portion of the luxury suite whose bedroom had been booked by Ferdinand and Frances Thieriot.

The Passantes told Peter that his parents must have departed earlier, and they persuaded him to leave the *Doria* with them. When they entered a lifeboat setting out for the *Ile,* Peter glanced back. He saw the spot his father had pointed out when they boarded in Gibraltar, the area where Ferdinand Thieriot thought their cabin would be. There was no porthole there now—only a massive hole in the *Doria*'s hull torn open by the *Stockholm*'s bow.

Margaret Sergio had clung to a railing, refusing to leave the *Doria* until she learned firsthand of her family's fate. A group of sailors grabbed her, but she kicked them, hoping to tear herself loose. They tied a rope around her waist and lowered her to a lifeboat leaving for the *Ile*. Her husband, Paul, would take a later boat.

Alba Wells had been skeptical when told that her nine-year-old Henry had already left the *Doria,* but she allowed her two daughters to be lowered into a lifeboat. Before she could slide down a rope to join them, the boat departed. Now she was separated from all her children.

When another lifeboat arrived for loading, Mrs. Wells gripped a rope, but as she slid toward the boat, the rope swung out over the water, then back toward the *Doria*. Her arm slammed against the hull and she lost her grip, went down the rope, out of control, and landed heavily in the lifeboat. It soon departed for the *Ile*. Whether her two daughters had been taken to the French liner as well, Mrs. Wells had no idea.

Leonardo Paladino's family had been waiting for a lifeboat for 3 hours. When they finally reached the front of the passenger line, the tailor from Bari handed daughters Tonya, two, and Felicia, three, to seamen who lowered them. As he was about to hand four-year-old Maria to the sailors, that boat departed. Maria, a playmate days earlier of Norma Di Sandro, the four-year-old who had landed unconscious in a *Stockholm* lifeboat when thrown by her frantic parents, was lowered into a second lifeboat. Just as Leonardo and his wife, Giovanna, were about to descend into that boat, it left.

The father and mother entered a third lifeboat, having no clue as to where the first boat had taken Tonya and Felicia and where the second boat was taking Maria. Mr. and Mrs. Paladino seemed headed for disaster moments later when the motor on their lifeboat conked out and it took on water. Another lifeboat, alerted by the crew's signaling with a light, threw the Paladino lifeboat a line and towed it to the *Ile*.

Angela Grillo dropped her three-year-old son, Anthony, into a blanket held aloft by lifeboat crewmen, but the boat departed for the *Ile* before she could make it down a rope ladder.

Hundreds of passengers were loaded onto lifeboats from the *Ile* or boats from the other rescue ships that took them to the French liner.

Jerry Reinert, the twenty-one-year-old from Brooklyn returning from his European tour, undertook a mission that lasted 3 hours—helping children and babies down the rope ladders. Reinert and a couple of other young men had a child placed against their forearms on each trip, a rope around the youngster's waist, its top point tied to a pipe. When one youngster was deposited into a lifeboat, the rope was removed and readied for the next child.

At 4:00 A.M. Reinert plopped into a lifeboat, utterly exhausted, his head spinning. "Don't go up anymore, you're out of it," a crewman told him. Reinert sat down, his night's work over. He was taken to the *Ile*.

If descending to a lifeboat was an impossible maneuver for children to attempt unassisted, the swinging out of the rope ladders and single

ropes—at times all the way to the horizontal—posed a forbidding avenue of escape to just about everyone.

When Istvan Rabovsky and Nora Kovach reached the *Doria*'s rail,
Nora looked down and announced that she could never make it to a
lifeboat. "If you're not going to climb down, I'm going to throw you,"
Istvan told his wife. With assistance from the crew, Nora managed to
go down a rope ladder. More than an hour later, Istvan got into
another lifeboat. They were both taken to the *Ile*.

Ann Dilworth, her eye blackened from her fall in sliding across the
deck, didn't want to leave the *Doria* without her husband, but the stewards insisted, and so she departed for the *Ile* at about 3:00 A.M. An hour
later, Mayor Dilworth left for the *Ile* in one of the last boats making the
trip. Dilworth prided himself on being physically fit, but had what he
would remember as a "terrible time" making it down the rope ladder.

Father Richard Wojcik and the two priests who had been waiting
for rescue with him—his cabinmate, Father John Dolciamore, and their
Scrabble partner, Father Paul Lambert—ultimately slid to the *Doria*'s
low side.

As Father Wojcik awaited his turn to descend into a lifeboat, he
witnessed parting rituals that touched him with their beauty. In several
instances, women ordered by crewmen to go down ropes would not depart without their husbands, saying they had spent their lives together
and would not end them separately.

That didn't sway the *Doria*'s sailors, who were giving women, children, and the elderly and infirm priority. The women and children
indeed left first in most instances, the husbands and fathers waving to
them. Father Wojcik noticed how even when the lifeboats were a few
hundred yards off, the men left behind could somehow see their loved
ones. It was the playing out of a "psychic bond," the priest concluded.

When it came time for the three priests to leave the *Doria*, Father
Wojcik and Father Dolciamore faced a mighty burden in Father Lambert, who had presumably—albeit inadvertently—saved their lives by
persuading them to play Scrabble with him. Had they not, they would
have been in the wreckage of their Cabin 58, the cabin into which
Thure Peterson had been thrown.

Standing at the opening where passengers were to descend to lifeboats, Father Lambert looked down, saw how the rope ladder didn't
reach the deck of the lifeboat below, and froze, grabbing the sides of
the doorway frame with a furious grip. The priest was an enormous
man—he weighed about 300 pounds (Father Wojcik remembered him

as "an Orson Welles type")—and it seemed to Father Wojcik that someone would have to cut off his fingers or break his arms to pry him loose.

Father Wojcik and Father Dolciamore took turns pleading with Father Lambert to go down the ladder. "I can't, I can't," he insisted.

The two priests weren't going to leave the *Doria* without Father Lambert, but crewmen persuaded them to do so, saying they would take care of him.

Father Wojcik and Father Dolciamore slid down ropes at another opening nearby, looked up from their lifeboat, and saw Father Lambert still perched at his spot, his hands in a viselike grip on the sides of the open doorway. They shouted encouragement to him once more. Finally he turned around and began backing down on the ladder, placing one foot on the top rung. But after he moved one or two rungs down, his weight pulled the ladder away from the side of the ship and he began spinning. Sailors in the lifeboat reached up and grabbed the bottom of the rope ladder, steadying it. Father Wojcik and Father Dolciamore expected Father Lambert to crash down on them, but he held on and gradually made it into the boat. It seemed to Father Wojcik that it had taken "forever."

And then the lifeboat departed, taking the three priests to the *Ile de France*.

For the particularly unlucky, the route to the lifeboats evoked World War II newsreels. When Jacob's ladders or single ropes weren't available, passengers had to climb down cargo nets. That was no easy task for the superbly conditioned soldiers who lowered themselves into landing craft for the approach to Omaha and Utah Beaches on D-Day. For middle-aged and elderly tourists, and especially for women, the prospect of negotiating these nets was almost inconceivable.

The cargo netting was the only means of descent for Gene and Freda Gladstone, the couple returning to Toronto from a realtors' convention in Vienna.

Freda went first. A crewman told her to step across the *Doria*'s railing—just knee-high because of the list—with one foot, then work her bare toes into the net's mesh. After she obtained a firm foothold, she was to lift her other leg over the rail, then keep going until she reached the bottom of the net.

She got one foot onto the netting, but then she looked down and saw that the net ended six feet above the lifeboat awaiting her. And it was flapping in a breeze that had blown away the fog. Freda froze in terror.

The sailor who had given the instructions told her to keep going. The passengers on line waiting to climb onto the net began shouting at her, and those already in the lifeboat, impatient to depart before the *Doria* toppled onto them, were yelling as well.

Gene Gladstone persuaded his wife to lift her other foot over the railing. "Freda, don't look down, look up," he pleaded. "You have to have courage."

He leaned over and kissed the top of his wife's head. "Start down, Freda, start down," he implored her.

Just as she summoned all her will to do that, an enormous woman began climbing down alongside her. When the woman's bulk hit the net, Freda's side lifted upward and the mesh tightened so severely that she couldn't pull her foot or hand out to take another step. She hung in midair, like a fly in a spider's web, the ropes cutting into her bare feet and hands. And then she evidently fainted. The next thing Freda remembered, she was hanging on to the net by one foot, her head down. When the fat woman got off the net and into the lifeboat, the mesh on Freda's side opened up again. She lost her grip and crashed headlong into the boat. Most of the impact was absorbed by her left shoulder, but she cut her face when it grazed a piece of machinery.

When Gene Gladstone descended on the net, he realized how truly difficult this was. It took dexterity and luck, not merely the courage he had urged upon Freda.

Simply finding the holes in the mesh and placing barefoot toes into them presented a daunting maneuver. And then, when Gene's full body weight bore down, the nylon cords felt like hard wires as they cut into the flesh of his toes. The pain was unbearable. When Gene tried to support himself by his palms, the netting bruised and bloodied them. At one point he slipped and just managed to grab the net again with his hands, but his eyeglasses were knocked askew and dangled from one ear.

All the while, a man above Gene was kicking him in the face as he tried to find the openings for his bare toes. Gene became dizzy, but he heard voices from the lifeboat yelling, "Hurry! Hurry!" He let go and landed sideways in the boat, his head and chest hanging overboard. Two men pulled him in while two others reached for the next man coming off the net.

Gene found Freda semiconscious near the rear of the lifeboat, her face and hair bloodied, the Dior outfit she had worn for the night's dancing in the Belvedere Observation Lounge torn to shreds. Not a crewman or fellow survivor was paying the least attention to her. He pushed her matted hair away from her face and kissed her on the cheek. Then a French officer came over and handed Gene a glass of cognac. He forced Freda to take a sip.

But Freda was not alone in her pain. Most of the people who had come down the net were injured, and now it seemed the *Doria* would land atop them, the lifeboat nearly underneath the severely listing starboard side.

"Let's go! Let's go!" Gene shouted to the officer running the boat, and others echoed the plea. But the skipper remained calm, continuing to receive passengers until an empty lifeboat arrived to take his place.

Helen Edwards of Hempstead, on Long Island, and Theresa La-Flamme of New York City, both registered nurses, spent more than 3 hours tending to the elderly, women, and children on the *Doria*'s decks. Then came their own ordeal when they descended to a lifeboat.

Mrs. Edwards was three quarters of the way down a cargo net when she slipped and fell 10 feet, into the lap of a French sailor. Miss LaFlamme had gone only about a quarter way down when she, too, fell, landing in the bottom of the lifeboat. She was knocked out but quickly revived.

They both became seasick on the trip to the *Ile de France*. "All I want to do is lay down and die," Mrs. Edwards thought. Miss La-Flamme decided to take one last look at the *Doria*. "I wanted to remember the sight," she would say.

One passenger passed up the lifeboats. Sarkees Kapriclian, a twenty-two-year-old Syrian, shed his clothes and swam to the *Ile*. When he got there he realized that the clothing he had left on the *Doria*'s deck contained $500 in cash to help pay his tuition at Geneva College in Beaver Falls, Pennsylvania.

At about 2:00 A.M., Bernie and Cissie Aidinoff descended on a rope ladder to a lifeboat belonging to the *Doria*, and Bernie grasped one of the levers that would propel the boat to the *Ile*.

A woman from Baltimore whom the Aidinoffs had met during the trip was in the boat and the epitome of high fashion. She wore a mink cape and sported a large ring. "Did you lose very much?" Bernie asked, quickly adding, "I guess it doesn't make much difference, you're probably insured." The woman's face dropped. "The only things insured were this mink cape and ring," she said.

The Aidinoffs were more fortunate. Cissie had a cousin in the insurance business who had persuaded Bernie to buy a personal-effects floater for $2,000.

Pat and Arlene Mastrincola and their mother were also in a lifeboat bound for the *Ile*. "Thank God we're saved," Mrs. Mastrincola remarked to a French crewman. But he peered up at the *Doria* and replied: "Ma'am, if this thing goes over, we're done. We're not saved yet."

For some, rescue was not at hand even when it seemed they would be aboard the *Ile* within the hour. Just before the lifeboat carrying Fathers Wojcik, Dolciamore, and Lambert was to depart, word came from the bridge that a doctor and a machinist in the boat were needed back on the *Doria*, evidently to aid in efforts to free Martha Peterson and Jane Cianfarra from the debris trapping them in Cabin 56. The two men arose and climbed back to the *Doria*. Father Wojcik thought that the bravest thing he had ever seen.

CHAPTER 19

"Get Your Cameras"

On the bridge of the *Ile de France,* Captain Raoul De Beaudéan got on the loudspeaker, hoping to coordinate the movement of his lifeboats. But his voice could not carry far enough. He would have to rely on his coxswains to bring his boats back safely amid the traffic jam that included lifeboats from the *Stockholm* and other rescue ships carrying survivors to his liner.

At one point, the *Andrea Doria* drifted toward the *Ile,* and the French liner had to adjust its position. Adding to his concerns, De Beaudéan realized that his returning lifeboats might run into his propellers. He dispatched an officer to check and was relieved to hear "all clear around the port propeller."

Most of the *Ile*'s passengers slept through the rescue, carried out between 2:00 A.M. and about 5:00 A.M., but a few had stirred and could hardly believe what they saw.

Back on Wednesday morning, as tugs guided the *Ile* into the Hudson River, Doris Sinness, traveling with her husband, Lester, a DuPont executive, and their son, Skip, spotted the *Stockholm* making its way out of the harbor as well. She remarked on the beautiful bow of the Swedish liner, as sharp, it seemed, as a razor.

Mr. and Mrs. Sinness had played bridge the first evening out, then went to bed shortly after midnight. At 4:30 A.M., Lester Sinness awoke with a start. Sensing the engines were still, he placed his hand on the wall of his portside cabin and felt no vibration. He realized the ship was dead in the water.

Hearing muffled cries, he scrambled from bed and looked out the porthole. He saw that the previous evening's fog had lifted, the sea now bathed in moonlight. And then he spotted a lifeboat just 30 yards from the *Ile,* jammed with people wearing orange life jackets. An officer was shouting instructions in French from the deck and seemed to be motioning that lifeboat to go to the other side of the liner.

"My God, the ship's sinking, and they didn't wake us up," Sinness thought.

"Get out of bed, now!" he shouted to his wife and son.

But it barely took a moment to realize it was not the *Ile* that was foundering. Sinness saw another ocean liner, this one leaning so heavily it seemed about to capsize. And he spotted at least a dozen lifeboats heading to or departing from the liner.

When they went to an upper deck, the Sinness family found a miserable band of people sitting in chairs, many half dressed and covered in oil. Doris Sinness came upon a nun wandering in shock, agitated over losing her black veil. She took the nun to the family's cabin, quieted her, and heard a chilling story.

The nun told of a collision in the dead of night, of shimmying 20 feet down a 3-inch-wide rope she could barely grip. She was filled with rage for the crewmen of her ship. "What horrible men," she said. "What a terrible crew." And then she confided: "I hear that they do not live very godly lives."

When the *Ile* had abruptly turned to embark on its rescue dash late the previous night, Dr. Louis Linn, a New York psychiatrist, had been dancing with his wife, Miriam. Dr. Linn had staggered, to the great amusement of friends. "You've gotten drunk early in this trip," one of them remarked. The Linns had no idea what caused the stumble until they awakened to find a rescue effort in full swing. Now Dr. Linn embarked on a professional research project. He brought a pencil and pad on deck and interviewed fellow passengers from the *Ile* and survivors from the *Doria,* curious as to their emotional state.

One *Ile* passenger told of being roused in the middle of the night by the sounds of crewmen scurrying on deck and the dropping of lifeboats, then telling his wife, "It's only a drill." The man had investigated further upon his wife's insistence that drills do not take place at two o'clock in the morning.

Several passengers told Dr. Linn they thought the commotion was late-night partying. One man who had gone on deck said that the *Ile*'s brilliant spotlights shining on figures in orange life jackets aboard bobbing lifeboats reminded him of "a carnival in Venice." The shouts of anguish coming from the lifeboats seemed to this *Ile* passenger to have been laughter. The man had returned to bed, concluding that Frenchmen were carrying their *joie de vivre* a bit too far. One should not carouse so raucously in the middle of the night, he thought. He was about to drift off to sleep, but then it all became clear. Stunned by the enormity of what he had seen, the man jumped out of bed and got dressed.

Dr. Linn concluded that his fellow *Ile* passengers were subconsciously trying to relieve anxiety that would disturb their sleep and had therefore interpreted their impressions in a way that would justify their return to bed.

Andrew Heiskell, the publisher of *Life* magazine, was aboard the *Ile* on vacation with his wife, the actress, Madeleine Carroll, their daughter, and his mother-in-law. When the *Ile* halted at the collision scene, Heiskell awakened, drew the curtain of his cabin, and saw what he thought was a brightly lit toy ship lying on its side. And he spotted three well-lit swimming pools that had lost most of their water. How strange, he thought. Then the fog of sleep cleared. "O my God, it's a shipwreck," he realized.

Heiskell dressed quickly, then remembered that one of *Life*'s most accomplished photographers, Loomis Dean, also was on the *Ile*. Dean was traveling with his wife, Mary Sue, and their three children to his new assignment in Paris after having worked out of New York and Hollywood.

Heiskell phoned the purser's office to get Dean's cabin number, but no one answered. Then he heard people running through the corridors—stewards and crewmen rushing to prepare for survivors. He went to the purser's office, found the door unlocked, then rummaged through the desk until he found Dean's name on the passenger list. He ran to Dean's cabin, banged on the door, and shouted, "Loomis, there's been a wreck. Get up. Get up. Get your cameras."

Dean might have slept through the rescue if not for Heiskell's summons. But once alerted, he sprang into action, grabbing two cameras and rushing topside. He saw what at first seemed to be a huge rowboat tipped over on its side. Then he spotted another ship, this one with a battered bow, seemingly sawed in half.

Heiskell set out to interview *Doria* survivors as they were brought aboard, leaving Dean to reflect on how "it's pretty good to have the chairman of the board for your reporter."

Holding his cameras against the side of the *Ile* for his time exposures since he didn't have a tripod, Dean clicked away, taking long shots of the *Doria* and the bobbing lifeboats as well as close-ups of survivors helped onto the *Ile*. The following week, Dean's photograph of the listing *Andrea Doria,* lifeboats nearby, became one of his thirty-one cover photos in *Life*'s American edition during a quarter century with the magazine.

The listing *Andrea Doria* in its final hours as lifeboats headed for the *Ile de France*. (Loomis Dean/TimePix)

Ken Gouldthorpe, the assistant picture editor of the *St. Louis Post-Dispatch,* also transformed a leisurely ocean voyage on the *Ile* into a professional coup. Gouldthorpe, a British native who was headed to Europe for a leave of absence, had been chatting in a bar at about 1:00 A.M. with a fellow passenger from San Francisco. The men were playing a little game inspired by the fog. Each time the *Ile*'s foghorn went off, the glasses on the bar jumped. The object of their contest was to catch the glasses before they hit the table again. Then Gouldthorpe happened to glance out a window. What he saw stunned him: a gang of crewmen were uncovering the lifeboats.

He ran onto the deck, and speaking in French, asked a sailor what was happening.

"I don't really know," the crewman replied. "I think we're going to the aid of a ship that's sinking."

Gouldthorpe raced down to his cabin and got his Leica 3F and an old Rolleicord, a twin-lens reflex that produced 2-by-2-inch photos. He donned an old Burberry raincoat—anticipating a long and chilly night of work—stuffed the pockets with film, and grabbed a notebook. But he had not taken a telephoto lens or flash equipment with him when he boarded the *Ile.*

He paced the deck for an hour, waiting for the *Ile* to reach the *Doria,* not another passenger in sight. When the *Ile* finally drew close, a scene unfolded that would remain etched in his memory: the lights still shining on the stricken ship, the *Ile*'s searchlights playing on tossing lifeboats, and above the silence of the ocean, screams from the deck of an ocean liner slowing dying.

Gouldthorpe first used his Leica in the sparse available light, clicking away and keeping in mind the news photographer's axiom to keep shooting and worry about what you've got later. When the *Ile* paused at the top of each roll, he counted 1 . . . 2 . . . and then snapped the shutter, holding the camera against the rail and hoping he captured more than a blur. He tried to get aboard one of the *Ile*'s lifeboats for a trip to the *Doria*, but was chased away by the crew, then snapped survivors as they were pulled aboard, pushing his camera against his face and hoping he could keep it still.

At one point Andrew Heiskell encountered Gouldthorpe and remembered that he also was a part-time contributor to his magazine. "Hey, kid, you're shooting for *Life*, aren't you?" said Heiskell. "I certainly am," replied Gouldthorpe. His first responsibility was to the *Post-Dispatch*, but he knew that his newspaper would make his photos available to *Life* and the Associated Press.

As the *Andrea Doria* survivors began coming aboard, Heiskell asked if anyone had taken photographs in the hours after the collision. The *Life* executive spoke Italian, German, and French, and tried them all.

He found a boy of about sixteen who said he had seen a man taking pictures.

"Can you find him for me?" Heiskell asked.

When the boy didn't seem interested, Heiskell pulled out his wallet and told him "fifty dollars."

He still wasn't particularly excited.

"A hundred dollars," Heiskell said.

The boy set off to find the survivor with the camera.

An Austrian named Heinrich Schneider appeared, opened a belted jacket, and showed Heiskell his camera. He reported having taken about a dozen photos, the film still inside. After a bit of haggling, Heiskell got the camera by promising to pay Schneider $2,500.

As the *Ile*'s lifeboats collected survivors, Coast Guard aircraft joined the rescue operation, illuminating the scene. A pair of World War II–era patrol bombers built for the Navy but converted to search-and-rescue craft and a couple of seaplanes arrived from Floyd Bennett Field in Brooklyn. Lieutenant Commander R. P. Cunningham and his crew of

five orbited in a PBY bomber, dropping a hundred miniature para-
chutes carrying flares in 6-foot-by-3-foot canisters, each flare possess-
ing the illumination of 5 million candles. The plane flew at 5,000 feet,
its flares igniting 500 feet below the craft. They burned for 5 minutes,
going out before they hit the water. While that plane was overhead, the
other PBY and the seaplanes swooped low, hoping to alert the rescue
ships to any survivors in the water.

Paul Grimes, the aviation machinist's mate serving as Cunningham's assistant flight engineer helping the ordnance man toss the para-
chutes out, would recall the somber mood as his plane headed to the
scene. "We didn't know how many people had gotten off and how
many were still on the ship," he remembered. "We didn't have a lot to
say. You had a helpless feeling, wishing you could do more."

When the lifeboats arrived at the *Ile*, they stopped in front of a large
loading door just above the waterline. The injured were carried to the
door on stretchers, but most survivors climbed to it on rope ladders or
single ropes.

When Jerry Reinert's lifeboat reached the *Ile* after a 35-minute trip,
he climbed a few steps up a ladder, went through the hatchway, and
then faced what, to his dazed psyche, seemed like yet another crisis
when a man placed a sharp knife on his chest. "O my God," Reinert
thought. "I've survived this thing and now they're gonna kill me with a
knife?"

The knife-wielder was an *Ile* crewman cutting away soggy life jackets.

Bernie and Cissie Aidinoff had been taken to the *Ile* aboard a *Doria*
lifeboat that was run by the Italian liner's chief deck steward in cabin
class. When the Aidinoffs reached the *Ile,* they were helped aboard
by an earlier arrival, their dining-room captain. "I haven't tipped any
of these guys," Bernie realized. The Aidinoffs had planned to do that
Thursday morning.

The lifeboat carrying Gene and Freda Gladstone and many other
badly injured passengers who had fallen from cargo netting was taken
out of the line of boats and brought to the *Ile*'s stern. Ropes with hooks
lowered from an upper deck lifted the lifeboat topside, where medical
personnel were waiting.

The *Ile*'s purser staff had prepared well. Wheelchairs, stretchers,
and crutches were assembled inside the doorway through which most
of the survivors entered. As passengers stepped aboard, crewmen placed
heavy blankets over their shoulders. The ambulatory injured and some
women were directed to elevators, but most survivors walked up to the

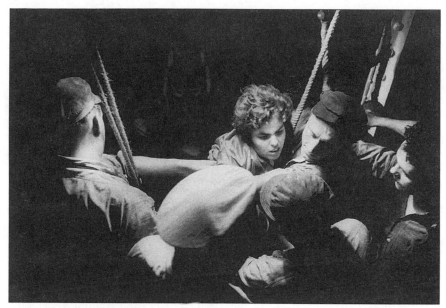

An *Andrea Doria* survivor is lifted aboard the *Ile de France*. (Loomis Dean/TimePix)

covered Promenade Deck, then were led to chairs that had been lined up. Stewards arrived with large cups of coffee and sandwiches. In the infirmary, doctors set fractures. Passengers in shock received special treatment. An Australian man gave his cabin to Walter Carlin, the elderly Brooklyn lawyer whose wife had been swept away.

Ken Gouldthorpe spotted Ruth Roman, who had arrived at the *Ile* not knowing where her three-year-old Dickie's lifeboat had taken him. The actress looked "utterly beautiful" despite her ordeal, Gouldthorpe thought. But he was moved by "the fear in her eyes."

"This was no longer some movie star reading her lines," he thought. "This was an ordinary woman who was very afraid and worried to death about her son."

CHAPTER 20

"Bulletin . . . Bulletin . . . Bulletin"

Newspapers on America's East Coast were going to press with their final editions when the first rumblings of a major sea disaster were felt.

All was quiet in the city room of the *New York Times* as the clock moved past midnight. Thursday's second edition closed in the composing room at 12:03 A.M., and in the alcove containing the wireless radio equipment, Barney Murphy, having sent out the *Times*'s Morse code nightly news summary for ships at sea, was doing what he did every night. He tuned to the 500-kilocycle shortwave ship-distress frequency, but with no great expectation of hearing anything urgent.

But this time Murphy's earphones caught a Morse code fragment: "Position 40.34 N, 69.45 W . . . but still undetermined our damage." That was from the *Stockholm*, signed off at 12:08 A.M.

Murphy, a former ship's radio operator, typed out the message and showed it to Tom Mullaney, the late-night news editor. Victor Lawn, a rewrite man, checked the latitude and longitude on charts in the ship-news office and traced the distress call to the waters near Nantucket, notorious for summer fog.

Murphy hurried from his listening post with another message, timed off at 12:21 A.M., again from the *Stockholm*: "Badly damaged. The whole bow crushed and No. 1 hold filled with water."

At 12:35 A.M., a third message arrived, from the *Andrea Doria*: "Please send lifeboats immediately."

Just about then, the Associated Press moved its first bulletin, the five bells signaling a dispatch of the highest urgency on teletype machines at newspaper and broadcast offices around the world.

Roused from sleep by the night editors, the *Times*'s managing editor, Turner Catledge, and the assistant to the publisher, Orville Dryfoos, hurried to the office, Catledge by cab from his apartment on

Manhattan's East Side, Dryfoos speeding from his home in Greenwich, Connecticut.

Forty-four years earlier, another managing editor of the *Times,* Carr Van Anda, had faced the formidable challenge of sifting elusive facts from rumors on deadline pressure in the face of an apparent disaster at sea.

It was 1:20 in the morning, Monday, April 15, 1912. The first-edition newspapers were coming off the presses underneath the *Times* Tower when a bulletin arrived in the eighteenth-floor wire room:

"CAPE RACE, Newfoundland, Sunday Night, April 14 (AP)—At 10:25 o'clock tonight, the White Star Line steamship *Titanic* called 'CQD' to the Marconi station here, and reported having struck an iceberg. The steamer said that immediate assistance was required."

Jack Paine, the *Times*'s acting night telegraph editor, rushed the bulletin to Van Anda, who ordered it placed on page one alongside a brief story on the *Titanic*'s departure from Southampton.

A half hour after the first distress call, the *Titanic*'s radio operator flashed an SOS, reporting the ship was going down by the head. After that, there was only silence from the great liner.

Editors at other newspapers in New York and London remained cautious through the night, emphasizing that the *Titanic* was unsinkable. But Van Anda was convinced there could be just one explanation for the radio silence: the *Titanic* was indeed sinking, was perhaps already on the bottom of the North Atlantic. Puffing on a large cigar, Van Anda moved through the city room, ordering a host of sidebar stories, placing a two-column photo of the *Titanic* on the front page, and overseeing the main story for the last edition, sent to press at 3:30 A.M., stating flatly that the *Titanic* had sunk. It was a *tour de force* for the *Times.*

Now Catledge was the editor facing the pressure, giving the directives. The *Times*'s picture desk found file photos of the *Andrea Doria* and the *Stockholm,* and the art department prepared a map pinpointing the collision site. The door to the locked ship-news department was broken open, the *Doria* brochures pulled out. They boasted of the ship's eleven watertight compartments and the double bottom, assuring stability "in the event of collision."

The *Times*'s top metropolitan reporters, Meyer (Mike) Berger, Peter Kihss, and Milton Bracker, were awakened, and upon arriving at the office were handed $200 apiece in travel expenses. They were sent to LaGuardia Airport, and at 3:45 A.M. they boarded an American Airlines Convair chartered by Catledge for a flight to Boston, where rescue ships were presumed likely to arrive.

The presses in the *Times*'s basement were shut down, only 31,000 copies of the late edition, with no news of the collision, having been run off. Some 15,000 copies were destroyed; only papers earmarked to meet train and plane schedules left the building.

At 2:34 A.M., a "postscript" edition rolled off the presses, and two more editions hit the streets by dawn. The final postscript went on the presses at 7:33, carrying a front-page "ear" reading "7:30 A.M. Extra."

At 8:29 A.M., Larry Heyer, the assistant press room foreman, flagged the presses to a final stop. A total of 740,000 papers had been printed, 540,000 of them with a fragmentary but exceedingly dramatic account of a developing disaster.

The lead article had been assigned to Max Frankel, a twenty-five-year-old late-night rewriteman recently returned from 2 years' Army service. Frankel wrote a few paragraphs for a "box" on page one in the delayed late edition, then built a vivid account that was reworked seven times, drawing largely on Barney Murphy's monitored radio messages. Since returning from military duty, Frankel had received perhaps half a dozen bylines. But now a rewriteman's byline appeared on page one, a rarity for the *Times*.

The eight-column headline proclaimed "all saved," based on a radio message from the *Ile de France*'s Captain De Beaudéan at 4:58 A.M. stating "all passengers rescued."

The *Times*'s city editor, Frank Adams, having reached the office at 4:00 A.M., typed up a preliminary list of reporters' assignments for Friday's paper before heading back to his home in Rye, New York, at about eight o'clock, for a few hours' rest. There were twenty-five assignments and the notation: "Every effort is being made to reach Cianfarra by phone or wireless."

For the *Times*'s editors, good fortune surely beckoned. They knew that Camille Cianfarra, their Madrid correspondent, was aboard the *Doria* with his wife and two daughters, and they anticipated a superb eyewitness account. Adams put in a telephone call for Cianfarra to the *Ile de France* at 5:00 A.M., hoping he was among the survivors taken to the French liner. But there was no response from the correspondent. The editors presumed he was aboard one of the other rescue ships, since it seemed that everyone from the *Doria* had been saved.

A high-profile journalist in broadcast news also was hoping to reach Cianfarra in the predawn hours, but for reasons far removed from deadline pressure.

Edward P. Morgan was the nightly anchor and commentator for the 15-minute ABC Radio evening news. The coming months promised to be a fulfilling time for Morgan, on both a professional and a personal level. Soon he would be off to report on the presidential campaign—first the Democratic National Convention in Chicago, where Adlai Stevenson was likely to launch a second bid for the presidency, and then the Republicans' convention in San Francisco, where Dwight D. Eisenhower would be nominated for a second term. Before that, there would be time away from the pressures of national political reporting, an opportunity for Morgan to renew bonds with his daughter, Linda, from his marriage to his former wife, Jane, now the wife of Camille Cianfarra.

Morgan would be taking fourteen-year-old Linda for a week's vacation on Martha's Vineyard and Nantucket, seeing her for the first time since the previous summer, when they had taken a two-week auto trip through Virginia.

On Wednesday evening, Morgan flew to New York from Washington, telling his colleagues he planned to meet Linda when she came down the ramp of the *Andrea Doria* the following morning.

At 5:00 A.M., the phone rang in Morgan's hotel room. It was Francis Littlejohn, the director of news at ABC. "We didn't want to wake you before, because everything was so confused," Littlejohn told Morgan in his North Carolina tones, "but it's all right now. The *Andrea Doria* and the *Stockholm* have collided off Nantucket in a fog, and the *Doria* is in a bad way, but the *Ile do France* has just radioed that everybody has been rescued. Nobody has been lost. I'll call you back if I get anything more."

In the blur of the moment, Morgan thought he was dreaming. Nothing made sense. Surely ocean liners equipped with radar wouldn't collide. And if they did, could there be no casualties?

Morgan phoned the *New York Times* to see if Camille Cianfarra had provided the paper with a first-hand report. He had not, but Morgan was assured he surely would before long. The editors promised to call as soon as they heard from him.

Despite the reassurance offered by his boss at ABC, Morgan grew increasingly uneasy. He called the Associated Press and United Press. The news agencies, too, were trying to reach the *Ile* and promised to phone Morgan as soon as they received news of the Cianfarra family. Morgan tried to phone the *Ile* himself but couldn't get through. He left for his offices at ABC to try again.

In Brooklyn's Sheepshead Bay section, Carmelo Grillo had gone to bed at about ten o'clock Wednesday night, planning to be up at 5:00 A.M. to meet the *Andrea Doria,* combining the obligations of his job with the joy of a family reunion.

While working as an officer on the Italian Line's *Conte Biancamano* after graduating from nautical college in Italy, Grillo had met an American-born passenger named Angela who happened to be celebrating her twenty-third birthday the very day he first saw her—April 28, 1950. A romance blossomed, and they married, settled in Brooklyn, and had a son. Now Grillo was an assistant manager for the Italian Line, helping handle passenger arrivals in New York.

He would be driving Thursday morning to Battery Park in Lower Manhattan to board a Coast Guard cutter that would meet the *Andrea Doria* as she entered the harbor. This time he would not simply be attending to his duties with the Italian Line, for Angela and their three-year-old son, Anthony, were returning on the *Doria* from a visit with family in Italy.

At 1:00 A.M., the phone rang. It was Irma Colombin, the secretary to Giuseppe Ali, the Italian Line's general manager in the United States. She was supposed to tell Grillo to report to the office immediately.

Colombin thought that Grillo had been advised of the collision, but realizing in the first seconds of their conversation that he was unaware of what happened, and knowing that his wife and son were aboard the *Doria,* she became unnerved. The secretary told Grillo she meant to phone someone else, apologized, and hung up.

Fifteen minutes later, the phone rang again. It was a man named Costa, whom Grillo assisted several times a week in meeting incoming ships. This time there was no avoidance of terrible news. The official told Grillo about the collision and asked that he meet him in the line's offices at 24 State Street in Lower Manhattan.

Grillo turned on the radio above his kitchen stove to hear the latest bulletins, then sped off in his new Ford Victoria. He was doing 80 miles an hour on the Belt Parkway along Brooklyn's south shore when a police officer pulled him over with a most unwelcome cliché.

"Where's the fire?" the policeman asked.

"There's no fire," Grillo replied, pulling out his credentials. "I work for the Italian Line. I just had a call from the office to report there. Two ships collided and I have a wife and son on board."

"I'm going in front of you," the policeman said, providing a one-car escort for Grillo to the Brooklyn Battery Tunnel.

Another speeder along the Belt Parkway drew a less sympathetic response from a police officer. Chief journalist Mel Abbott, a Coast Guardsman headed for the search and rescue headquarters on Manhattan's Lafayette Street from his Brooklyn home, was stopped at 1:30 A.M. while doing 70 miles an hour. He explained his haste, but the officer spent 10 minutes shuttling between his car and Abbott's, then wrote out a summons.

When Grillo arrived at the Italian Line's offices at 2:30 A.M., newspaper reporters were camped outside, but no one else from the line had come in. Grillo said nothing to the reporters—he didn't know whether his own family was alive, much less have word on the *Doria*'s fate— and unlocked the door.

A teletype message arrived from Captain Carlo Fava, the manager of the Italian Line's New England office. It relayed a report from the Coast Guard that it had been asked by Captain Calamai to provide tugboats to tow the *Doria* to shallower waters, where it might be beached. From what little information he had, Grillo doubted the cutters would arrive in time to save the ship.

Looking for some way to keep busy, to keep fears for the safety of his wife and child from overwhelming him, Grillo made photocopies of a passenger list received from the home office in Genoa, a useful enough task for want of anything else he could do. As dawn arrived, the office was filling up, twenty Italian Line employees fielding phone calls from passengers' families.

The phone rang as well in the middle of the night for Lena Alfano, a homemaker in White Plains, New York.

Almost two months earlier, Lena's husband, Charles, a barber, had left New York on the *Doria,* accompanying his parents on a visit to his mother's birthplace, the Sicilian village of Cattolica Eraclea. When the ship left the pier, Lena Alfano had become teary. She feared that something terrible might happen to Charles, leaving her with four children to raise. But the rest of the Alfano family simply laughed.

"Nothing happens on ocean liners," she was assured.

Charles Alfano was returning on the *Doria* alone, his mother wanting to spend more time with her four brothers and four sisters. He was traveling in tourist class, his cabin next to that of a father and his young daughter. The little girl always wore a beautiful cross on her neck, Alfano noticed, and she was invariably holding an orange. He presumed she had come from a poor village in Italy where fresh fruits were a luxury.

The man and his daughter had gone to sleep early on Wednesday night. Alfano was preparing for bed as well, but his roommate persuaded him to partake in a final round of partying. "Let's go up on deck, we'll have a good time—it's the last night," the roommate said.

The two men went to the tourist-class lounge to see the impromptu musical show. When the *Doria* rocked, Alfano was momentarily blinded by the *Stockholm*'s lights, then thrown to the floor. It seemed that as many as thirty passengers had fallen atop him, but he scrambled to his feet. He tried to return to his cabin for a life jacket, but the corridor was blocked with passengers fleeing for the upper decks. So that's where he went, too.

At just about that time, Lena Alfano, back at their home in New York City's Westchester suburbs, was about to make a second attempt at getting to sleep.

She had gone to bed early, planning to be up at dawn for the car ride to mid-Manhattan to meet the *Doria*, but sleep would not come. She turned on the television, hoping it would bore her enough to surmount the nervous energy occasioned by the anticipated family reunion. After an hour of TV, Lena Alfano had indeed become drowsy and reached for the dial to turn the set off. Just then a crawler moved across the screen: "Bulletin . . . Bulletin . . . Bulletin."

When she heard the news flash, her heart began to pound. She thought it was going to jump out of her chest. She turned on the radio, hoping for some word on survivors, but it was too early to know. Before she could decide whether to wake the children—Connie, seventeen, Nicky, sixteen, Sal, nine, and Bunny, eighteen months old—the phone began to ring. The first callers were her brothers-in-law, Al and Frank Alfano, White Plains firemen, relaying what they, too, had heard. Then came a call from friends who worked at an all-night bakery. After that, the Alfano cousins began phoning.

Lena Alfano was no longer drowsy.

On Booth Street in the Forest Hills section of Queens, Elizabeth Boyd was alone at home, her husband, Joseph, the captain of the freighter *Cape Ann*, at sea, and their eleven-year-old daughter, Vickie, at summer camp. Mrs. Boyd was taking an early-morning shower when she caught a brief mention of the *Cape Ann* on the radio. She assumed the freighter had been in an accident and she thought back to June 1942, when her husband's ship had escaped an attack by a German submarine while on North Atlantic convoy duty.

At 7:00 A.M., a reporter for the *Long Island Press,* a daily newspaper based in Queens, phoned the home. Mrs. Boyd learned that her husband and his crewmen were not victims. They were, in fact, saviors, in the vanguard of a massive rescue effort.

Dawn was about to break in Italy when the first bulletins arrived. In Genoa, Piero Calamai's wife, doing her morning shopping, saw a banner newspaper headline in an extra edition at a newsstand. She rushed home to find a group of neighbors at her door. Such was her turmoil that she barely noticed them. Her older daughter, Maina, eighteen, was traveling to London that morning, but fifteen-year-old Silvia was at home and sought to comfort her mother.

Straining to keep her emotions in check and having no idea of her husband's fate, Mrs. Calamai broke the news of the collision to her mother-in-law, telling what she would recall as "a white lie"—Piero was safe. In what she would term "hours of torture," she listened through the day to the radio bulletins, placed phone calls to the Italian Line, and prayed for her husband and his passengers and crew.

"I knew my husband's temperament and his dedication to the Navy code of honor," she told a reporter for the International News Service on Thursday. "I knew he would go down into the sea with his ship unless he were ordered to leave it by someone higher up. I mentally went down with him a hundred times."

CHAPTER 21

"You May Go, I'm Staying"

The scintillating arrival of the *Ile de France* and the parting of the fog had turned the tide. By 2:30 A.M. it appeared that all of the *Andrea Doria*'s passengers who had survived the collision would surely be saved.

Now Captain Calamai and his senior officers turned their full attention to the fate of their ship.

Operating on emergency power, the *Doria* had only a limited reach for its radio messages, forcing it to rely on the *Stockholm* or the other ships nearby to send these messages to shore. At 2:38 A.M. the *Doria* asked the *Stockholm* to relay a request to the Coast Guard for tugboats, Captain Calamai still hoping his listing liner could be towed before it capsized.

The *Private William H. Thomas* responded to the message sent to the *Stockholm*, saying it had been designated as the connection with the Coast Guard and would pass on the *Doria*'s request. At 3:08 the *Thomas* relayed a reply from the Coast Guard stating that the cutter *Evergreen*, which would arrive in 4 to 5 hours, and other cutters en route would be equipped with towing hooks.

In the *Doria*'s engine rooms, conditions were spinning out of control.

The portside turbodynamo had stopped functioning, deprived of cooling from its circulation pump. That pump had overheated because the *Doria*'s sea intake valves on the high side, having risen out of the ocean, could no longer suck in water to cool it. And the seawater continued to rise on the starboard side of the engine rooms.

All electrical power was lost except for the 250 kilowatts supplied by the battery-powered emergency generator on A Deck, which kept the ship's lights functioning. With the progressive loss of electrical power, the boilers had to be shut down, since it became impossible to pump water to cool them.

At 2:45 A.M., with the *Doria*'s list at 33 degrees and the crewmen in the bowels of the ship exhausted, unable to keep their footing, and blinded by steam, the engine rooms were abandoned.

Fifteen minutes later, Captain Calamai approached Guido Badano, his second officer junior, on the starboard wing, with an ominous message: "If you are saved, maybe you can reach Genoa and see my family. Tell them I did everything I could."

Calamai had evidently decided to go down with his ship.

The *Stockholm*, its rescue role largely over by 2:00 A.M., remained immobile. Its anchor chains were still entangled on the ocean floor. At 2:30 A.M. Captain Nordenson asked the *Ile de France* if she could accompany him to New York as a precaution once he was able to get under way. But Captain De Beaudéan, having already fallen far behind schedule and carrying many severely injured survivors, was in no mood for a slow trip back to the city. He told the *Stockholm* that another ship would have to keep her company when she limped back to her Hudson River berth, perhaps at no better than 5 or 6 knots.

"Will proceed New York full speed when all are rescued," De Beaudéan told Nordenson. "Please ask another ship. My schedule is imperative."

Upon reading his message later, the *Ile*'s captain was remorseful over the tone. His response seemed callous, something he would attribute to the fatigue of the moment and his awkwardness in English.

Even if he had been able to free his ship from the ocean floor, Captain Nordenson was hardly ready to leave. He had five grievously injured persons aboard—four crewmen who had been trapped in the wreckage of his bow and four-year-old Norma Di Sandro, knocked unconscious when her father threw her into a *Stockholm* lifeboat before its crewmen could spread a blanket to catch her. At 3:50 A.M. Nordenson radioed the Coast Guard in Boston, requesting evacuation helicopters.

At 4:00 A.M.—just before Martha Peterson died in the wreckage of Cabin 56—the *Doria*'s staff captain and second in command, Osvaldo Magagnini, advised Captain Calamai that no passengers remained on the decks. Calamai told the remaining crewmen they could abandon ship, but asked for volunteers to stay on board until the Coast Guard tugboats arrived.

Most of the stewards and waiters had long since left, fleeing in lifeboats without permission, or manning the levers propelling those boats. The crew members remaining with Calamai were the true seamen.

About twenty stayed on board, the others lingering in lifeboats alongside the liner.

After receiving the report from Magagnini, Calamai dictated a message for the Italian Line offices in Genoa and New York: "Run down in mist by Swedish ship. Passengers transferred to rescue ships. Vessel in danger." He handed it to Guido Badano, who added "*Stockholm*" after the words "Swedish ship" and took it to the wireless station. But with the *Doria*'s electrical power nearly gone, she would have to rely on the *Stockholm* to relay a message that clearly blamed the Swedish ship for the collision unless one of the other rescue vessels passed the message on.

As five o'clock neared, twelve officers remained on the *Doria*. Magagnini reported that all accessible cabins had been searched, that the crew had evidently reached everyone who could be saved, and that it was time to abandon ship. "There is nothing more to be done," he told Calamai.

The captain was determined to stay on board at least until the Coast Guard tugs arrived, although they were three or four hours away, but Magagnini pointed out they could all wait for the tugs in a lifeboat.

"You may go," Calamai told Magagnini, "I'm staying."

"If you stay, we will stay with you," Magagnini said.

At that, Calamai seemed ready to depart. As dawn approached, the senior officers climbed down the Jacob's ladder to lifeboat No. 11, leaving in reverse order of rank. But when Magagnini reached the lifeboat and looked up, he saw Calamai leaning against the deck rail, making no move to leave a ship that was listing 40 degrees.

"Come down," Magagnini pleaded.

"I remain," Calamai insisted.

Magagnini told his captain that if he didn't come down, his officers would return to the *Doria*. When Magagnini began to climb back up the ladder, Calamai finally relented. Magagnini went back down, followed by the captain, and they took seats in their lifeboat. It was 5:30 in the morning.

What the captain and his senior officers did not know was that at least one passenger who was very much alive had been overlooked.

A thirty-five-year-old merchant seaman from New Orleans named Robert Lee Hudson had been taken aboard the *Doria* at Gibraltar with back injuries and a severe gash on his right hand incurred in accidents on a freighter named *Ocean Victory*. He spent most of the trip in the *Doria*'s hospital but had gone to bed early Wednesday evening in his A Deck cabin, portside amidships, with the aid of a painkiller. It worked so well that he slept through the collision and the chaos it spawned.

When Hudson awoke, he found, to his bewilderment, that he was not in his bed but sprawled against his cabin wall on a ship that was tilting. Clad only in undershorts, he crawled into a deserted hallway flooded with water and oil.

"Is anyone there?" Hudson shouted. No one answered. The remaining *Doria* officers, high on the ship, could not hear him, and all the other passengers had gone.

How his plight had come to pass, Hudson had no clue, but he knew he was stranded on a deserted ship that was about to sink. He had little idea of the *Doria*'s layout, his injuries having confined him to bed for most of the trip, but he ventured toward the stern, then made his way, slowly and painfully, to the Upper Deck. Still, there was not a person to be found. He could see rescue ships out there and a few lifeboats still in the water, their spotlights shining. But no one saw him.

And then a wave swept him overboard. He thrashed in the water, on the brink of drowning, but managed to clutch on to a swimming pool netting that had been hung over the side for passengers to descend into lifeboats. Virtually naked, his shorts hanging by a thread, freezing, and in intense pain from his injuries, Hudson began to scream, cursing the lifeboats oblivious to his plight.

The last rescue ship to arrive, the tanker *Robert E. Hopkins,* had stopped a half mile from the *Doria* and had launched one of its four lifeboats, rowed by ten crewmen with space for seventy-five people.

It was this boat that finally spotted Hudson while some 300 yards from the *Doria.* Rowing furiously, the crewmen reached the netting, and the boat's chief mate, Eugene Swift, snatched the seaman to safety— at just about the time the *Doria*'s senior officers were abandoning ship.

Wrapped in a blanket, Hudson was taken to the tanker and placed in the care of the radio operator, Ray Maurstad. "Sparks, I want you to take charge of that man and see that he gets clothing and a good night's rest," Captain René Blanc ordered.

Supported by two crewmen, Hudson was taken first to the radio room. Maurstad asked him if he wanted to lie down. He said he didn't, then sat in the radio operator's chair. He seemed to want to relate what he had gone through, but at times he was reduced to mumbling, weary from the ordeal.

"Do you have a drink?" Hudson asked.

"Do you mean whiskey?" asked Maurstad.

"Yeah."

Maurstad had a bottle stashed away, opened it, and set a water glass down. Hudson was shaking so severely that he couldn't hold it, so

Maurstad poured the whiskey an inch high. Hudson reached up and held Maurstad's hand until the glass was full. Then he drank it dry and passed out.

Maurstad didn't want to chance taking Hudson up a stairwell to the infirmary, fearing he would fall. So he brought him to his quarters, almost dragging the seaman. Maurstad placed Hudson under the sheets and covers and got out a clean khaki shirt and trousers, socks, and underwear for when he awoke.

Robert Lee Hudson was taken to New York later that day, the only *Andrea Doria* passenger the tanker *Robert E. Hopkins* had saved.

CHAPTER 22

"Seaworthiness Nil"

In an exceedingly efficient operation bolstered by the fog blowing away, the *Ile de France* picked up 576 passengers and 177 crewmen from the *Andrea Doria*, most of them arriving by 4:00 A.M. The *Stockholm* had saved 308 passengers and 234 crewmen before leaving the completion of the rescue to the *Ile*.

The military transport *Private William H. Thomas*, in charge of the rescue operation pending the arrival of the Coast Guard, gave the *Cape Ann* permission to depart shortly after 5:00 A.M. The freighter left for New York with 91 *Doria* passengers and 38 crewmen.

Captain De Beaudéan of the *Ile* was hoping to salvage something from his tattered schedule. He had wired Captain Calamai at 3:55 A.M., asking whether he had any passengers left to evacuate and whether he and his senior officers intended to remain on board, saying he wished to return to New York at full speed as soon as Calamai released him. Calamai had replied 20 minutes later, telling De Beaudéan that it the *Thomas* remained in the area until Coast Guard ships arrived, the *Ile* could depart.

When the *Thomas*, having taken aboard 112 passengers and 46 crewmen, radioed that she would remain at the scene, the *Ile* began collecting its lifeboats. In the process, one of the *Ile* crewmen received an unexpected bonus.

The director of the French Line, Jean Marie, who happened to be aboard the *Ile,* went back to his cabin as the last returning lifeboat was being hoisted on its davits. When Marie noticed a lifeboat sailor outside his porthole, he grabbed a bottle of whiskey left on his dresser the previous night by a visitor as a farewell gift and offered it.

When the sailor went on deck, the bottle in his belt, he encountered De Beaudéan's second in command.

"Where did you swipe that?" the officer asked.

"I didn't swipe it," the sailor protested.

"Come now, did it fall from the skies?"

"Some jerk handed it to me through his porthole."

That bit of comic relief aside, a moment of high solemnity transpired as the *Ile* prepared to depart at 6:00 A.M., a half hour after Captain Calamai and the last of the *Doria* crew entered their lifeboat, No. 11, to await the Coast Guard and, they hoped, a towing line.

The survivors and the *Ile*'s passengers and crew jammed the rails of the French liner. Some 1,000 feet away, the *Doria* seemed near its end. Gene Gladstone, the ordeal on the cargo netting behind him, thanked God for sparing him and his wife, Freda. But the Canadian real estate man was consumed by guilt as he watched the *Doria*'s death throes. When he had fled up the stairs of the *Doria* with Freda after returning to their cabins from the Belvedere Lounge to retrieve their life jackets, he heard muffled cries from an elevator stuck between decks. He planned to notify crewmen that passengers were trapped, but in the excitement he never did. "Were they still there, trapped beneath the sea in a cage-tomb?" he wondered. With tears in his eyes, he turned his gaze from the *Doria*.

Captain De Beaudéan faced one final task before departing. He wired Captain Nordenson, asking if he had found an escort to New York. Nordenson replied that two Coast Guard cutters would accompany him.

De Beaudéan now directed the *Ile*'s helmsman to circle the *Doria* three times. Each time, the *Ile* dipped the Tricolor and sounded her siren in tribute. At 6:05 A.M., her farewell completed, the *Ile de France* headed back to New York.

In the *Doria*'s lifeboat No. 11, Captain Calamai sat up front with Staff Captain Magagnini, the two dozen or so Italian crewmen with them keeping their distance, an Aldis searchlight and a megaphone beside them. Guido Badano, the second officer junior, sat at the rudder tiller. The other two *Doria* lifeboats still astride the liner marked time as well, awaiting the Coast Guard. Each of those boats carried twenty to thirty crewmen—exhausted, soaked, and dispirited.

On the *Stockholm,* Captain Nordenson was waiting for the helicopters he had requested to evacuate four severely injured *Stockholm* crewmen and the unconscious *Doria* survivor, four-year-old Norma Di Sandro, her identity still unknown.

At Otis Air Force Base in Falmouth on Cape Cod, Lieutenant Claude G. Hess was in his eighth month of wondering whether his training in search-and-rescue operations would ever be put to use.

The twenty-six-year-old helicopter pilot from El Dorado, Kansas, had spent a year commanding an H-19 'copter search-and-rescue unit based at Keflavik, Iceland, but he never had a rescue mission. His only operation since being transferred to Otis had been an exceedingly tame affair. When an elderly man, evidently senile, had not turned up for two or three days after wandering from his home on Cape Cod, Lieutenant Hess's helicopter was summoned. He spotted the man lying in bramble bushes, invisible to ground searchers, and alerted the police. The man died a month or so later, but his daughter had sent Hess a thank-you note.

Since the previous December, Hess had been assigned to a helicopter unit servicing the Texas Tower platform 100 miles off Cape Cod. The platform served as an outpost of America's Air Defense Command, a Cold War lookout for Soviet bombers. But Hess was determined to be prepared for any search-and-rescue operation that might come his way and had conducted voluntary drills with his men, their goal to be ready to move within 15 minutes by day, 30 minutes by night.

When Captain Nordenson asked for evacuation helicopters, all that scrambling practice proved to no avail. Hess and his two crewmen were awakened, but had to wait an hour or so for the fog to lift. At first light, they finally set off for Nantucket Island, where they picked up an Air Force doctor, Captain Edward Murray, and a medic from Nantucket Cottage Hospital. The 'copter, a twin-rotor II-21 from the 33rd Air Force Hospital, normally seated twenty-two, but it held six to eight litters now, its capacity when carrying flotation gear.

Hess's helicopter linked up at Nantucket with a Coast Guard helicopter from Salem Air Station in Massachusetts. The Air Force 'copter was 20 miles an hour faster than the Coast Guard 'copter and had more lifting capacity. So the Coast Guard 'copter departed first. The Air Force would pick up whatever victims the Coast Guard couldn't rescue.

Hess circled the collision scene at 7:30 A.M., evaluating his chances of landing on the *Stockholm*. Peering down at the *Andrea Doria*, intent on taking personal photos, he was struck by how strange the great liner looked, almost turned over, deserted, its swimming pools empty.

Hess was worried by the presence of small planes carrying reporters and photographers over the *Doria*, fearing a collision with his helicopter, but he would not have a close call. His overriding problem was the *Stockholm*'s fantail, where he wanted to land. It was too small and had too many obstacles to accommodate either the Air Force or the Coast Guard helicopter. They would have to lower baskets and stretchers to hoist the injured. But the breeze, which Hess estimated at 10 to 15 knots, was adequate to allow hovering.

A small, yellow Coast Guard helicopter, piloted by Airman James W. Kieffer of Ipswich, Massachusetts, hovered first. The hoist operator,

Aviation Technician John Fachko, dropped a basket on a line perhaps 50 feet long and lifted up Norma Di Sandro, her eyes puffed and closed. The *Stockholm*'s physician, Dr. Ake Nissling, had attached a tag of brown wrapping paper affixed to a blanket covering the four-year-old's white woolen jersey. It read: "Italian child born, is recommended treatment at nearest surgical clinic. Consequence of fractured cranium. Remarks: Collision between motor ship *Stockholm* and *Andrea Doria*."

Fachko lowered a stretcher that picked up Alf Johansson, Bill Johnson's cabinmate. Johansson had been alert for a time, but had lapsed into a coma. He was given intravenous solutions to restore his blood volume as the helicopter flew to Nantucket.

Ten minutes later, the Air Force helicopter began hovering. Technical Sergeant Vernon Gleason dropped stretchers attached to a 25-foot line and hoisted the other injured *Stockholm* crewmen, Wilhelm Gustavsson, forty-eight, who had lost his left eye and had suffered fractures of the collarbone, right elbow, and upper-right leg; Arne Smedberg, thirty-six, with a broken lower-left leg; and Lars Falk, twenty, who had suffered a broken neck.

When the Air Force helicopter arrived at Memorial Airport on Nantucket, photographers crowded around the injured as they were transferred on stretchers to ambulances taking them to Nantucket Cottage Hospital. Hess regarded the placement of a camera 2 feet from the anguished face of a grievously injured person unseemly, and so he left the 'copter without speaking to the reporters.

Commander Thomas Dixon, a Coast Guard doctor, met the four *Stockholm* seamen and Norma Di Sandro at the airport. But help had arrived too late for Alf Johansson. Suffering from a fractured skull and leg injuries, he died within minutes of reaching the island.

After emergency treatment at the Nantucket hospital, the other survivors were driven back to the airport, flown by a Coast Guard Albatross Amphibian plane to Boston's Logan International Airport and then transferred by ambulances to the U.S. Public Health Service's Brighton Marine Hospital in Boston.

The *Stockholm* seaman Arne Smedberg told of his ordeal from his hospital bed. "It was like a streak of lightning out of a clear sky," he said. "I was in my cabin and I fell asleep. The next thing I knew, everything seemed to cave in. Things were falling all over us."

At the collision scene, the *Private William H. Thomas* sent a message to the Coast Guard at 7:40 A.M.: "No communication with the *Andrea Doria*. Has 45-degree starboard list. Large gash below starboard bridge wing. List increasing. Seaworthiness nil. Last report captain and 11 crew still on board. No passengers."

The *Thomas* did not know that Captain Calamai and his senior officers had finally abandoned ship. It had not spotted them waiting for the Coast Guard together with some sixty other seamen in three lifeboats alongside their dying liner.

After aborting their training cruise, the Navy destroyer escorts *Edward H. Allen* and *Heyliger* had arrived as dawn was breaking. To Seaman Joseph Coviello, an eighteen-year-old reservist on the *Allen* from Port Chester, New York, the *Doria*'s lights looked like a string of pearls in the mist. The *Allen* stood about a half mile off and sent an 18-foot motorized boat with half a dozen crewmen to the *Doria* to find out what assistance it needed. But that proved to be a misadventure; the boat's propeller became entangled in a line hanging from the *Doria* and another boat had to free it and tow it back to the *Allen*. Learning that the *Doria*'s passengers had been removed, the *Allen*'s skipper, Lieutenant Commander Boyd H. Hempen, allowed the *Heyliger* to continue on to New York. The *Doria* asked the *Allen* for pumps, but she didn't have any large enough to handle the awesome task of pumping out the tons of seawater still pouring in through the shattered starboard hull. The *Allen* invited Captain Calamai to come on board, but he declined, hoping the Coast Guard would soon arrive with its towing equipment.

The Coast Guard buoy tender *Hornbeam* encountered spotty fog, with occasional heavy patches, en route from Woods Hole, Massachusetts, and had been plagued by the periodic overheating of an engine. Each time the engine balked, the cutter had slowed from its maximum of 14.5 knots to about 13 knots. But it arrived at about 8:00 A.M.

The *Stockholm* came into view first, the site of its smashed bow horrifying the *Hornbeam*'s acting executive officer, Ensign Robert Boggs. Then the *Hornbeam* passed along the port side of the *Doria,* its eight high-side lifeboats still attached, one screw out of the water, ropes hanging from the fantail. The cutter moved next to the starboard side, where it came upon Captain Calamai and his senior crewmen in their lifeboat, a quarter mile to a half mile from their ship. Coast Guardsmen boarded the boat, tied it to the *Hornbeam,* and Calamai and his men climbed aboard. Some 30 or so crewmen on lifeboat No. 5 also came onto the *Hornbeam,* while 30 others from the third Doria lifeboat transferred to the *Allen.*

One of the *Hornbeam* bosun's mates, Joseph De Chane, heard Captain Calamai plead: "Coast Guard, save my ship," and De Chane thought he saw tears in Calamai's eyes. The captain was utterly defeated and forlorn. He still wore his jaunty blue beret, but a white stubble of beard lined his face. He had seemingly aged overnight.

Calamai and his senior officers climbed to the *Hornbeam*'s bridge to confer with its skipper, Lieutenant Roger Erdmann. Calamai was hoping to get a tow, and Erdmann was willing enough. He sent Elmer Lee, his warrant bosun, to the buoy deck to round up volunteers to go aboard the *Doria* to handle the towing lines.

Erdmann phoned the cutter *Evergreen,* which had arrived by then and had been placed in charge of communications with Coast Guard headquarters in Boston as the on-site commander. He asked the *Evergreen*'s skipper, Lieutenant Commander L. F. Lovell, the ranking Coast Guardsman on the scene, to relay Calamai's request.

Notwithstanding Calamai's visions of the Coast Guard saving his ship, the Italian Line had been busy with alternate towing arrangements. Even while passengers were being rescued, it had contacted Moran Towing, which had two large tugs ready to go, one at the Battery in Lower Manhattan and the other at Port Jefferson, Long Island. If the *Doria* could be towed to Davis South Shoal, 22 miles northwest of the collision scene, where the waters were only 38 feet deep, or Asia Rip, 28 miles to the northeast, where the ocean depth was less than 50 feet, the liner's superstructure could remain far enough out of the water for salvage efforts to proceed.

At 9:20 A.M., the *Evergreen* advised the Coast Guard in Boston of Calamai's towing request, but the cutter also relayed a grim report.

"Master SS *Andrea Doria* has requested *Hornbeam* attempt to tow *Doria*. *Doria* listing badly to starboard. Main deck line at water's edge."

At 9:45 A.M. the *Evergreen* sent a message to the Coast Guard command in New York. Now, said the cutter, the *Doria* was too far gone for a tow.

"*Andrea Doria* settling rapidly. Not possible to tow or to board. Master advises there are three deaths. Names not known."

The 1st Coast Guard District in Boston wanted no part of a towing operation for its men, replying that "*Hornbeam* should not attempt to tow." It advised that the Italian Line had contacted Moran and another commercial firm, Merritt, Chapman, and Scott, for towing assistance.

Calamai was subdued when he returned from his meeting with Lieutenant Erdmann. Now Ensign Boggs undertook a most prosaic task in the midst of high drama: he began to fill out an accident report.

Calamai told Boggs that his ship was valued at more than $20 million, but provided little information when asked about the cause of the collision. He said he had seen the *Stockholm* on radar, but when Boggs

The *Hornbeam* (W394), a Coast Guard buoy tender, picked up Captain Piero Calamai and his senior crewmen from their lifeboat as the *Andrea Doria*, a few hundred yards away, tipped ever closer to the end. (AP/Wide World Photos)

asked if he had plotted the approach of the Swedish liner, he did not receive much of a response. Calamai may have decided to say little in anticipation of a formal inquiry and lawsuits, but there also was a language barrier between the captain and the Coast Guard officer, and at times they resorted to sign language.

As Calamai waited for the end, the *Hornbeam* crewman Joseph De Chane noticed one of the *Doria*'s senior officers peering in the direction of the *Stockholm,* barely visible some 2 miles off in the morning haze. The officer muttered, "You ugly son of a bitch."

CHAPTER 23

"That Thing's Going Down in Five Minutes"

The *Andrea Doria*'s list grew more calamitous as the sun came up, though in some ways she seemed the lesser victim of the collision. Her lights continued to gleam along the Promenade Deck on her intact port side, and her eight high-side lifeboats remained securely in place, as if there had been no need for their use. The enormous gash in her starboard side was mostly hidden, in contrast to the wrecked bow of the *Stockholm*.

Overhead in a small plane, Milton Bracker of the *New York Times* thought the *Doria* looked "tired but serene" through the haze of early morning, while the *Stockholm* "stood as if foreshortened by a dull and clumsy ax wielded by a giant."

Later that morning, a CBS newsman whose prominence foreshadowed the emergence of the celebrity TV network anchorman, arrived in another small plane. In the mid-1950s, most of the TV news coverage came from newsreel companies, which made little attempt to cover breaking stories, gravitating instead to anything easy to plan for—sports events, fashion shows, ribbon-cuttings. Live news coverage by the networks was rare. But that would begin to change with the *Andrea Doria* story, as told by Douglas Edwards, whose dramatic account illustrated television's vast potential.

Edwards, the nightly news anchor for CBS—his only rival NBC's John Cameron Swayze, anchor for the *Camel News Caravan*—flew up from New York City with Don Hewitt, the producer-director for *The CBS Evening News with Douglas Edwards,* and Tony Petri, their cameraman. They were among the newsmen who rushed to Quonset Naval Station on Rhode Island, where the Coast Guard had set up a press headquarters. But the CBS men arrived late.

"Everybody had finished shooting and were rushing back to New York to get their film on the air," Hewitt would recall. "We were even pondering whether to give it up when a Coast Guard pilot recognized Doug and said: 'Hang around. That thing's going down in five minutes.'"

The pilot took the broadcast crew over the scene in a seaplane, Edwards providing the narration, CBS the only network still filming. Its coverage of the *Andrea Doria* story would long be remembered.

Harry Trask, a twenty-eight-year-old photographer for the *Boston Traveler,* also caught a huge break by being late.

Trask was summoned from home by his editors and sent to the airport in Revere, where he rented a Piper to take him to Nantucket. But that's as far as the small plane went. Arriving at 4:00 A.M., Trask now had to find another plane to take him over the collision scene.

A DC-3 rented in Boston by other papers had flown photographers to the *Doria,* and they had returned to Nantucket with their pictures while Trask was still trying to get his ride. When the Air Force and Coast Guard evacuation helicopters arrived at the island's airport, Trask took pictures of the injured *Stockholm* crewmen and four-year-old Norma Di Sandro as they were transferred to ambulances. But he was still stuck on the island with not a single disaster picture. He feared he was about to lose his job.

The *Traveler*'s aviation editor had given the phone numbers of private pilots in the area to John Dowd, the reporter accompanying Trask. Unable to get a ride over the *Doria* from the Coast Guard, they began phoning and eventually persuaded a pilot on Martha's Vineyard named Bob Walker to fly to Nantucket and then take them to the scene.

But Trask had other problems. Although he had been the *Traveler*'s airplane photographer for a few years, he was prone to airsickness. He kept Dramamine pills in his photo bag, but each time he went up he decided, "Maybe this time I'll be okay, I won't take them."

When Trask finally got his ride to the collision scene at about 9:30 A.M., as usual he had no pills with him. And he was apprehensive about the plane itself, a Beechcraft Bonanza. A few months earlier at a party in his hometown of Cohasset, he met a doctor who had broken his back in a crash of that model.

Trask's woes mounted when the plane was aloft. He made a tactical error by sitting up front with the pilot and placing his reporter in the back. The front area was so cramped that there was little room for Trask to focus his Speed Graphic, a large camera used by press photographers, with 4-by-5-inch-cut film. To made matters even worse, Trask's plane had a low wing, so the pilot had to tip it over on its side to give Trask the field of vision he needed. That kicked in his customary airsickness.

When Trask's plane arrived over the *Doria,* just about everyone else had taken their photos and left. There were two other planes in sight. One was from the Coast Guard—carrying Douglas Edwards—and the other evidently from a Providence, Rhode Island, television station.

Trask took a couple of shots of the *Stockholm,* and then his plane circled over the *Doria.* After he took his first picture, and the plane continued circling, Trask saw how the *Doria's* smokestack was noticeably closer to the water.

"I think it's going under," he told the pilot. "Fly around as close and as fast as you can go, and I'll keep on taking pictures." He was the only still photographer to capture the *Doria's* final moments.

On the deck of the Coast Guard cutter *Evergreen,* a twenty-year-old bosun's mate named Robert Wallace got out his Speed Graphic. The *Evergreen* had a photo lab on board, its crewmen using it simply as a hobby, and Wallace was hardly a seasoned photographer. But now he began shooting the *Doria,* using up two or three rolls, taking at least twenty photos. As he snapped away, watching the *Doria's* starboard side tip farther and farther into the sea, hearing what seemed like groans as debris popped loose, Wallace felt an overpowering sadness. His fellow crewmen stood alongside, silently. It seemed to the young crewman as if they were attending a funeral.

As ten o'clock neared, the *Doria's* starboard decks almost reached to the sea, and the bow slowly dipped. The three lifeboats that had held the last of her crewmen to depart now drifted empty. The port propeller emerged along its entire shaft.

At 10:01, water seeped into the single funnel carrying Italy's national colors of white, red, and green. The three swimming pools refilled with seawater.

By 10:04 the *Doria* was completely on her side, water licking over the bow.

On the *Stockholm,* surrounded by a large oil slick, on the destroyer escort *Allen,* on the military transport *Thomas, Doria* crewmen and survivors crowded the rails.

As the *Doria's* bow nosed down, a huge swell came up over the fantail. Five or six of the eight portside lifeboats ripped loose and floated freely. Geysers arose from the sides of the ship, air pressure having blown out portholes, and debris flew high in the air.

The *Andrea Doria* sinks, one of the final photographs in a sequence shot from a small plane by Harry Trask of the *Boston Traveler*. (AP/Wide World Photos)

The *Doria* keeled over, both screws and her rudder free of the water. Her nose plunged completely into the sea and her stern rose, the legends "*Andrea Doria*" and "Genoa" now visible.

She could still be glimpsed for 3 or 4 minutes. And then she was gone.

The force of the suction created a whirlpool, and then objects rose to the water's surface as the *Andrea Doria* settled into the muck 225 feet below. Huge bubbles mixed with a heavy oil slick, the blue sea churning to green.

Captain Calamai, still wearing his blue beret, Staff Captain Osvaldo Magagnini, and an engineering officer had been watching together from the port side of the *Hornbeam*. Forty or so officers and crewmen from the *Doria* were spread out along that side or on the buoy deck.

Lieutenant Erdmann and Ensign Boggs of the *Hornbeam* stood beside Calamai and his officers. Magagnini was misty-eyed but Calamai shed no tear, so far as Boggs could observe.

Calamai turned to Boggs and said, "I'd like to send a telegram."

The ensign handed him a piece of paper.

The captain wrote out a message for the Italian Line. It may have been the most succinct description ever sent of a wreck at sea.

"*Doria* sank 10:09—Calamai."

At 10:15, a small plane from Boston carrying Carlo Fava, the New England representative of the Italian Line, flew overhead. Except for the oil slick and scattered debris, there was nothing for him to see.

CHAPTER 24

"It Is Incomprehensible"

Piero Calamai's terse message announcing the loss of his ship went nowhere for the better part of an hour. Ensign Boggs of the cutter *Hornbeam* radioed the *Evergreen,* the Coast Guard's communications conduit, asking it to relay the word to shore. But each time Boggs called via two-way radio, the *Evergreen's* operator replied: "We've got emergency traffic. We've got other stuff we're doing."

By the time the ensign prevailed on the *Evergreen* to send the captain's four-word dispatch, that cutter had long since announced the end.

At 10:19—ten minutes after the *Doria* disappeared—the *Evergreen* radioed: "SS *Andrea Doria* sank in 225 feet of water at 261409Z [2:09 P.M. "Zulu" or Greenwich time, four hours ahead of Eastern time] in position 40.29.4 North 69.50.5 West. *Evergreen* will search debris. *Hornbeam* has remaining survivors aboard."

Those 46 "remaining survivors" reboarded the two *Doria* lifeboats from which they had climbed into the *Hornbeam,* and at eleven o'clock Captain Calamai and the last of the officers and seamen to abandon the *Andrea Doria* rode the boats to the destroyer escort *Allen,* joining the thirty-one *Doria* crewmen already there. Some of the *Doria* sailors on the Navy ship emptied their pockets of articles they brought from the liner—keys, flashlights, and the like—and threw them into the sea, wishing to retain no mementos.

The *Allen's* skipper, Lieutenant Commander Hempen, brought Calamai to his stateroom and said he could use it for whatever purposes he needed. Calamai asked for writing paper to draw up a report for the Italian Line. In midafternoon he returned to the bridge and gave Hempen an account of the collision, repeatedly telling how he kept track of the *Stockholm* on his radar while the ships approached each other.

It was late afternoon Thursday in Italy when bulletins flashed around the world by international news agencies, radio, and television told of the *Andrea Doria*'s end. This was the worst maritime accident to befall the Italian nation in peacetime since the *Principessa Mafalda* sank off the Brazilian coast in 1927 with the loss of 314 lives. But it was more than that. The sinking of the *Andrea Doria,* a symbol of Italy's resurgence from the devastation of World War II, amounted to a national calamity.

The news was met with disbelief.

"With all the instruments that all ships, big and little, possess nowadays, it is incomprehensible," said Angelo Costa, president of the Italian Confederation of Shipping Lines.

Gennario Cassiani, the minister of Merchant Marine, had earlier wired Captain Calamai instructions to save himself as soon as the *Doria* found itself in a "serious state." Now he called the loss of the *Doria* a "cruel disaster."

"Italy considered that beautiful ship one of the most expressive symbols of its reconstruction," said the Italian president, Giovanni Gronchi. The *Doria*'s loss, he said, "plunges the whole Italian nation into sadness."

Pope Pius XII was notified at his summer villa in Castelgandolfo, south of Rome, and Premier Antonio Segni's cabinet received updates throughout Thursday. The Italian government had more than an emotional stake in the *Doria:* it was part owner of the Italian Line and had contributed 5 percent of the *Doria*'s $29 million construction costs.

Early reports telling how many of the *Doria*'s crew—albeit waiters, stewards, and the like—had left the ship in the first lifeboats brought protests from the Italian press. The Italia news agency said the allegations could not be true. Some Italian newspapers appearing on Friday afternoon omitted the reports, choosing instead to tell of courageous actions by the *Doria*'s sailors. The following Monday, the Italian cabinet, having received a summary of a report on the collision submitted by Calamai, expressed "complete solidarity" with the *Doria*'s crew. But it would not make the report public.

Italy's left wing exploited the disaster to fuel anti-American propaganda. *Avanti,* the newspaper of Socialists allied politically with the Communists, speculated that the collision was caused by the testing of America's hydrogen bombs over the Pacific Ocean. The radioactive particles, said Avanti, "blind ships' radar."

Italy's Treasury Ministry and Foreign Office arranged quickly for a preliminary fund of 10 million lire ($16,300) to meet survivors' needs, and the cabinet, acting at the behest of the Italian Line, said it favored construction of a liner to replace the *Doria.*

"The Italian merchant fleet is today in mourning, but not beaten," said the Communist newspaper *Unità* in a rare display of accord with all sectors of Italy's ideological spectrum. "The *Andrea Doria* must rise again. The Italian fleet must again become great and strong."

But in the North Atlantic, 45 miles south of Nantucket Island, all that remained of the *Doria* were deck chairs, waterlogged suitcases, and assorted debris floating in her wake together with a dozen or so of her lifeboats. By afternoon, the Coast Guard's task turned from search and rescue to recovery.

The cutter *Legare* would bring three *Doria* lifeboats to New Bedford, the *Yeaton* would take another three to New London, while the *Hornbeam* would carry two to Woods Hole. But several of the lifeboats had overturned and could not be picked up. Since they presented a hazard to navigation, they had to be destroyed.

The *Legare* pumped two magazines from its 20-millimeter gun into one of the lifeboats, but it wouldn't go down. The cutter's skipper, Lieutenant Philip G. Ledoux, resorted next to his 40-millimeter gun, but that accomplished nothing except for opening more holes. While the futile bombardment went on, sharks seemed to be checking every piece of paper, every sliver of wood, cigarette cases, and bits of clothing left floating.

The *Legare* finally gave up on its guns, took on a couple of floating deck chairs and a cocktail table along with three upright lifeboats, and departed. The task of destroying the overturned *Doria* lifeboats fell to the cutter *Yakutat,* which had launched four lifeboats of its own during the search-and-rescue operation.

When *Yakutat* bosun's mate Richard Worton took his lifeboat over the spot where the *Doria* sank, he could almost spot its outline 225 feet below. Every so often, a compartment popped and a rush of air came up, spawning turbulence that resembled a depth charge's wake. When Worton looked over the sides and saw a bubble of air start to rise, he had to move quickly. If his 26-foot-long lifeboat had been hit by a bubble, it might have capsized. After dodging the air bubbles, Worton returned to the *Yakutat* and took aim at three or four *Doria* lifeboats floating upside down, the cutter *Yeaton* having failed in an attempt to flip them over with a hook. The boats, 60 to 70 feet long, were like glasses stuck upside down by their suction.

Worton riddled each of the lifeboats with a dozen rounds from the *Yakutat's* port side 40-millimeter gun, aiming at spots several feet apart in an effort to break up air pockets. Each boat took about 15 minutes to finish off, but Worton completed the mission.

Deck chairs and a life ring from
the *Andrea Doria* aboard the
Coast Guard cutter *Campbell*.
(Courtesy of Norman Cubberly)

The *Yakutat* later picked up floating suitcases with tags marked
Ruth Roman and Betsy Drake but also cardboard boxes, presumably
belonging to third-class passengers, that had split open.

The cutters took the luggage to the Coast Guard's Castle Hill sta-
tion at Newport, Rhode Island, for inspection by the U.S. Customs
Bureau and then shipment to New York in vans hired by the Italian
Line. At the center of one pile, a red and white life ring stenciled
Andrea Doria stood out. A battered, inexpensive black suitcase con-
tained a brand-new black-and-white accordion.

Helping sort the suitcases, Coast Guardsman Leon Scarborough
was puzzled to find gold wedding bands. They probably belonged to
nuns, his Catholic buddies told him, representing their symbolic marriage to Christ. As Scarborough sifted through the baggage, he wondered whether the people who owned all this soggy clothing were still
alive.

A profile of the battered *Stockholm*, taken from the cutter *Campbell*. (Courtesy of Norman Cubberly)

Soon after the *Andrea Doria* capsized, the *Hornbeam* secured a makeshift marker over the spot where she went down—a couple of life preservers and heavy shackles anchored to the ocean floor by a rope.

At 3:15 in the afternoon, the cutter *Evergreen* placed an official marker. It anchored a yellow 50-gallon drum over the *Andrea Doria*'s ocean grave.

CHAPTER 25

"How Good God Is to Me"

When the *Ile de France* departed for New York just after 6:00 A.M. Thursday, Captain Raoul De Beaudéan returned to his cabin and collapsed on a sofa, having been on his feet for 11 hours. He was hungry, thirsty, and utterly exhausted. He had carried out a triumph of seamanship, but like his dispirited counterpart Captain Calamai, a stubble of beard lined his face, accentuating his weariness.

Too many decisions lay ahead for De Beaudéan to get any sleep just yet. Now that the rescue had been carried out, he pondered the financial consequences to the French Line of further delays. He envisioned arriving at anchor off the quarantine station outside New York Harbor between noon and 2:00 P.M., then placing the *Andrea Doria* survivors onto tugs over the course of an hour or two. That would put the *Ile* facing eastward, south of Ambrose Light, the harbor's entrance, by late afternoon.

If he sailed at that time, he would be just over 28 hours behind schedule. By applying extra speed, he would arrive at Plymouth, England, one full day late. The *Ile* had been scheduled to remain there for 48 hours. If that layover were cut in half, she might arrive at her final destination, Le Havre, exactly on time.

But De Beaudéan had become a celebrity. When he phoned a French Line official in New York to outline his plans for turning around without so much as stepping foot on shore, he was politely asked if he had "gone crazy."

The hero of the hour would not be allowed to quash a publicity windfall for the French Line, would not be permitted to disappoint the newspaper reporters, broadcast crews, and newsreels, let alone the grateful friends and relatives of the survivors waiting at the pier to hail him.

There was, meanwhile, a more immediate matter to deal with. The scene in the *Ile*'s radio room had become frantic. Survivors crowded it, sending reassuring telegrams to families in New York or Europe. And messages were flowing between the *Ile* and the other rescue ships among family members who had become separated. Amid all that clamor, phone calls were arriving from reporters seeking interviews with De Beaudéan before he arrived on shore. And the *Ile*'s officers needed to compile a list of survivors for transmission to New York, no easy task since they were scattered throughout the ship, some having been given beds by the liner's regular passengers.

De Beaudéan decided the newspaper and broadcast interviews could wait. He would first tour his ship.

On the Promenade Deck, he saw survivors still in shock, clad in makeshift outfits donated by passengers, many bundled up in gray woolen blankets, only a few wearing shoes. Many reached out to shake his hand, offering thanks in a variety of languages. The captain spotted two nuns whose white habits were so immaculate it seemed they had just arrived from their convent's laundry. He asked the nuns if they had come from the *Doria*. Indeed they had. A monk in a well-worn cassock showed off two solidly built ankle boots. "Everything is fine," the monk said, smiling. "I was able to save them, thanks to God. If I had lost them, I wouldn't have had another pair for at least five years."

At times De Beaudéan became confused, trying to speak Italian with survivors who were, in fact, American.

The infirmary was jammed, every cot filled, more than twenty surgery cases beginning to emerge from anesthesia. De Beaudéan visited the patients, accompanied by a nurse describing the injuries.

His most somber moment came when he saw Jane Cianfarra, her face covered with violet cuts, her body racked with fractures. Sobbing, she told the captain she had lost her husband and two daughters. Neither knew that Linda Morgan had been found alive on the mangled bow of the *Stockholm*.

During the morning, a clothing display was set up with contributions from the *Ile*'s passengers. The garments were sorted by size, and the slippers and shoes were laid out on a long counter. The *Doria* survivor Neil Gebhardt was given a pair of blue jeans with an orange belt, a white shirt, a new sleeveless sweater and a light-colored sport jacket. Everything fit.

Ruth Roman, taken to the *Ile* after her three-year-old son, Dickie, had been placed aboard a lifeboat bound for the *Stockholm*, received a change of clothing from a tennis pro named Eddie Hand, a former fiancé of the glamourous tennis player Gussie Moran, known for her lace panties. Hand gave the actress a pair of blue trousers tied with a yellow ribbon, a white polo shirt, and woolen socks. The evening gown she wore in the *Doria*'s Belvedere Lounge had been ripped and soiled.

After shooting his photos for *Life* magazine, Loomis Dean brought Roman to his family's cabin. The actress still did not know where her son had been taken, but it seemed to Dean that she was in charge of her emotions.

Dean's wife had bought clothing for their children at Macy's in New York just before they sailed on the *Ile,* figuring that would be less expensive than a shopping expedition in Paris when her husband began his assignment there. But the Deans gave all that clothing away to children evacuated from the *Doria.*

The psychiatrist Dr. Louis Linn interrupted his interviews of survivors to make a quick trip back to his cabin. Dr. Linn's wife, Miriam, had bought him a light bathrobe for the trip, but its texture had annoyed him. When he saw an elderly Italian woman with nothing to ward off the morning chill, he fetched the bathrobe and draped it around her to a flutter of applause saluting his ostensible generosity.

Dr. Linn sensed exhilaration among the *Ile*'s regular passengers on the trip back to New York. They would be enjoying an extra day of *haute cuisine* aboard the *Ile* while "unexpectedly thrust into a wonderful adventure."

Amid the best efforts of the *Ile*'s passengers and crew to clothe the survivors, mismatches were inevitable. Robert Young, the official with the American Bureau of Shipping, had been given a pair of waiter's black trousers and bedroom slippers at least three sizes too small. At 11:00 A.M. Young borrowed a razor and went to a public bathroom to shave and wash. One of the *Ile*'s regular passengers came in and was startled to see a waiter using the facility—and with ridiculous slippers.

"Where did you come from?" the man asked.

"From the *Andrea Doria.*"

"From the what?"

The man had awakened 10 minutes earlier, after having slept soundly through the rescue.

Throughout the early morning, the *Ile*'s regular passengers had been stunned to come upon hundreds of new arrivals. When the passengers arrived on deck expecting to sit in their favorite lounge chairs, they found them occupied by a miserable but thankful band of strangers in all manner of makeshift clothing, drinking hot coffee.

In midmorning Captain De Beaudéan went on the public-address system to announce the sinking of the *Andrea Doria*. Father Richard Wojcik said Mass with his fellow survivors. He told Catholics participating that they need not be concerned about fasting before communion. In view of the circumstances, said the priest, "there are no laws now."

For many, emotional reunions were at hand.

Having left the *Doria* in separate lifeboats, Nora Kovach and her husband, Istvan Rabovsky, walked the *Ile*'s decks, each hoping the other had been taken to the French liner. Suddenly they found each other, they hugged, and Istvan's heart began to race.

Just after the Hungarian refugees embraced, they heard someone moaning—a cry of pain in unmistakable Hungarian. Nora looked down and saw an elderly woman with a broken leg lying on the deck, no one paying attention to her. She spoke to the woman in Hungarian and found she was indeed a countrywoman from the *Doria*.

"My dear, how good God is to me," said the woman, who had been coming to America to visit a son. "God has sent a Hungarian to me, that I can tell you how much pain I'm in. Please help me." Nora ran to summon a doctor.

Leonardo Paladino, the tailor from Bari, and his wife, Giovanna, both still barefoot, found daughters Felicia, three, and Tonya, two, being cared for by another family from their hometown whom they had met on the *Doria*. Tonya was still sucking on the pacifier in her mouth when her parents had placed the girls in a lifeboat, remaining aboard the *Doria* with four-year-old Maria. But Maria, later put into a separate lifeboat before her parents had taken yet a third boat to the *Ile*, was not on the French liner.

Jerry Reinert was walking along the *Ile*'s deck when an Italian woman he didn't know reached out and kissed his hand. The woman recognized him as the man who had taken her child down a rope ladder. Reinert was annoyed rather than gratified. He wondered where the woman's husband had been when he was rescuing her youngster.

Betsy Drake, taken in a lifeboat to the *Ile*, was presumably the only *Doria* survivor who had once been a guest of Captain De Beaudéan on a different ship. A few years earlier, Drake and Cary Grant had enjoyed a lunch of Normandy sole and white wine with De Beaudéan when they toured his cargo-passenger ship the *Winnipeg* while it was docked in San Pedro, California. De Beaudéan had been struck by the enormous popularity of movie stars. As Grant and Drake toured the *Winnipeg*, longshoremen shouted to them, a reception that in De Beaudéan's mind "would have made the great Charles de Gaulle himself green with envy."

But De Beaudéan did not know that Betsy Drake was aboard the *Ile*. She had received no favors from the liner's officers and had, in fact, been frustrated in trying to reach Grant from the ship, its telephone lines tied up by the swarm of survivors.

Angela Grillo paced the *Ile*'s decks for 2½ hours, searching for her three-year-old son, Anthony, who had departed the *Doria* just before she could climb down to his lifeboat. Mrs. Grillo had taken another boat to the *Ile*, but she had no idea whether Anthony had gone there as well. And then she found him sitting in a lounge chair, eating an orange.

Her husband, Carmelo, the Italian Line official who helped oversee the arrival of passengers in New York, would not have to wait at the pier for word of his family. Late Thursday afternoon, he boarded a Coast Guard cutter that headed out to meet the *Ile* at the entrance to the harbor. Whether his wife and son were aboard—or on another rescue vessel, or had gone down with the *Andrea Doria*—he had no idea. As the cutter approached the *Ile*, a former coworker of Grillo's who was aboard the French liner spotted him. "Grillo," he called out, "your wife and son are here."

Angela and Anthony, still in nightclothes and bundled in blankets, were sitting in lounge chairs on the Promenade Deck alongside the first-class swimming pool when Carmelo Grillo found them. Overcome by emotion, Angela remained silent. Not so for Anthony. "Daddy," he said, "don't leave me anymore."

CHAPTER 26

"Oh, What a Climax"

Arriving in New York Harbor with 753 rescued passengers and crewmen, the *Ile de France* received a splendid tribute rivaling the reception accorded her maiden voyage 29 years earlier. So many boats tooted their whistles that the *Ile*'s helmsman didn't know which one to acknowledge first. Repeatedly answering with his own whistle, he seemed embarrassed by the clamor. White streamers glinting in the sunlight billowed in salute from skyscraper windows along the waterfront.

When the *Ile* eased into her berth at Pier 88 off West Forty-eighth Street shortly after five o'clock Thursday afternoon, a representative of the Italian Line went to Captain De Beaudéan's cabin to thank him. Jean Marie, the director of the French Line, intervened with a little joke he hoped would ease the official's distress. "Good-bye till tomorrow," the Frenchman said. "We'll probably come aboard one of your ships wrapped in a blanket and barefoot."

The Italian managed only a slight smile.

The *Doria* survivors would soon tell their stories to the reporters jamming the pier, but photographs of the rescue were already en route for processing.

Ken Gouldthorpe, the *St. Louis Post-Dispatch* assistant photo editor who had been a passenger on the *Ile*, provided an eyewitness account to his newspaper by radiotelephone while the liner was at sea. Now he had to get his photographs into the paper quickly. Having given his passport to the *Ile*'s crew for processing, it would be difficult for him to leave the ship and then return. He solved the problem by tossing his film to newsmen on the pilot boat that met the *Ile*. The photos would make page one and bring him a Pulitzer Prize nomination and a $2,500 bonus.

Gouldthorpe wasn't the first *Post-Dispatch* man thrust by happenstance into an epic disaster at sea. Carlos Hurd, a reporter for the paper, had been on the *Carpathia*, en route to a European vacation, when it

The *Ile de France*'s captain, Raoul De Beaudéan (center), and two crewmen with an early headline that proved far too optimistic on the casualty toll. (AP/Wide World Photos)

came to the aid of the *Titanic*. Hurd had interviewed survivors and tossed his article—perhaps five thousand words—into a tug for transfer ashore when the *Carpathia* approached New York Harbor.

The photos taken aboard the *Ile* by *Life* magazine's Loomis Dean and the pictures bought by his fellow passenger and *Life*'s publisher, Andrew Heiskell, from a survivor appeared in a fifteen-page spread the following week. Dean, meanwhile, had enjoyed a little joke at the expense of the *Life* photo desk while the *Ile* was returning to New York. He phoned an editor not known for his sense of humor to express regrets that he had slept through the entire rescue. The editor was not amused.

More than three thousand people, held behind barricades by two hundred policemen, jammed the streets alongside the *Ile*'s pier. Some were gawkers, but most were evidently hoping that a parent, a husband, a wife, a child were among those saved by the *Ile*. Many survivors had been able to send messages to family members from the *Ile*'s radio room, but a goodly number of the people at the pier had no idea whether a reunion beckoned.

An Italian-speaking police officer at a loudspeaker called out the names of survivors who were to arrive later in the evening aboard the freighter *Cape Ann* at a pier four blocks to the south. A third rescue ship, the *Private William H. Thomas,* would be docking in Brooklyn that night, and the *Stockholm* was due the next day at its mid-Manhattan berth.

The Red Cross provided facilities for heating baby bottles and baby formulas, and Gimbel's department store brought free clothing for four hundred. Many survivors jamming the rails of the *Ile* were still disheveled, some in bathrobes, others in coats over pajamas.

Dorothy Haywood of San Pedro, California, fashioned a skirt out of a plaid-patterned carrying bag used to cover topcoats, the gift of an *Ile* passenger. Rose Adragna of Pittsburgh held her two-year-old daughter, Olivia, who was nibbling on a donut and fingering a heavy, black wool sweater reading "Italian Line," placed on the child by a *Doria* crewman who had carried her down a rope ladder. Neil Gebhardt waved red pajamas he was carrying, and his son, Neil Jr., waiting behind a barricade, waved a white handkerchief so they could keep each other in sight as the Gebhardts made their way to the pier.

Pat Mastrincola's father, who had learned of the collision only when he picked up the New York *Daily News* that morning, tearfully embraced his nine-year-old son and his eight-year-old daughter, Arlene. It was the only time Pat would see his father cry.

Watching the reunions—the hugging, the touching of faces—Ken Gouldthorpe thought back to the newsreels of servicemen returning home from World War II.

The Philadelphia mayor, Richardson Dilworth, and his wife, Ann, were greeted aboard the *Ile* by New York City's mayor, Robert F. Wagner. Dilworth told reporters of "the tireless and courageous work" of the *Doria*'s crew in getting passengers into the lifeboats "without apparent thought for themselves." Whatever his private views, Philadelphia had a large Italian population. Dilworth's remarks would be well received at home.

The Italian immigrants rescued by the *Ile* were a pitiful lot. They were cold, ill-clothed, bearing no identity papers, they had fled a rising tide of seawater and oil from the lowest decks of a sinking liner, and they were unable to make their needs known, since they spoke little if any English.

Nicandro Caranci, a forty-five-year-old farmer from Campobasso, Italy, was coming to America to live with a brother he had never seen. He had hoped to find him when the *Andrea Doria* docked by shouting their family name. Now there was no *Andrea Doria* and no brother. When he came down the gangway of the *Ile,* he encountered a confused scene, and his shouts were to no avail.

The farmer was taken in hand by a Travelers Aid Society volunteer named Eileen Sweeney who had once visited Italy, had remembered the kindnesses of Italians, and hoped to do something in return.

She met with the man in a room at the Hotel Roosevelt reserved for survivors, but she spoke almost no Italian. Caranci scrawled the name of his brother, Antonio, and an address of sorts: "Saut Bar." Sweeney began phoning telephone information, a search that took her through operators in three states before she found a listing for a Tony Caranci in South Barre, Vermont. She learned that he had indeed gone to New York to meet his brother and that he might be staying with one of his married daughters, in Stamford, Connecticut, or Bloomfield, New Jersey. Sweeney called the Stamford number, but it was busy. When she dialed the Bloomfield number, Caranci's niece, Evelyn Neri, answered. The brother was at her home, and soon there would be a belated family gathering.

The U.S. Immigration and Naturalization Service worked to speed foreigners through with a minimum of formalities, but for a Yugoslav-born resident of Toronto named Milan Babic, Cold War fears intervened when he arrived on the *Ile*.

Babic, a Canadian citizen, was held overnight at a federal office building in Manhattan "in the interest of national security," as an immigration official put it, then allowed to return home the next morning after clearance was received from headquarters in Washington. "They started questioning me," Babic told reporters. "Had I or did I now belong to any Communist party? How long had I been in Europe? I denied that I had ever belonged to any Communist organization and then told them I had been in Italy and France for fifteen months on a business trip."

The following week, Lester Pearson, the Canadian foreign secretary, told the Parliament in Ottawa that Babic hardly seemed a threat to American national security. Pearson asked Canadian officials in New York to investigate the detention.

Fifty-seven *Doria* survivors arriving on the *Ile* were admitted to Roosevelt, St. Vincent's, and St. Clare's Hospitals in Manhattan.

Freda Gladstone was being taken on a stretcher to an ambulance, having suffered multiple injuries in her plunge to a lifeboat from a cargo net, when a well-dressed man approached. "I'm so sorry that you're hurt," he said. "Can I do anything to help?" Without waiting for an answer, the man took off his silk jacket, folded it over twice into a makeshift pillow, and placed it under Freda's head.

Alba Wells was taken to St. Vincent's Hospital, having injured her spine and shoulder when the rope ladder she was climbing down whipped against the *Doria*'s hull. In the next bed was her three-year-old daughter, Rose Marie, whose hand had been caught between her berth and a cabin wall. Mrs. Wells's husband, Charles, who had not accompanied his family on the *Doria*, arrived at the hospital and assured his wife that their son, Henry—off watching a movie when the ships collided and not seen by his mother since—had been rescued. Wells was simply trying to keep his wife calm. He had not seen his son's name on any survivor list. But late Friday afternoon, a nurse told Mrs. Wells that Henry was indeed safe. He had just arrived on the *Stockholm* with the missionary Ernest LaFont, who had stayed with him during those hours of waiting for rescue.

Betsy Drake was met at the *Ile*'s pier by a friend named Judy Quine. "Her hair was very neatly combed," Quine would remember. "Since she never wore much makeup, she didn't look much different from when she wore the minimum amount. She was wearing a charming little Ben Zuckerman silk suit with a little pin on the lapel. It was all adorable except that on her feet were huge, bulky white sweat socks loaned to her by a sailor. Betsy had lost her shoes."

Bernie Aidinoff and his bride, Cissie, returning from their prolonged European honeymoon, had just gotten off the *Ile de France* when Mrs. Aidinoff spotted someone from Travelers Aid she knew.

The Aidinoffs' anxiety was growing and they were eager to be off the pier.

"Can you get us out of here?" Mrs. Aidinoff asked her friend.

"Yeah, if you'll agree to a TV interview on your way out."

Officials were delaying the departure of the survivors from a holding area to complete their processing, but were willing to release anybody who was going to be interviewed on television or radio. Ruth Roman was right in front of the Aidinoffs. After she was interviewed on TV, they volunteered to tell their stories.

The interviewer asked: "Were you in Europe on business or pleasure?"

The Aidinoffs said they had been on their honeymoon, which brought a big smile from the reporter.

"What was your reaction to the collision?" he asked.

While in Europe, the couple had received a letter from Mrs. Aidinoff's father saying he was sure the trip on the *Andrea Doria* would be anticlimactic.

The honeymooners responded to the interviewer's question in unison: "Oh, what a climax."

This being the mid-1950s, the unintended double-entendre brought an abrupt end to the live interview.

The Aidinoffs lived in New York City, so they were home within minutes. For Margaret Antonacci, a fifty-two-year-old housewife from Slateford, Pennsylvania, the trip home brought only further anxiety.

Mrs. Antonacci, returning on the *Doria* from Rome, where she attended the wedding of her daughter, Ann, had been given a room at the Hotel Commodore by the Italian Line after leaving the *Ile*. Her son, Emery, driving in from Pennsylvania to meet his mother, had not put his car radio on and knew nothing of the collision until arriving at the *Doria*'s pier Thursday morning. Later that day, he got in touch with his father, Luigi, back in Pennsylvania, who told him that his mother had called from her hotel.

Emery picked her up that afternoon. While they were driving through the Lincoln Tunnel, their trip back barely under way, traffic suddenly stopped. The son told his mother—her nerves already frayed—that there was nothing they could do but wait it out. For more than an hour they remained in the tunnel, their car without air conditioning. "We thought we were going to suffocate," Emery would remember. "It was a nightmare."

When they arrived home at midnight, Mrs. Antonacci found she had become a local celebrity. Reporters and photographers from the *Easton Express* and the *Pocono Record* were at her doorstep.

By early Thursday evening, the 753 *Doria* survivors had departed the *Ile,* and Captain De Beaudéan had obliged the newspaper reporters and photographers. A barge replaced the fuel the *Ile* had consumed in returning to New York, and at 8:00 P.M. she sailed once again for Europe.

Only four of her original passengers were no longer aboard. Two people switched to an airline to make an appointment. An elderly couple, unnerved by the night's events, decided this was not exactly the right time for a voyage at sea.

CHAPTER 27

"It's My Baby"

Newspaper reporters crowded the tugboat *Martha Moran* as it drew alongside the *Cape Ann* in New York Harbor Thursday evening, hoping for shouted interviews with survivors on the deck of the freighter. But the reporters came away with much more. As the United Fruit Company boat headed toward its pier at West Forty-fourth Street shortly after seven o'clock to a horn-tooting salute from ships in the harbor, survivors lowered a rope to the tugboat, and reporters hauled the rope in. Attached to the line was a typewritten statement drawn up on the *Cape Ann* and signed by some ninety survivors, accusing the *Andrea Doria* crewmen of "complete negligence."

They charged that the evacuation drill early in the trip had been perfunctory, that no instructions were provided over the public-address system following the collision, and that crew members took no organized action to help them. The statement, drawn up largely by Mike and Meryl Stoller, did credit a small number of crewmen for aiding passengers on their own initiative.

This was the opening salvo in a controversy that would linger for months. Still to come were accounts of the *Doria*'s abandonment by many waiters and stewards in the first lifeboats going to the *Stockholm* while more than a thousand passengers had yet to be taken off.

When the *Cape Ann* docked, Mike and Meryl Stoller were met by Mike's partner, Jerry Leiber, who had flown in from Los Angeles to attend a music convention with him.

Leiber had exciting news.

"We have a No.1 hit," he reported. " 'Hound Dog.' "

"The Big Mama record?" Stoller asked, thinking that their song, recorded three years earlier by Willie Mae (Big Mama) Thornton, had been reprised by her.

"No," Leiber replied. "Some kid named Elvis Presley."

Hours after the *Cape Ann* docked, a hugely emotional reunion played out.

Leonardo Paladino; his wife, Giovanna; and their daughters Felicia, three, and Tonya, two, having arrived on the *Ile de France,* went to the home of Leonardo's sister, Antoinette Misciagna, in the Elmhurst section of Queens. The family still had no idea what had happened to four-year-old Maria, last seen departing the *Doria* in a lifeboat whose destination was unknown.

The father went to the *Cape Ann*'s pier when the freighter docked but was told that Maria had not been aboard. Mrs. Paladino sat by the television and the phone at her sister-in-law's home, an evening filled with tears and anxiety, while her other two daughters slept.

At midnight, there were tears of joy. Giovanna Paladino saw Maria on television, being cared for at a municipal shelter in East Harlem. Soon the phone rang. It was Leonardo, reporting he had a lead to Maria's whereabouts and hoped to bring her home.

The child had, in fact, been aboard the *Cape Ann*. A seventeen-year-old boy named Antonio Ragina, who was from Bari, the Paladinos' hometown, and had become acquainted with the family aboard the *Doria,* had cared for Maria on her lifeboat and aboard the freighter. But he didn't know her last name. When the *Cape Ann* arrived in New York, the boy's brother, Ralph, offered to watch over the child at his home in Queens until her parents could be located. But immigration officials said she could only be turned over to a parent. So she was taken to the New York City Welfare Department's children's center.

Red Cross officials dressed the child in blue jeans, a shirt, and new shoes, and canvassed Manhattan hotels for her parents, hoping they might have been put up overnight by the Italian Line. Leonardo, having failed to locate Maria at the *Cape Ann*'s mid-Manhattan pier, went to the Brooklyn Army Terminal with a brother-in-law, hoping she was aboard the two military ships arriving there later Thursday evening, the *Thomas* and the *Allen*. When he got to the pier, a New York City police detective who knew of the Red Cross inquiries advised Leonardo that a little girl at the shelter might be his daughter. So he was driven by his brother-in-law to East Harlem, and shortly after 1:30 A.M. Friday he was reunited with Maria.

The staff was reluctant to release the child at such a late hour, but Leonardo persisted. Maria slept all through the car ride to Queens.

Leonardo had just gone to bed when NBC phoned, asking him to come to its Rockefeller Center studios that morning. A limousine was

Four-year-old Maria Paladino, separated from her parents and two sisters, is comforted by a nurse at a New York City shelter after being rescued by the freighter *Cape Ann*. (Courtesy of Leonardo and Giovanna Paladino)

dispatched, and Leonardo Paladino—who spoke no English—headed off to be interviewed on national television through a translator on his second day in America.

Another reunion of parent and child came when the *Private William H. Thomas* arrived in Brooklyn.

Anna Coppola of Genoa, traveling on the *Doria* to visit a sister in the Bronx, had gone down a rope ladder with her sons Frank, eight, and Philip, four. When Mrs. Coppola had reached up for her sixteen-month-old son, Luigi, "One of the crew told me not to worry, that he'd bring the baby to me," the mother recounted. "But the lifeboat pulled away. I looked up and couldn't see my baby. My baby was gone."

Mrs. Coppola and her two older boys were taken to the *Ile de France*. The Red Cross eventually learned that Luigi had been taken later to the *Thomas* and notified the New York City police. Mrs. Coppola was escorted to the Brooklyn dock by Police Commissioner Stephen Kennedy, an agreeable public relations touch for the police. A nurse named Mary Green came off the *Thomas* holding Luigi, only his blond hair showing out of his blanket. Mrs. Coppola ran to take the child, crying, "It's my baby, it's my baby," to cheers from the crowd on the pier.

At 11:30 that night, the *Allen,* carrying Captain Calamai and seventy-six *Doria* crewmen, arrived at the Brooklyn Army Terminal. The ordeal had taken a physical and emotional toll on the seamen, who had been treated by the *Doria*'s chief physician, Dr. Bruno Tortori-Donati, for cuts, sprains, burns, respiratory problems resulting from stress, the effects of cold, and cramping in their calves from their exertions aiding passengers. Some had fainted from fatigue or vomited from anxiety.

A half-dozen Italian Line officials and lawyers boarded the Navy ship and spent an hour with Calamai while scores of reporters and photographers waited on the pier.

Still in his blue uniform and beret, Calamai stepped off the ship flanked by Navy officers and Italian consular officials. He posed at the foot of the gangplank for motion picture and still photographers, then read a three-paragraph statement from a single page of handwriting. It praised the rescuers and hailed the supposed calm displayed by his passengers and "the sense of duty of my officers and crew." But the captain shed no light on why the ships collided. He refused to answer questions, then left to spend the night at the Manhattan home of his brother Mario, a banker.

The next morning, Calamai was admitted to Presbyterian Hospital for treatment of phlebitis.

The *Allen* moved on to its regular pier, at the Brooklyn Navy Yard, the following day. When it arrived there, a car belonging to Admiral M. E. Miles, the commander of the 3rd Naval District, was waiting for the *Allen*'s skipper, Lieutenant Commander Hempen, who was handed a message saying the admiral wanted to see him immediately. When Hempen arrived at Miles's office, a captain in an anteroom remarked, "Boy, are you in trouble."

"Why didn't you tell me what you were doing?" the admiral asked heatedly.

Miles had never been notified that the *Allen* was going to the aid of the *Doria*. But the destroyer escort's skipper possessed evidence in his defense. Hempen reached into his pocket and pulled out his two messages—one sent at about 11:30 P.M., saying he was responding to the scene, and another, upon arrival, stating he was canceling gunnery practice and doing what he could in the rescue operation.

The admiral spouted a few epithets, but this time his anger was directed at the failure of Navy communications to relay the messages to him. He told his chief of staff to find out what happened. (Someone at the Navy radio station in Washington, D.C., had failed to pass Hem-

Captain Piero Calamai stepping off the Navy destroyer escort *Edward H. Allen,* which brought 77 *Andrea Doria* crewmen, including all her senior officers, to a pier in Brooklyn. (AP/Wide World Photos)

pen's messages along to Miles and to the commander for destroyers of the Atlantic Fleet, at Newport, Rhode Island.)

Miles told Hempen: "You did your part. Now I've got another job for you."

WOR-TV in New York wanted the Navy to send someone to talk about its participation in the rescue.

"You're going," Miles said.

"What do I say?" Hempen asked.

"Don't get the Navy in trouble."

A sailor walked in with a TV set and hooked it up.

"I'll be watching," said Miles.

Hempen was asked by the television interviewer what might have been done to avoid the collision. He said he was far away at the time, didn't know the circumstances, couldn't say. That was good enough for Admiral Miles. Not long afterward, Lieutenant Commander Hempen received a commendation for his role in the rescue.

CHAPTER 28

"I Lost My Love for Italians"

Hundreds of *Andrea Doria* survivors had lined the decks of the *Stockholm* Thursday morning, watching the *Doria*'s single funnel lay on its side and then disappear. Antonio Ponzi, the fourteen-year-old who had barely escaped the water rushing into the cabin he shared with another Antonio, thought of his sister, Marcella, as he saw the *Doria* go down. Where she had been when the ships collided, he did not know. What had happened to her afterward, he had no idea. His fears overwhelmed him. He was convinced his sister had perished, and he wept.

Whatever his private emotions at seeing another ocean liner die, Captain Nordenson of the *Stockholm* had a very practical problem to deal with. The Swedish ship was still stuck at the spot where it had been trapped since the collision.

Since 5:30 Thursday morning, when Captain Calamai and his senior crewmen finally abandoned the *Doria*, Nordenson had been trying to free the anchor chains entangled on the ocean bottom. He ran his engines full speed ahead and ran them in reverse, but the chains would not budge. Bobbing alongside the *Stockholm*'s mangled bow in lifeboat No. 7, officers sought to burn through the 75-pound steel links with an acetylene torch. But the bow's jagged edges endangered the lifeboat, and they finally gave up. It wasn't until midmorning—just after the *Doria* sank—that the chains were finally burned away by torches operated from the deck. But when the captain rocked the *Stockholm* one more time, to shake off the remnants of one of the chains, almost 70 feet of the wrecked bow fell into the ocean.

Just then, the *Doria* survivor Father Raymond Goedert spotted a body floating past, catapulted into the sea when the shreds of the bow gave way. This was Jeanette Carlin, who had been flung onto the *Stockholm*'s bow from the *Doria* together with Linda Morgan. She was the woman Linda thought was her mother when the girl heard cries before being rescued by the Spanish seaman Bernabe Polanco Garcia. Mrs. Carlin had lain behind wreckage, and by the time a *Stockholm* crewman reached her, she had died. That crewman, terrified by the corpse, had not retrieved her body, and now it was gone.

The *Stockholm*'s officers radioed the Coast Guard cutter *Legare,* which had been standing alongside, to ask that it recover the body. The *Legare* searched for a while, but all its crewmen saw was blood in the water. The sharks had evidently gotten there first.

The *Stockholm* started back to New York at a woeful 8 knots, accompanied by the cutters *Owasco* and *Tamaroa,* the latter involved in its second rescue operation in 3 days. Early the previous Monday, the *Tamaroa* had picked up seamen from the crippled American freighter *Fairisle* after it collided with the Panamian tanker *San José II* in fog outside New York Harbor. The *Stockholm* was returning with the loss of five crewmen. Three had been swept to their deaths in the collision, Karl Osterberg had died of injuries aboard the liner, and Alf Johansson had died after being evacuated to Nantucket.

The collision soon claimed another life. Frank Russo, the teenager who had been coming to America with his family friends and future employers Giuseppe and Antoinette Guzzi, sat in a chair on the *Stockholm*'s deck in his oil-stained shirt as the ship made its way to New York. As Frank pondered what had become of the Guzzis—his search aboard the *Doria* had been futile, and they seemed to be nowhere on the *Stockholm*—a fellow survivor reading a newspaper alongside the boy collapsed. Doctors were summoned, but nothing could be done. Carl Watres, a fifty-four-year-old sales manager from Manasquan, New Jersey, who had been returning on the *Doria* from a European trip with his wife, Lillian, succumbed to a heart attack.

The *Stockholm*'s kitchen staff, meanwhile, scrambled to provide meals for the 308 passengers and 234 crewmen rescued from the *Doria* while also serving the Swedish liner's 534 regular passengers. The *Doria* passengers and crew ate cafeteria-style in the main lounge while the regular passengers were seated in their dining room. Carl Geser, the chief chef, served pot roast as the main dish with potatoes for the *Stockholm* people and spaghetti for *Doria* survivors who preferred it.

Bill Johnson was put to work in the kitchen after returning from his lifeboat rescue mission with a bloody head and a concussion suffered when his cabin had been crushed. The kitchen was receiving requests for salads, Johnson noticed, something Swedes seldom ate but Italians coveted. The *Stockholm*'s supply of vegetables, used mostly to make sauces, was now heaped onto plates to accommodate the Italian guests.

There were many *Doria* waiters on board, but it seemed that not all of them would be serving those salads. The *Stockholm* waiter Stig Oscarsson saw how some of the Italian waiters balked when asked to help serve passengers from the *Doria,* considering themselves simply survivors who should be served by the Swedish staff. But after a while they were prevailed upon to perform their duties, albeit on a Swedish ship.

Other *Doria* survivors were unhesitant in taking up their callings. Father Thomas Kelly was approached by a Lutheran minister who he assumed was the *Stockholm*'s chaplain. "There's a lot of people in sick bay," the minister told the priest. "I think some of these sailors aren't doing well." The priest blessed the injured and spoke to those who were well enough to respond.

Father Kelly grew uneasy when he saw the crumpled bow, wondering whether the *Stockholm* was still seaworthy. He was given a blanket, and that night he slept on deck beneath a warming air vent. David and Louise Hollyer slept with their life jackets tied to their wrists, worried that the battered *Stockholm* might founder. Some of the survivors and the *Stockholm* crewmen who had rescued them relieved the tension by gathering in a salon to sing the Swedish hymn "No One Is as Safe as When in God's Hands."

But the anxiety could hardly be eased for survivors who remained separated from family members, especially when a burden of guilt bore down. After Elisabeth Hanson and her three children got some sleep in the cabin a *Stockholm* stewardess had given them, Mrs. Hanson saw the man who had been in her lifeboat, averting his eyes from the *Doria*'s rail, where his wife and child remained while he saved himself. The man approached her, wringing his hands and crying for his daughter. "*Mia figlia, mia figlia,*" he lamented. Mrs. Hanson wondered what their family reunion in New York would be like.

At 8:30 Thursday evening, Johan-Ernst Bogislaus August Carstens-Johannsen was once again placed in charge of the bridge watch. After making a rescue run to the *Andrea Doria* soon after 1:00 A.M. Thursday and bringing back survivors in a lifeboat whose steering was damaged when it smashed into the *Doria*'s hull, Carstens had called it a night so far as saving any more passengers went. He spent the overnight hours passing on orders from Captain Nordenson and accompanying rescue crews to the wrecked bow where seamen had been trapped. At one point he became drenched on a flooded staircase. Not until 2:00 P.M. Thursday did Carstens return to his cabin for a few hours' sleep.

When he returned to the bridge during the evening, Carstens thought that Nordenson and perhaps another officer or two would be joining him on watch in view of the severe damage suffered by the *Stockholm* and, perhaps, questions concerning his judgment in those final minutes before the crash. But when Carstens relieved Second Officer Lars Enestrom on watch, he was alone, just as he had been the sole officer on the bridge during the hours preceding the collision. Back then, Nordenson had told Carstens to call him if he ran into fog. Never suspecting that the *Stockholm* was approaching a fogbank that was hiding the ship he had been tracking on radar, Carstens had not called the captain. This time Nordenson instructed him to summon Chief Officer Herbert Kallback if fog were encountered. If there were any other problems, Nordenson wanted to be advised directly. By now exhausted from overseeing efforts to keep the *Stockholm* afloat, free its anchor chains, and bring hundreds of *Doria* survivors on board, the sixty-three-year-old captain of the *Stockholm* finally went to bed.

Carstens was heartened, if not a bit surprised, by the confidence Nordenson was showing in him. "To let a guy twenty-six years old go up and take watch on the bridge again after such a thing like this collision, and then to go to bed himself, I think this is a very calm person," he reflected long afterward.

When the *Stockholm* entered New York Harbor late Friday morning—48 hours after her departure for Scandinavia—she was greeted with a cacophony of horn-tooting from boats large and small that echoed the receptions accorded the *Ile de France* and the *Cape Ann*. But the mood was somber at the offices of the Italian Line on State Street in Lower Manhattan. Frank Braynard, a maritime historian who was there when the *Stockholm* passed, observed how "the Italians stood silently at their harbor-view windows, just staring, daggers in their eyes."

The Swedish liner was a sorry sight. As she made her way up the Hudson River, sections of her steel skin peeled away from what remained of her once-graceful bow, dropping in chunks, and the residue of a large brown oil slick smudged her white hull.

Escorted to the Swedish-American Line berth at Pier 97 off West Fifty-seventh Street by three police helicopters, the Coast Guard, and three tugs, her flags were still flying and her twelve lifeboats had been reattached, but only the last six letters of *"Stockholm"* remained on the port side of her wrecked prow.

As the *Doria* survivors began telling their stories to newsmen, it seemed that no one had experienced more hard luck at sea than Nicola

Difiore, a fifty-year-old machinist from Matnazzoli, Italy, who had been aboard two troop transports sunk in the Mediterranean while serving in the Italian Army during World War II. "I never want to see another ship," said Difiore, who had been thrown against a bulkhead, injuring a shoulder, but had made it to a lifeboat by going down a rope ladder.

For many, joyous reunions were at hand.

Ruth Roman, having learned that her son, Dickie, was aboard the *Stockholm,* waited in the throng at the pier. She glimpsed the boy while he was on the deck, waved to him, and within minutes was carrying him through a horde of photographers, reporters, and newsreel cameramen.

Elisabeth Hanson, her three children in tow, spotted her husband, Alfred. The University of Illinois physics professor had met each of the earlier arriving rescue ships. For Albert Hanson, as for all the family members at the pier, the *Stockholm* represented the only remaining hope.

Ten-year-old Donnie Hanson rushed to greet his father. The boy held his left wrist in the air with wonderment and glee and shouted, "It runs, it runs." The wristwatch he was wearing when his pregnant mother dropped him into the sea was still working.

The Hansons walked along a barrier lined on the other side with reporters calling out the names of their papers, looking for hometown people to supply a local angle. Mrs. Hanson was wearing a pair of brocade slippers given her aboard the *Stockholm;* her children were barefoot. Within minutes they all had their choice of footwear, the Red Cross having provided boxes upon boxes of shoes.

Antonio Ponzi was reunited with his mother in a tearful embrace. And he learned that his sister, Marcella, had already arrived aboard the *Cape Ann,* among the first passengers rescued.

Some families had not been aware of the collision until arriving at the *Doria*'s pier when she was due to dock.

Father Raymond Goedert's brother, Father Robert Goedert, and his parents had driven from Chicago to bring him home. When they came to the pier Thursday morning, Robert Goedert approached a policeman and asked, "Where do we go to meet the ship?"

"Apparently you haven't heard," the officer said.

"Haven't heard what?"

"There was a collision between your ship and another one."

The parents hadn't overheard the exchange, and now Robert Goedert had to figure out how to keep them calm while they waited. He told them there had been some sort of accident, but didn't say there had been a collision.

Having arrived the day before on the *Ile de France*, Ruth Roman was reunited with her three-year-old son, Dickie, when he came off the *Stockholm*. (AP/Wide World Photos)

To pass the time, the Goederts chose one of New York's more popular tourist attractions, albeit a strange way to spend their day in view of the circumstances: they took a boat ride around Manhattan.

In the early afternoon, Robert Goedert and his parents were in a cab.

"Did you hear the news?" the taxi driver said. "The *Andrea Doria* sank."

So much for Father Goedert's hopes of keeping his parents calm.

The priest called the Italian Line a little later, but it could tell him only that there were many survivors. There was no word on which people were on which rescue ship.

The Goederts met the *Ile de France*, the *Cape Ann*, and finally went to Brooklyn to meet the *Thomas*—but Raymond Goedert was on none of these ships. Upon returning to their hotel late Thursday night from the *Thomas*'s Brooklyn pier, they received a phone call from the Italian Line—Raymond Goedert would be arriving the next day on the *Stockholm*. He was one of the last survivors coming down the gangplank, still wearing the black pants and T-shirt in which he had fled his cabin. The trousers were stained with oil and his shoes were tied around his neck.

When David and Louise Hollyer arrived on the *Stockholm*, they were bemused by a curious scene. Two Italians greeted each other with great emotion in a room reserved for survivors and their families. When these people emerged, they spotted news cameras and, without prompting, reenacted the hugs and kisses.

But for some, the arrival of the *Stockholm* brought no embraces— only confirmation of their fears.

Louis Guzzi had left his family's home in Easton, Pennsylvania, to meet his parents, and he arrived at the *Stockholm*'s pier with high hopes. The morning after the collision, his hometown paper, the *Easton Express,* reported that Giuseppe and Antoinette Guzzi had been spotted by friends aboard a lifeboat headed for the *Stockholm.*

When the *Stockholm* came in, Louis found Frank Russo, whom they had accompanied.

"Where's my parents?" Louis asked.

Frank had looked everywhere on the *Stockholm* for the couple, to no avail. "They're not on this ship," he told Louis, "and this is the last one."

It was evident to Frank that the Guzzis had returned early from the party they invited him to and had perished in the flooding of C Deck, the third-class section where they had taken a cabin so they could be close to him.

Margaret Sergio had been taken to the *Ile de France* after being assured that her sister, Maria, and four nephews and nieces had been rescued earlier. She was reunited on the French liner with her husband, Paul, who arrived in a later lifeboat. But they found no sign of Maria or her children on the ship. Their sons Tony and Joe had driven in from South Bend. Joe took his mother back to Indiana while Paul and Tony stayed behind, hoping that their extended family had been picked up by one of the other rescue ships. But Maria Sergio and her children were not on the *Cape Ann* or the *Thomas* or the *Stockholm.*

Father and son decided to wait one more day, in case another ship should arrive with survivors. They had dinner in Manhattan's Little Italy the night the *Stockholm* docked, then returned to their hotel. But Maria and her four children had gone down with the *Doria.*

Francisca D'Alesio of Queens searched in vain for her brother Michael Russo, his wife, Maria, and their children, Giovanina, fourteen, and Vincenza, ten, who had boarded the *Doria* in Naples, planning to settle with another sister in the Bronx. "Someone must have seen him," Mrs. D'Alesio insisted after calling hotels, hospitals, and even the Coast Guard in Boston, hearing that some survivors might have been brought there. "He's got a little mustache and he's a skinny fellow. He was jolly and would meet everyone with a big smile." But the cabinetmaker and his family had perished.

Antonio Diana and his nineteen-year-old daughter, Mary, of Hartford, Connecticut, having preceded the rest of the family to America to earn money for their passage, also found their last hopes gone with the arrival of the *Stockholm*. Angelina Diana, son Biaggio, eight, and daughter Victoria, six—traveling in tourist class like the Russos—also had died in the wreckage of the *Doria*'s lowest deck.

Sam Iazzetta of Brooklyn came to the *Stockholm*'s pier in search of his mother and his aunt. His seventy-year-old father, Benvenuto, had been persuaded to flee topside by a *Doria* crewman after he tried to break down the jammed door of the third-class cabin in which his wife, Amelia, and her sister, Christina Covina, had been trapped. Benvenuto Iazzetta had already returned on the *Ile de France*. So far as could be determined, no one from the *Doria*'s crew had ever gone back to the women's cabin in an effort to save them.

Lillian Zangrando, twenty-seven, of Clark Township, New Jersey, also waited in vain at the *Stockholm*'s pier. She was hoping to see her mother, Anita Leoni, fifty-four, of Rome, who had taken the *Doria* to be with her for the arrival of her baby in 2 months. The next day, Mrs. Zangrando received a letter mailed by her mother in Naples just before she went aboard the *Doria*. "I know that I will never live to see you again," her mother had written.

"Mother was afraid of the sea, but she put aside her fear because she wanted to see my baby," said her daughter.

Floyd Bremmerman, thirty-two, of Fort Worth, Texas, an Army Air Force pilot in World War II, came to the *Stockholm*'s pier searching for his thirty-one-year-old wife, Laura, an Italian war bride who had been returning from a visit to her family in Rome. The Italian Line had no record that Laura was on the *Doria*. But Bremmerman had proof, a radiogram his wife sent from the liner timed at 4:07 P.M. the day before the collision.

Replying to a message her husband had sent, saying he would meet her at the Belmont-Plaza Hotel in Manhattan, Mrs. Bremmerman had wired: "Bring blue and red dress and high-heeled shoes." Floyd Bremmerman came to New York with the dress and the shoes, but his wife never arrived.

Josephine Blanco of Tampa, Florida, carried a souvenir postcard of the *Doria* that her mother, Angelina Gonzales, had mailed from Gibraltar. She, too, was lost at sea.

Upon stepping off the *Stockholm*, Lillian Watres had plenty to say about the events leading to the death of her husband, Carl, from a heart attack aboard the *Stockholm*.

"Right after the crash, crewmen in our first-class area got out bot-tles of whiskey, which they passed around among themselves and started drinking," she said. "Then they disappeared. I asked the head steward where I should go. He said 'anywhere' and ran off. We waited on the deck for more than 2 hours. No one told us what to do. The only instructions over the loudspeaker were in Italian, and Italian-speaking passengers said they just were instructions to the crew."

Mrs. Watres said her husband had no history of heart problems but wore himself out helping other passengers. And she told of how an eld-erly man helped people keep their footing on the slippery deck, telling them, "On this ship it's everyone for himself, but I'm old and it doesn't matter."

"We enjoyed Italy," Mrs. Watres said. "But I lost my love for Ital-ians fast that night."

Frank Clifton, a city legislator from Toronto, who had been aboard one of the first lifeboats to depart the *Doria,* stepped off the *Stockholm* with an account that fueled the charges against the *Doria*'s crew. "From out of nowhere lots of the crew got into one of the boats," he said. "There were about forty crew members to four passengers in the boat."

The fact that more than two hundred *Doria* crewmen had been picked up by the *Stockholm,* which assumed much of the rescue burden in the early going, suggested that many had indeed saved themselves while leaving passengers behind.

Some of these crewmen had handled the *Doria*'s lifeboats, and they were quick to defend their actions when approached by reporters.

"Look at my hand," said a first-class steward named D'Alessandro Egislio, displaying a large broken blister painted with an antiseptic. "I rowed the first lifeboat to the *Stockholm* and rowed No. 9 lifeboat two or three times to the *Ile de France.* In four hours, we saved them all." The steward said he had carried children into lifeboats and calmed pas-sengers, singing and praying with them.

John Vigano of Genoa, the chief steward in tourist class, said he helped sixteen passengers down rope ladders.

When the *Doria* survivors and the *Stockholm*'s regular passengers had departed his ship, Captain Nordenson, speaking slowly and softly, met with reporters in a *Stockholm* lounge. He told of containing the damage the *Stockholm* had suffered and ordering the rescue operation that had plucked hundreds from the *Doria.* And he said his radar was in "tip-top" shape when he left New York. But on the advice of the Swedish-American Line lawyer Charles S. Haight, sitting beside him, Nordenson declined to speculate on how two ships with radar came to collide.

Gunnar Nordenson, the captain of the *Stockholm,* meeting with reporters upon the Swedish liner's arrival in New York. (AP/Wide World Photos)

"I don't want to boast and I don't want to blame anybody," he said.

Nordenson also refused comment on the allegations that many *Doria* crewmen were aboard the first lifeboats arriving at the *Stockholm.* "I don't know anything about that," he said. "We took off survivors. We couldn't tell what kind of people came off."

On Saturday evening, three tugboats towed the *Stockholm,* stern first, to the Bethlehem Steel Company drydock in Brooklyn for restoration of her bow. She looked a bit neater than when she had arrived in New York the day before, the jagged steel edges of her crumpled bow having been cut away.

All through Friday, the *Stockholm's* regular passengers had begun booking cabins on other Scandinavia-bound liners, eager to resume their vacations or business trips. Late that day, two *Doria* survivors were setting off on a far different kind of trip, a wild automobile ride through New England in search of the child who had been evacuated from the *Stockholm* by helicopter, her identity a mystery.

Tullio and Filomena Di Sandro had last seen their four-year-old daughter, Norma, fading into the North Atlantic night aboard the lifeboat she had been tossed into by her panic-stricken father in the first hour of the rescue operation. Where the lifeboat had gone, whether the child had survived her fall into the boat—and in what condition—her parents did not know.

The Di Sandros had been rescued by the *Ile de France.* When they came down its gangplank Thursday afternoon, Mrs. Di Sandro was hysterical, calling repeatedly for the little girl.

A New York–based reporter for the Italian weekly *Espresso,* Mrs. Friedl Orlando, heard the Di Sandros' story at the pier and received a

The *Stockholm* about to undergo restoration of its bow at the Bethlehem dry dock in Brooklyn. (Bethlehem Steel Corporation)

description of the girl from them. Norma was wearing a gold bracelet with a ram's horn good-luck charm on her left wrist and had a scar on her left knee.

The reporter phoned the Public Health Service hospital in Boston, having learned that an unconscious little girl had been flown there.

The description she relayed to the hospital matched that of the child. The reporter passed the news on to Mrs. Di Sandro's brother, Alfred De Matteo of the Bronx, who had met the Di Sandros at the pier. They set out for Boston by car Thursday night, picking up escorts from the state police in Rhode Island and Massachusetts, and arrived at the hospital five hours later.

Norma had undergone surgery to relieve pressure on her brain but had failed to regain consciousness. Mrs. Di Sandro tried to embrace the child in her bed as her husband and a nurse attempted to calm her, and then she fainted.

At 9:15 Friday night, Norma died. An Italian-speaking priest broke the news to the parents.

The evacuation of the little girl—her identity unknown to the public until late Friday—struck an emotional chord. Early in the day, the hospital switchboard was jammed with calls offering blood transfusions. Some people offered to adopt the girl in the event her parents had perished on the *Doria*.

Tullio and Filomena Di Sandro at the Boston hospital where their four-year-old daughter, Norma, was flown after being knocked unconscious when her father tossed her into a lifeboat. (Gordon Parks/TimePix)

After learning of Norma's death, the Di Sandros left for the home of a relative, Nicholas Di Sandro, in Providence, where they had planned to settle, having saved 10 years for their new life in America.

Soon after they departed from the hospital, an envelope arrived there, addressed to "the parents of little Norma Di Sandro."

Inside was a $10 bill and an unsigned note on a torn sheet of yellow paper reading: "The money's not important, but we'll pray for her." It was turned over to the Red Cross for delivery to the Di Sandros.

Norma was to have enrolled in September at the day nursery school of St. Ann's Church in Providence. At 9:30 the following Tuesday morning, a small white casket was carried up the church stairs by six cousins of the child as Filomena Di Sandro, supported by her husband and a friend, and escorted by seventeen girls from the nursery, entered the chapel. Hundreds of people gathered on the street. Inside, an Italian consular official, Guido Leopizzi, and the New England representative of the Italian Line, Captain Carlo Fava, were among the mourners.

Monsignor Anthony L. DiMeo sang a Solemn High Mass and the Litany of the Angels, and then the funeral procession left for St. Francis Cemetery in Pawtucket, filing out of a church honoring the saint whose life is commemorated on July 26—the day the *Andrea Doria* went down.

CHAPTER 29

"This Is a Jumbled Story"

Edward P. Morgan's predawn phone calls to the *New York Times* and the wire services from his Manhattan hotel seeking word on the Cianfarra family had led nowhere. When daybreak arrived, Morgan went to the ABC newsroom in New York, hoping he would soon receive news, but when none came by early Thursday afternoon, Morgan boarded the Coast Guard cutter meeting the *Ile de France* outside New York Harbor. He had never missed a broadcast, and he was determined not to do so now, but he arranged with Francis Littlejohn, ABC's news director, for someone to replace him if he did not arrive back by his 7:00 P.M. deadline.

When Morgan boarded the *Ile,* he sought a survivor list, but was told it was incomplete. Then someone said his former wife was aboard ship. Soon he found Jane Cianfarra in the *Ile*'s hospital, swathed in bandages.

"Cian is dead," she said, using her husband's nickname. "I heard him die. Where are the children?"

Morgan sought to reassure her, saying she couldn't be certain about her husband and that the two girls had no doubt been taken aboard other rescue ships.

He went to the purser's office to recheck the survivors list and then walked the decks. Nothing. It seemed obvious now—Linda Morgan, her half-sister, Joan Cianfarra, and Camille Cianfarra were all dead. And yet, if Jane had survived, perhaps there still was hope.

Morgan accompanied the crewmen maneuvering Jane on a stretcher through the *Ile*'s narrow corridors, then helped take her down the gangplank and onto the pier. An ABC reporter and his cameraman approached him for a live interview. Vaguely aware that he was breaking a journalistic code, Morgan declined, then hustled Jane into an ambulance that took her to St. Clare's Hospital for treatment of facial injuries, a fractured right hand, and a broken right leg and ankle.

When they arrived at the hospital, it was past six o'clock, less than an hour before airtime. Morgan phoned Littlejohn to say he would arrive at the studio in time for his 15-minute network newscast, but there would be no script: he would speak from his notes. Littlejohn was kindly but adamant—it wasn't necessary for Morgan to do the program, it didn't seem possible. Morgan was undeterred, and when he arrived at the studio 20 minutes later, his boss relented.

Ten minutes before airtime, while Morgan was going through his notes, the *New York Times* called. Did he have a photograph of Linda? Yes, he had a snapshot. Why?

The *Times* man paused. Then, apologizing for brusqueness, he told Morgan, "Of course, you know she and Joan and Cian are dead."

"Who the hell said so?" Morgan shouted. "I've just come off the *Ile de France* and I couldn't find anybody to confirm anything."

"Harrison Salisbury found the doctor who rescued your ex-wife, and he saw the bodies."

Salisbury, a distinguished correspondent on the Russian front in World War II, was one of the *Times*'s senior reporters. His source could not have been more authoritative. And yet . . .

Morgan told the *Times* it could send a messenger for the snapshot and hung up. Then he walked into the studio and approached his microphone, having no idea what he would say.

"Good evening," he began. "Here is the shape of the news: Tonight, it is the shape of disaster."

Morgan told of reports that seventeen hundred people had been rescued from the *Andrea Doria,* that "five or six" people were dead, scores of others injured. He told of having returned from the *Ile de France,* where he interviewed survivors. Then he put a human face on the disaster.

"This is a jumbled story—a story told in the faces of the persons that you see on the ship. Perhaps the best way to tell it, from notes and from memory, is just to jog down through the notes informally as I go.

"Take, for instance, a particular case: the case of a person who had persons, relatives, aboard the *Andrea Doria,* and was notified this morning about five o'clock that the two ships—the *Andrea Doria* and the *Stockholm*—had collided in the fog last night.

"There is the numbing, the wait, the confusion, the conflicting reports. And then in the afternoon the news that correspondents would be picked up by the Coast Guard and taken down the harbor to board the *Ile de France.*

"A lump comes in one's throat as one sees this vessel, a vessel of mercy. As we push under the starboard side, one looks up and sees a line—a necklace of faces—looking down from the rail. Somebody wants to know who are the passengers and who are the survivors. Soon one is able to tell. Here a shirttail sticking out. Here a nightshirt. Here a bandaged head."

Morgan told of encountering a survivor he knew, a broadcast executive named Morris Novik, who had described a "hideous crash" in the "worst fog he could think of." He told of Betsy Drake, having left her shoes behind, arriving aboard the *Ile* wearing borrowed cotton socks.

"But there were other people," Morgan continued. "There was Camille Cianfarra, the Madrid correspondent of the *New York Times;* his wife, Jane; and his stepchild, and another child. 'Where were they?' I asked. I was told that Mrs. Cianfarra was badly hurt. One finds her. She has multiple fractures and cuts. She asks about her husband. It is reported, but it is not confirmed, that Camille Cianfarra of the *New York Times* is among the dead. The children may be aboard another ship. It is not proved. It is not certain.

"Slowly, little by little, torturously for the persons who don't know, happily for the persons who do, the whole pieces of the disaster will be fitted together."

Morgan left his listeners to surmise that he had a connection with the Cianfarra family, but he never mentioned his daughter, Linda Morgan, by name. She was Camille Cianfarra's "stepchild." It seemed improper to identify her, Morgan would say later, "as if I would be soliciting condolences in a public place."

Morgan returned to his hotel room and phoned Thure Peterson, the chiropractor who had been interviewed by Harrison Salisbury after helping save Jane Cianfarra and laboring for 6 hours, together with the waiter Giovanni Rovelli, to free his wife from the rubble of Cabin 56, only to see her die.

"Doctor, I apologize for bothering you now," Morgan said, "but I need your confirmation that Linda and Joan are dead."

"There is no doubt of it," Peterson said in an even voice showing little emotion. "I saw their bodies."

For Morgan, there was a certain comfort, an end to his doubt. He went back to St. Clare's Hospital to tell Jane. Betsy Drake, who had met the Cianfarras in Spain, when Jane Cianfarra was writing a magazine article on Cary Grant, and had spent time with them aboard the *Doria,* was visiting the hospital room. "The girls had such an utterly happy time on the voyage—you can remember that," she told Morgan.

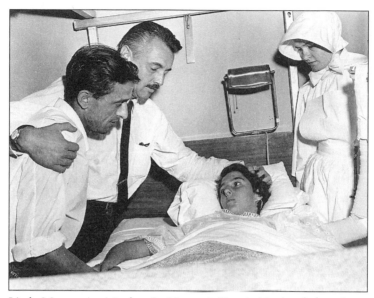

Linda Morgan is visited at St. Vincent's Hospital by her father, the broadcast commentator Edward P. Morgan (second from left), and Bernabe Polanco Garcia, the *Stockholm* crewman who carried her from the liner's wrecked bow. Sister Marita Rose is at right. (AP/Wide World Photos)

Morgan was numb, his eyes were dry. But walking back to his hotel with a friend, he broke down and cried.

On Friday morning, ABC's Littlejohn phoned to say the *Times* was now reporting there was a Linda Morgan on the list of survivors aboard the *Stockholm,* which was about to dock.

Morgan thought someone was playing a cruel joke on him, or if there really was a Linda Morgan aboard, it was not his daughter; perhaps an elderly schoolteacher from Detroit with the same name. He grabbed a taxi and got to the pier just as the *Stockholm* was tying up. Despite his press passes and frenzied explanations, Morgan couldn't get aboard at first, but a company official eventually escorted him onto the ship just as the injured were being wheeled onto ambulances.

He was taken to the chief purser, Curt Dawe, who confirmed that Linda Morgan had been saved. "You ought to know where we found your daughter," Dawe said. "In the wreckage on the bow."

A crewman told Morgan that Linda had been taken to Roosevelt Hospital in midtown Manhattan, but when Morgan arrived in a cab, she was not there. The nurses made some phone calls and found that she had been taken to St. Vincent's Hospital, in Greenwich Village.

"The drive downtown seemed like a trip across the continent," Morgan would recall. He finally found Linda at 1:15 P.M. as she was being wheeled into an X-ray room before surgery for a fractured bone in her upper left arm. She also had suffered injuries to both knees, and a piece of tape was wound around her forehead reading "M.S. Gr. 1/4," signifying she had received a quarter gram of morphine sulfate while aboard the *Stockholm*.

Morgan phoned Jane Cianfarra at St. Clare's Hospital. "Something's happened that some people call a miracle," he told her.

By now the newspapers were reporting the rescue of his daughter, notwithstanding Thure Peterson's certainty that he had seen the bodies of the sisters, an account that was never explained. Edward P. Morgan's first impulse was to once again forgo a revelation of his personal stake. But with the word of Linda's survival—she soon would be known as "the miracle girl"—this no longer made sense.

On his Friday evening ABC broadcast, Morgan told America: "Within the space of 24 hours, this reporter has been pushed down the elevator shaft of the subbasement of despair and raised again to the heights of incredible joy, washed, one suspects, with a slightly extravagant rivulet of some heavenly champagne."

PART IV

The Questions

CHAPTER 30

"The Passengers Were Highly Excitable"

The first formal step toward finding out why the *Andrea Doria* and the *Stockholm* collided was taken the day after the *Doria* sank, when the U.S. House of Representatives authorized an investigation by its Merchant Marine and Fisheries Committee. But before the issue of blame was addressed in a legislative or legal forum, a public relations skirmish was joined.

The *Doria*'s survivors seemed largely in agreement that the crew's actions in the aftermath of the collision had been disorganized. While some passengers praised individual crew members, others condemned the Italians for no help whatsoever.

Responding to the charges, the Italians launched an offensive to win over public opinion, and at the center stood a dispirited Captain Calamai.

Newsmen were called to the Italian Line offices in Lower Manhattan on Saturday—three days after the collision—to meet with the *Andrea Doria*'s captain, who had last been heard from upon arriving aboard the destroyer escort *Allen* Thursday night, when he read a statement at a chaotic session with reporters.

Calamai seemed far removed from the aura surrounding the captain of a magnificent ocean liner when he gathered with reporters a second time. He had shed his uniform for civilian clothes—a blue blazer, white shirt, and gray trousers—and he spoke softly and haltingly in uncertain English. He appeared to be under severe strain, and the Italian Line's chief lawyers, Eugene Underwood and Morgan Burke, often had to repeat his answers during a session that lasted 55 minutes.

Calamai denied that crew personnel took most of the spots in the first lifeboats, pointed out that he and his senior crewmen stayed aboard until it seemed the *Doria* was about to capsize, and expressed "gratitude to passengers who spoke highly of the conduct of my crew."

He maintained that "nearly all the deaths were caused at the moment of impact," evidently dismissing the possibility that some passengers were trapped alive in cabins that crewmen could not or would not enter. And he insisted that loudspeaker announcements had been made in English and Italian.

Italian Line officials refused once more to allow questions about Calamai's actions on the bridge in the moments preceding the collision, pointing out that Captain Nordenson of the *Stockholm* had declined to discuss the circumstances surrounding the crash when he met with reporters aboard the Swedish liner the day before.

When reporters persisted, the Italian Line lawyer Morgan Burke flushed in anger. "We have a theory but are not prepared to discuss it now," he said.

In a radio interview that day, the *Doria*'s chaplain, Monsignor Sebastian Natta, added his voice in defense of the crew, saying that many crewmen in the first lifeboats were there only to aid the passengers. He was quoted by the *Boston Globe* as calling it "a sin" to have criticized the seamen. An Italian Line spokesman maintained that most of the ninety survivors on the *Cape Ann* who signed the statement criticizing the *Doria*'s crew believed they were simply signing a survivor list or joining in a petition praising the *Cape Ann*'s seamen for rescuing them.

While Calamai was defending his crewmen's behavior, they were out on a shopping trip, many having barely enough clothing to venture from their hotel rooms. On Saturday afternoon, the seamen toured Macy's and Gimbel's in groups of ten with interpreters, buying clothes and luggage with a $60-per-seaman allotment from the Red Cross. Shoppers gawked as the crewmen fanned out, many still wearing oil-splattered blue denim trousers and torn shirts.

On Sunday, Calamai spoke at Manhattan's Hotel Governor Clinton at a rally for crewmen organized by the Italian embassy, reportedly out of concern for morale in light of the negligence charges.

Reporters were barred from the rally, leaving them to rely on an account offered by Giuseppe Ali, the Italian Line's director-general in New York. He reported that Calamai expressed his support for his men, saying, "I, as well as you, have a broken heart. You did all that you should have done to save the passengers, and I thank you all." Ali said that the crewmen had given Calamai a standing ovation, shouting, "Long live our captain."

Both the Italian Line and the Swedish-American Line paid passengers' expenses for hotel accommodations and meals in New York while they made alternative arrangements, but the Italians were especially eager to compensate *Doria* survivors who had spoken highly of the crew.

Referring to the Italian Line's payment of $24.18 to Margaret Dwight, an eighty-one-year-old Boston woman, for one night's stay and meal costs at the Hotel Sulgrave on Park Avenue, Captain Carlo Fava, the line's New England representative, wrote to his New York office: "Mrs. Dwight was one of the first passengers to declare through radio and television that the conduct of the crew of the *Andrea Doria* was commendable for the prompt attention given the passengers during the entire rescue operation."

Crewmen staying at the Hotel Commodore were eager to defend themselves when approached by reporters. "Why don't you ask Ruth Roman whose baby I saved?" said Cadet Giuliano Pirelli, who had taken the actress's three-year-old son, Dickie, down a ladder to a lifeboat.

"The passengers were highly excitable, fighting among themselves," said another cadet, Mario Magracci, who maintained that he told passengers to walk to boat stations, single file, then wait because help was coming.

The Italians were seen as sympathetic figures the following Thursday when a noon Mass for the dead and missing was offered at St. Patrick's Cathedral by Cardinal Francis Spellman, assisted by twenty-five Italian American priests in black vestments. Captain Calamai and four hundred crewmen were among the fifteen hundred in attendance, gathering alongside a catafalque draped in black in the middle aisle, three candles burning on each side in memory of the victims.

Cardinal Spellman received Calamai and Italian Line officials on the cathedral's terrace afterward. "I am sure the Italian spirit will rise from its sorrow and triumph over this disaster," the cardinal told the captain.

And the victims were remembered in a ceremony at sea. When the *Cristoforo Colombo,* the *Andrea Doria*'s sister ship, left Genoa for New York five days after the *Doria* went down, she flew her flag at half mast, a gesture joined in by eighty-nine ships in the harbor. On the final night of her voyage, as she approached the spot where the *Doria* plunged to the bottom, Captain Filippo Rando canceled the farewell ball and all other entertainment. Eight Maltese nuns threw a wreath overboard in tribute to two sisters from that order who perished on the *Doria,* and a fifteen-minute prayer service was held in the ship's chapel.

When the *Doria* crewmen began arriving back in Italy, they were treated as heroes. Forty-four crew members reaching Milan by air were welcomed in the name of the Italian government by Mayor Frederico Lomonaco of Verase. While three hundred onlookers cheered, he said the crewmen deserved the highest praise and had confirmed "the valor of Italian seamen."

The Swedes had no need to defend themselves as far as the rescue went. They had, by all accounts, acted valiantly, saving more than five hundred *Doria* passengers and crewmen while the *Stockholm* remained entangled in its anchor chains. But the Swedish-American Line would soon be facing questions of blame for the collision. Before that happened, its managers worked to create an aura of confidence in its crewmen while joining in criticism of the *Doria*'s crew.

The Italians weren't the only ones who could stage a crewmen's rally. Exactly one week after the ships collided, Erik Kronvall, the Swedish consul-general in New York, hailed the *Stockholm*'s 276 crewmen for their rescue efforts in a rally staged by 200 of them aboard the *Stockholm* at its Bethlehem Steel dry dock in Brooklyn.

At a news conference aboard the Swedish-American Line's *Kungsholm* at its Manhattan pier, the line's resident director, G. Hilmer Lundbeck, said that "Nordenson and his crew all did a swell job and they have our one hundred percent support and one hundred percent confidence."

And the Swedes were happy to draw a contrast with the *Doria*'s crew. Carl Quant, the *Stockholm*'s chief first-class steward, who supervised the arrival of lifeboats at the *Stockholm*'s starboard side, said that most of those arriving on the first three *Doria* lifeboats were kitchen help. He said that each boat had forty to fifty people aboard and "not too many were women and children."

Concerned with their image, the Swedes were none too happy when someone spoke without official permission, as the seaman who rescued Linda Morgan learned.

On Saturday, August 4, Bernabe Polanco Garcia visited Linda at St. Clare's Hospital, posing for pictures with the girl he had carried from the *Stockholm*'s bow. He had visited her before, but now he was saying good-bye, for he was scheduled to leave the next day with sixty-nine fellow crewmen on a chartered flight to Sweden and a reunion with his Swedish wife, Margit, and four-year-old daughter, Luisa.

Garcia brought Linda three carnations and told her *"Mi casa es tu casa"* (My home is yours). That made for splendid publicity as far as the Swedes were concerned, but soon it became evident that all was not well between Garcia and Captain Nordenson.

Garcia left the Brooklyn dry dock where the *Stockholm* was undergoing repairs at 3:00 P.M. Sunday on one of three buses carrying *Stock-*

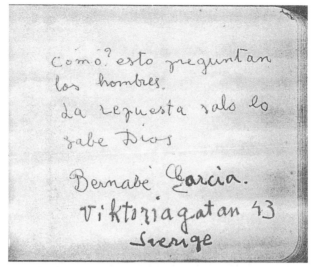

Bernabe Polanco Garcia signed Linda Morgan's autograph book, which had been catapulted with the fourteen-year-old girl onto the *Stockholm*'s bow from her *Andrea Doria* cabin. The inscription reads: "How this ask the men? The answer comes out God knows." (Courtesy of Linda Morgan Hardberger)

holm crewmen to Idlewild International Airport, but he disappeared upon arriving there. The Scandinavian Airlines System plane was held briefly as officials conducted a search, then left without him. The next day, Garcia turned up at the Spanish Benevolent Society in Manhattan.

According to newspaper reports, in a meeting with crewmen the previous Monday, Captain Nordenson had expressed his unhappiness with non-Swedes in the crew who had discussed the crash in print, and had mentioned Garcia by name. Garcia had reportedly told friends, as well as Edward P. Morgan, Linda's father, that he was offended by the remarks and that he was thinking of leaving the ship.

When the Spaniard was located at his countrymen's offices, high officials of the Swedish-American Line assured him that the captain had not insulted him—it was all a misunderstanding—and that he remained in Nordenson's good graces.

Garcia agreed to return to Göteborg on the freighter *Braheholm*, sailing the following Friday, a spokesman for the line said. By then the sparring to create a favorable public image had run its course. Now the Italians and the Swedes would be called to account for their actions at a U.S. courthouse.

CHAPTER 31

"It Could Have Been
a Patch of Fog"

When the accusations hurled by the Italians and the Swedes for public consumption died down, when the outrage of many *Doria* survivors over the crew's supposed neglect had run its course, it seemed evident that the last word would come in the courts.

The inquiry announced by the House of Representatives' Merchant Marine and Fisheries Committee was expected to shed light on the causes of the collision, but the committee did not have the power to summon witnesses. Its mandate was simply to look into safety considerations involving ships carrying Americans, with an eye toward legislation. The U.S. Coast Guard inspected foreign ships coming into American ports, but it lacked the authority to investigate the *Andrea Doria–Stockholm* collision since it involved foreign-flag liners on the high seas. And no international agency was empowered to investigate accidents in international waters.

The opening legal moves came a few weeks after the collision when the Italian Line, the Swedish-American Line, and some *Doria* passengers went into U.S. District Court for the Southern District of New York. Since many of the *Andrea Doria*'s passengers were American citizens, and since both lines had assets in the United States that could be seized to pay judgments, court action would be played out under American maritime law.

Both the Italians and the Swedes asked the federal court to give them exoneration from liability for the collision or, failing that, a limitation on liability for damages. The limitation concept dated back to the 1850s, when every sea journey was a perilous venture. Subjecting a maritime company to loss of all its assets through a legal judgment arising from a single accident would have played havoc with commerce. So the United States and other countries enacted laws limiting a maritime firm's liability for damages from an accident to the value of the ship involved unless it could be proved that the company had knowingly sent out an unseaworthy vessel or had known that the ship was being operated in a negligent or unlawful manner.

The Swedish-American Line put up a bond of nearly $4 million covering the appraised value of the *Stockholm,* hoping the courts would rule that it could not be held liable for damages exceeding that. The *Andrea Doria* was worth nothing, since it lay at the bottom of the Atlantic Ocean. In the case of a sunken ship, admiralty law limited a shipper's liability to $60 per gross ton unless negligence could be proved. Since the *Andrea Doria* was almost 30,000 gross tons, the Italian-American Line put up a bond of nearly $1.8 million.

The Italians and the Swedes, meanwhile, sued each other. The Italian Line filed a $25 million claim for the loss of the *Andrea Doria* (later increased to $30 million to reflect lost business), while the Swedish-American Line sought $1 million to cover repairs to the *Stockholm* and another $1 million for business losses. The Italians charged that the *Stockholm* caused the collision by making a right turn into the *Doria*'s path and that it had been traveling improperly on a track reserved for United States–bound ships. The Swedes maintained that the *Andrea Doria* had made an illegal left turn across the *Stockholm*'s bow and that even if the *Stockholm* were responsible for the collision, the *Doria* sank because it was not seaworthy or had been operated incompetently

More than a thousand lawsuits were filed ultimately against the two shipping lines. *Andrea Doria* survivors and heirs of *Doria* passengers and *Stockholm* crewmen who died in the collision brought claims totaling $53 million for death, injury, or property loss. Companies whose cargo went down with the *Doria* sought $33 million in damages.

All the lawsuits were consolidated into one action under federal judge Lawrence E. Walsh, who appointed four lawyers as special masters to preside over hearings designed to lay out each side's contentions before trial. These men—Louis M. Loeb, president of the Association of the Bar of the City of New York; Mark W. Maclay, an admiralty-law specialist; Benjamin A. Matthews, president of the New York County Lawyers Association; and Simon H. Rifkind, a former federal judge— were to ensure the orderly presentation of testimony and make rulings subject to the judge's final determination.

The hearings opened on September 19 at the U.S. courthouse in Lower Manhattan, the site a few years earlier of two sensational cases of the Cold War era, the perjury trial of the former State Department official Alger Hiss, and the espionage-conspiracy trial of Julius and Ethel Rosenberg.

Taking the stand as the first witness, Johan-Ernst Bogislaus August Carstens-Johannsen, the officer in charge of the *Stockholm*'s bridge when it collided with the *Andrea Doria,* looked out onto two banks of benches. Some fifty lawyers—representing the Italian and Swedish liners, passengers, cargo carriers, and insurance companies—were arrayed in front of him. The *Doria*'s captain, Piero Calamai, sat on one side, wearing a brown suit, his hands folded in his lap, "on his face the pale dust of fatigue," as Horace Sutton of *Saturday Review* put it. On the opposite side, two rows forward, sat the *Stockholm*'s captain, Gunnar Nordenson, wearing his blue uniform, two strands of gold on his sleeve, three rows of ribbons on his chest, the courtroom lights reflecting off his bald head. At the bench, the special master Simon Rifkind presided, slouching back in his green leather chair.

Carstens was taken through the events leading to the collision by the Swedes' chief lawyer, Charles Haight, a tall, soft-spoken Harvard Law School graduate and a prominent member of the Swedish-American community.

Although Carstens spoke and understood English, the questions and answers were translated to and from Swedish. Occasionally Carstens arose to examine his charts, illustrating a point he was trying to make. His face grew flush at times, and pulling a handkerchief from his side pocket, he swabbed at his brow and patted his mouth, but his evident nervousness soon passed and he grew self-assured.

He told of spotting the *Doria* on radar at 12, 10, and then 6 miles away—each time to the *Stockholm*'s left, or port side; of plotting the Italian liner's course on a board beside his radar screen; and of seeing the *Doria*'s lights to the *Stockholm*'s port side at a little less than 2 miles' distance. (The plotting board was not produced, since Carstens had erased the readings.) He told how he had ordered a turn of some 20 degrees to the right to create a wider expanse between the ships, expecting them to pass at a separation of at least 1 mile. And finally Carstens related how after answering a telephone call from a lookout, facing away from the bow when he picked up the receiver, he was startled to see the *Doria* turn left and veer into his path. He testified that he did not hear a whistle signal from the *Doria* signifying a turn until the liner had begun to cross his bow and that he could not identify the precise nature of the signal because the noise of his engine telegraph or the din of the collision had partially drowned it out.

Johan-Ernst Bogislaus August Carstens-Johannsen at the federal court pretrial hearing in New York where he testified on his actions preceding the collision. (AP/Wide World Photos)

Before the opening day had ended, Carstens came under cross-examination from the Italian Line's chief lawyer, Eugene Underwood, a specialist in admiralty cases with a zest for courtroom combat and an aggressive manner. Like Haight, he would not let a single detrimental nuance go unchallenged.

Much of Underwood's questioning of Carstens focused on the *Stockholm*'s failure to reduce speed in the moments preceding the collision.

Carstens maintained that he had no cause to slow from his customary 18.5 knots, or to call Captain Nordenson to the bridge from his cabin, or to sound his foghorn periodically, since he was not running in fog. In fact, the moon was shining brightly to the *Stockholm*'s right, he said. But he conceded that the *Doria* might have been temporarily obscured by a fog bank shortly before the ships collided, although insisting that he had no indication of that at the time.

Since ships' lights were said to be visible for 4 to 5 miles on clear nights, Carstens was asked by Underwood why he thought he had not been able to see the *Doria*'s lights until she was less than 2 miles away.

"I'm also wondering about that," he replied.

"Was it because of fog?" Underwood asked.

"There was no fog around me," Carstens answered.

"What did you think was around her so you couldn't see her?" Underwood asked.

"It could have been a patch of fog," Carstens said.

Underwood was seeking to show that Carstens's inability to see the *Doria*'s lights at 5 miles off should have led him to realize he was entering fog and that he should therefore have reduced speed.

Carstens's testimony in regard to time and distance in the minutes before the collision was challenged by Underwood.

In notes that Carstens made just after the collision, he reported having picked up his first radar observation at 11:00 P.M.—"on the even hour"— when the *Doria* was 12 miles away. But he testified that 11:00 P.M. was merely the approximate time he made the entry, that he had first picked up the *Doria* on radar some minutes earlier. And Carstens testified that the *Doria* was, in fact, 10 miles off at about 11:00 P.M. The collision came 9 minutes later, he said.

Underwood noted that the *Stockholm*, going at about 18 knots, would have traveled 2.7 miles between 11:00 P.M. and 11:09 P.M., meaning that the *Doria* would have had to travel 7.3 miles in the 9-minute span, or at an impossible speed of 47 knots, for the crash to have occurred at 11:09.

"You don't think any ship can go that fast, do you?" Underwood asked.

Carstens acknowledged the impossibility of such a speed and calculated that the *Doria* would have been about 5.5 miles away at 11:00 P.M., not 10 miles off, as he had stated. But he said that the 11:00 P.M. time he gave for the 10-mile reading was an approximation. "I haven't said anything about a definite time," he told Underwood.

Through cross-examination by a host of lawyers, the *Stockholm*'s third mate remained adamant that he had followed all the maritime rules of the road and that he had used good judgment. An employee of one of those lawyers had, meanwhile, been engaged in black humor. Somebody at the Lower Manhattan offices of Jacob Rassner, who represented many clients suing the Italian and Swedish shipping companies, placed a ship model on its side in the bottom of a 50-gallon fish tank and labeled it *Andrea Doria*.

Carstens was followed to the stand by Captain Piero Calamai. By then, the hearings had been moved to the New York County Lawyers Association building on Vesey Street in Lower Manhattan, its gray facade looking out on Trinity Church and its graveyard bearing the remains of Alexander Hamilton. A sense of history also permeated the crystal-chandeliered hearing auditorium, a long room adorned with red drapes.

Along the walls, oil paintings of twenty-one figures of the American legal profession overlooked the foreign mariners who were being called to account in an American legal proceeding.

Carstens and Calamai presented a stark contrast. Carstens had testified in a strong voice, his demeanor assertive. Calamai spoke softly and appeared depressed.

"Calamai sat glum, dour and ashen on the dais," Horace Sutton wrote in *Saturday Review.* "At times his face seemed to disappear into the yellowish beige of the walls, and the ordeal of his time showed in the vertical gorges that run like a pair of parentheses from his nose to his sharp chin. The thoughts weighed his head and he rested it now and then in the vise of thumb and forefinger pinched against the bridge of his nose.

"Sometimes his fingers spread like a restraining web against his cheek, and his eyes narrowed to slits as he focused, as if focusing would help him translate the lawyer's words before they could flow in friendly Italian from the translator who sat at his feet below the dais."

Under direct questioning from the Italian Line's Underwood, Calamai told of coming up to his bridge when fog rolled in during the afternoon of the final full day at sea and remaining there through the evening as the *Doria* continued at nearly full speed, the radar constantly observed, the foghorn sounding. He told of the *Doria*'s radar having first spotted an oncoming ship 17 miles away and 4 degrees to the right, or to starboard, and of eventually ordering a 4-degree turn to port to create a wider passing distance. He testified to having spotted a glow of lights from the other ship when it was a bit more than 1 mile away and still to starboard, and then of his astonishment at seeing the ship making a right turn—into the *Doria*'s path—without sounding a warning whistle. Calamai recounted how he then sounded his own turning whistle and ordered a sharp left turn, full speed ahead, in a futile effort to avoid a crash.

Calamai maintained that the two ships would have completed a right-side-to-right-side passage if the *Stockholm* hadn't turned into the *Andrea Doria*. And he said that if the *Stockholm* had sounded its whistle to warn it was about to make its right turn, he would have steered the *Doria* to the right, allowing the ships to pass safely. Moreover, said Calamai, the *Stockholm* had been traveling in the track reserved for westbound ships, 20 miles north of the track for eastbound vessels. He said that in his dozens of transatlantic trips, he had never encountered a European-bound ship in the New York–bound track.

Amid the host of allegations from each side, one overriding and irreconcilable issue remained: Carstens had testified that the *Stockholm*'s radar showed the two ships were about to pass left-side-to-left-side, but Calamai testified that the *Doria*'s radar showed they would be passing right-side-to-right-side.

When the Swedes' chief lawyer, Charles Haight, cross-examined Calamai, he focused at first on the fate of the *Andrea Doria*'s logs, whose contents presumably could have thrown light on culpability for the collision.

At issue were navigation logs kept by the watch officers on the bridge, containing data about a ship's course, the weather, currents, and drift; the engine-room logs, recording a ship's speed at any instant as well as orders from the bridge; and the wireless logs, recording messages sent and received.

Calamai testified that he had given orders at 2:30 A.M. that all the *Doria*'s books and papers be saved, but that this was only a general directive to the officers and seamen on the bridge at the time—that no specific officer was told to save a particular log. Calamai said he removed his personal log, containing administrative data, and two secret code books of the North Atlantic Treaty Organization from his cabin safe and had taken these materials with him when he boarded a lifeboat at 5:30 A.M. He said that his only specific directive concerning documents had been to an officer told to save the course-recorder printout, giving the ship's heading at every moment, and that the portion of the recorder detailing the *Doria*'s final day at sea had, in fact, been taken to the lifeboat.

But no one saved the navigation, engine-room, or wireless logs, Calamai testified. He said he realized they had not been removed only when he and his senior officers were in their lifeboat and that he decided against asking crewmen to return to the *Doria* and retrieve the logs out of fear the ship might capsize at any moment.

Haight expressed skepticism over this account, since the Italian Line had reported on July 31 that the logs had been saved. Asked by the Swedes' lawyer why he had not publicly contradicted that report, Calamai said there were so many incorrect statements arising back then that he felt no need to refute each one.

Calamai was also asked whether the crew had fulfilled its responsibility to the *Andrea Doria*'s passengers in the hours following the collision.

"What measures did you take to determine if any passengers had been catapulted or slid into the sea after the collision?" asked Leon Silverman, a lawyer for the Cianfarra family. Eight-year-old Joan Cianfarra, her body never found, could well have been hurled into the sea at the moment of impact, when her half sister, Linda Morgan, was tossed onto the *Stockholm*'s bow.

"We put on all the lights and could have seen anyone in the water," Calamai replied.

Silverman then asked Calamai if he had ordered a search of the seas around the hole in the *Doria*'s hull before his abortive effort to bring his liner to shallower waters for a possible beaching.

"No," Calamai said, "at that moment I had other thoughts, pre-occupations."

"Did you at any time before you left the ship give any orders for that area to be searched?" Silverman asked.

"I didn't give this order," Calamai answered, "but the lifeboats in the water could have ascertained if there was anyone in the water."

Some of the lawyers who cross-examined Calamai suggested that a number of passengers were left trapped in their cabins when the captain and his senior officers abandoned ship at 5:30 A.M.

Calamai testified that at about 4:00 A.M., and again just before he left the ship, he had received reports from Staff Captain Osvaldo Magagnini that all passengers who could have been saved had been rescued.

"The staff captain reported that all parts of the ship that were accessible had been visited by the stewards, and that all passengers had been disembarked in lifeboats, naturally with the exception of persons who remained in cabins hit by the collision," Calamai said. Wreckage and flooding by seawater had made some cabins impossible to enter, he maintained.

Calamai was asked by Nathan Baker, one of the lawyers for claimants, "Were you satisfied with the staff captain's report without making any further effort to determine whether any persons still living were left behind?"

Calamai said that in view of the severe list, "When I left the ship it was impossible to go from one side of the ship to the other to check all cabins."

Asked whether he could have done this earlier, he replied, "How could I personally make the rounds of the ship myself? I was occupied with many duties on the bridge."

The crewmen purportedly searching for passengers had missed at least one person who was decidedly not trapped—Robert Lee Hudson, the ailing seaman who slept through the collision and was plucked from a cargo net by a lifeboat crewman from the tanker *Robert E. Hopkins*.

There was, in particular, the question as to what happened in A Deck's Cabin 230, whose occupants—Margaret Carola, Christina Covina, and Amelia Iazzetta—had perished. This was the cabin where a steward had tried in vain to help Mrs. Iazzetta's husband, Benvenuto, break down the door, then had persuaded the man to leave the ship while promising he would seek help.

Calamai had indeed received a report of women trapped in that cabin, presumably from this steward. But no one from the *Doria*'s crew ever entered that cabin. Under questioning by Leonard Matteson, another of the lawyers representing *Doria* passengers, Calamai said he had sent a rescue squad to Cabin 230, but that those crewmen reported that a mistake had been made in the cabin number, that the call had actually come from Cabin 236. That was where three-year-old Rose Marie Wells had caught her hand between her bed and a cabin wall. These rescuers may, in fact, have been stopped by the girl's mother before they ever got to No. 230, freed the child, and then forgotten about the original rescue call.

Had the three women in Cabin 230 died instantly when their cabin was struck by the *Stockholm*'s bow? Had they been swept to sea at that moment? Or were they still alive, and trapped, when the *Doria* sank? No one would ever know.

Another vexing issue for Calamai was the fact that so many passengers had remained on upper decks along the port—or high side—of the *Doria* for a couple of hours without any idea that lifeboats were loading from the low—or starboard—side.

Calamai was asked whether the passengers were notified on the public-address system that the portside lifeboats could not be used because of the ship's list and that only the starboard lifeboats could be launched.

"No," he replied, "I did not want to frighten them."

He said that ship's officers were ordered to explain the situation to passengers as they assembled in response to loudspeaker instructions.

His first instructions, he said, were given in Italian through loudspeakers in the crew's quarters: "Personnel in charge of lifeboats should go to their stations."

A few minutes later, Calamai said, directives were given in Italian, and then in English, over loudspeakers, saying, "Passengers are instructed to go to their stations," and asking them to remain calm.

Some passengers later reported hearing these instructions, others told of hearing only garble from the loudspeakers, some said they heard only the plea *"calmi,"* and yet others maintained they heard no instructions whatsoever.

Calamai was asked under cross-examination to defend his decision to run at nearly full speed—only 1.2 knots below his maximum of 23 knots—while proceeding through fog for 8 hours and even after spotting an oncoming ship on radar.

He testified that without radar, 12 to 14 knots would have been his maximum safe speed on a foggy night. Since he had radar, it was his practice, he said, to make only a slight reduction of speed in fog unless he were in crowded waters or the radar showed the possibility of collision. Although the stretch of sea where the accident occurred had been called "The Times Square of the Atlantic," Calamai maintained "we were not in crowded waters." And he said that the other ship was proceeding on a parallel route that clearly would have resulted in a safe passing if not for its right turn.

That last assertion was challenged by Haight, the Swedes' lawyer, who asked Calamai and Curzio Franchini, the officer who had been manning the *Doria* radar and testified later in the hearing, to plot the *Stockholm*'s approach. They drew plots showing that the separation between the *Doria* and the *Stockholm* was, in fact, narrowing as the two ships approached each other, that the vessels would have cleared each other by less than half a mile if they had continued on without any turns. The suggestion was that Calamai would have slowed down had he known the passing distance was decreasing, and that the only reason he didn't know that was that he had neglected to use his plotting device.

Calamai was also asked about the *Doria*'s stability, an issue that went to the heart of the puzzle over why she had listed so severely. He said he couldn't remember the technical details relating to stability in the days preceding the crash. The Swedish-American Line's lawyer raised that matter to suggest that the *Doria* capsized because it was structurally unstable and/or because proper measures to keep the liner afloat were not taken by engine-room personnel after the collision. If the Swedes could prove that, then the *Stockholm* presumably could not be held liable for the *Doria*'s sinking even if the *Swedish* liner were shown to have caused the collision.

As the days wore on, the chief lawyers for the Italians and the Swedes clashed repeatedly.

When the Swedes' Haight asked Calamai to fix the time at which he abandoned ship, the Italians' Underwood broke in: "I object to that as a matter of simple arithmetic."

When Haight sought a precise translation of the Italian word for fog, Underwood complained: "This is not a semantical exercise."

When Haight asked if the *Doria* lost buoyancy after the collision, Underwood rose to say: "It should be unnecessary for me to tell Mr. Haight that the *Doria* sank."

Calamai, his face paling, seemed increasingly mired in depression as lawyers for the long string of claimants subjected him to repetitive questioning. After he had been on the stand for more than a week,

Underwood complained of "this medieval trial by ordeal," prompting Benjamin A. Matthews, the special master presiding that day, to cut short questioning he found repetitious or irrelevant.

Captain Nordenson was called to testify after Calamai and spent much of his first two days defending his decision to place the *Stockholm* on a path creating the prospect of a head-on collision with ships coming to New York.

Nordenson said he had been with the Swedish-American Line for 36½ years, had made 423 Atlantic crossings, and that except for periods when there was ice near Nantucket, had always followed an eastbound route to *Nantucket Lightship* that was 20 miles north of the path recommended by the U.S. Coast and Geodetic Survey for vessels going to Europe. He said that his route was the shortest one to Scandinavia, was commonly taken by ships heading there—and even by some ocean liners going to other European destinations—and that his route was the safest one for him.

Nordenson said that if he had taken the recommended eastbound track—a path that would have had the *Stockholm* pass 20 miles south of *Nantucket Lightship*—he would have then had to turn north and cross the lanes of westbound ships as he headed toward Nova Scotia and Scotland. That, he said, would have taken him a distance of 10 or 15 miles across the bow of ships bound for New York from Irish, English Channel, and Mediterranean ports.

"Meeting ships head-to-head, or nearly so, is safer than to meet them crossing," he maintained.

In Nordenson's third day on the stand, the hearing took a distressing turn.

Focus had shifted to the calculations of time and distance made by Carstens in the moments preceding the crash, specifically his statement that the *Doria* and the *Stockholm* were 10 miles apart about 9 minutes before the collision, an impossibility in view of the two ships' speed.

Nordenson was directed by the Italian Line's lawyer to do some arithmetic of his own relating to the combined distance that could have been traveled by the *Andrea Doria* and the *Stockholm* over a 9-minute span at their combined speed of about 40 knots, an exercise that Underwood knew would buttress his contention that Carstens's testimony was unreliable.

While Nordenson was working with pencil and paper on the witness stand, he seemed to have difficulty making his calculations. Leonard Matteson, one of the cross-examining lawyers, stood over him, watch in hand, alongside the Italian Line lawyer Underwood. Matteson announced that 2 minutes had gone by without an answer from Nordenson and then that 5 minutes had elapsed.

"I ask that Mr. Matteson sit down and not hold his watch on the captain," the Swedes' Haight interjected.

"Captain, do you know how to figure that computation?" Underwood asked.

Nordenson did not answer. He stopped his figuring. His usually ruddy complexion turned white and he put his hand to his head. Then he turned to Mark Maclay, the special master presiding, and told him in a low voice, "I do not feel well."

The hearing adjourned, Nordenson went back to his quarters on the *Stockholm*, undergoing repairs in Brooklyn, then entered St. Luke's Hospital in Manhattan shortly after midnight. Nordenson's doctor found that he had suffered a cerebral spasm that interfered with blood supply to the brain, then reported to the court a few days later that he had, in fact, experienced a small brain clot.

Nordenson returned to the courtroom six weeks later, the hearings having continued with testimony from other officers and engine-room personnel. But now the *Stockholm* captain's vigor was gone. He spoke in an almost inaudible voice in expressing full agreement with the actions Carstens had taken as the *Stockholm* approached the *Doria*.

The hearings seemed destined to drone on until February—the court-imposed deadline for testimony to end—with a full trial scheduled to begin in April. But the myriad allegations, the conflicting accounts, and the explanations of highly technical navigation data were soon cut short.

CHAPTER 32

"The Stability of the Ship Was Low"

The courage and skill of the crewmen who manned lifeboats and led passengers down ropes, ladders, and cargo nets, and the confluence of good fortune—calm waters and the evaporation of the Nantucket fog—averted a huge loss of life.

A total of 1,660 passengers and crewmen of the *Andrea Doria* were saved by the *Stockholm*, the *Ile de France*, the freighter *Cape Ann*, the military transport *Private William H. Thomas*, the Coast Guard cutter *Hornbeam*, the Navy destroyer escort *Edward H. Allen*, and the tanker *Robert E. Hopkins*. Only the rescue of some 1,500 people in the *Republic-Florida* collision of 1909 and the saving of a similar number of British servicemen and their families from the burning troopship *Empire Windrush* off the Algerian coast in the predawn hours of March 28, 1954, had approached the massiveness of the *Andrea Doria* operation in the annals of peacetime rescues at sea.

Nevertheless, forty-six *Andrea Doria* passengers and five *Stockholm* crewmen died in the collision or its immediate aftermath, and a magnificent ocean liner was lost.

In early January 1957, while the federal court hearings were entering their fifth month, the House of Representatives' Merchant Marine and Fisheries Committee, chaired by Herbert Bonner, a North Carolina Democrat, sought to provide some explanations for the collision and the rapid listing of the *Andrea Doria*.

The committee report, drawn up by four maritime specialists, including Edward L. Cochrane, a retired naval vice admiral who once served as chairman of the U.S. Maritime Commission, did not attempt to apportion blame. And the committee was limited by lack of authority to subpoena witnesses. But it found that the collision raised "serious questions" as to whether the *Andrea Doria* and the *Stockholm* "were being operated in accordance with the precepts of good seamanship."

The report noted that the *Stockholm* was running 20 miles to the north of the recommended path for European-bound liners. Nevertheless, the report stated, the collision "would have been prevented if the information provided by radar had been properly used."

The report's especially controversial findings related to the *Andrea Doria*'s construction. Referring to the ship's arrangement of watertight compartments, it found that the *Doria* "met the subdivision requirements of the 1948 Safety of Life at Sea Convention by a very narrow margin." And those requirements, the committee said, were less strict than the standards set by American authorities for United States–flag ocean liners.

The issue of the *Andrea Doria*'s stability was particularly troublesome for the committee's investigators, who noted that the ship's Stability Report assured it could meet the requirements of the 1948 convention "provided she was kept ballasted with substantial and specified quantities of liquids in her various tanks."

"It does not appear possible to account for the behavior of the ship following the collision on July 25, 1956, except on the assumption that she was not in fact ballasted in accordance with this information at that point," the report said.

It continued: "The stability of the ship was low, else she would not have taken the immediate heavy list reported as 18 degrees. . . ."

The onrush of seawater into the nearly empty deep starboard fuel tanks pierced by the *Stockholm*'s bow while the empty portside fuel tanks remained undamaged—was presumably the prime factor causing the *Doria* to list. Had seawater been pumped into all-empty fuel tanks as the ship approached the end of its trip, its stability would have been enhanced. But that was not done for understandable reasons. Had water been put into the fuel tanks, it would have had to be pumped into a barge—a lengthy and expensive procedure—before the *Doria* refueled in New York. The mixture of fuel oil residue and saltwater could not have been discharged into the harbor because of pollution regulations.

In its report, the House committee noted that all ocean liners faced this predicament. But it said that American-flag ships surmounted the problem by being built in accordance with particularly high construction standards and, if necessary, by carrying solid ballast to replace expended fuel oil.

The Italian Line was predictably indignant over the report. It maintained that the *Doria*'s having remained afloat for 11 hours despite

receiving a "tremendous blow" was "the best proof of the positive stability of the ship."

Three weeks after the House committee issued that report, the Italian
Line and the Swedish-American Line ended their legal wrangling. Following talks with their insurance underwriters in London, they reached
a settlement approved by the U.S. District Court in New York. The
congressional report questioning the *Andrea Doria*'s stability may have
prompted the Italians to settle, although that meant dropping their
claim of $30 million in damages against the Swedes for the loss of the
Doria. But neither the Italians nor the Swedes would say why they
reached an accord.

Under the settlement, the Italian Line and the Swedish-American
Line were granted the limited liability they sought and were to negotiate settlements with the more than one thousand parties who had filed
$86 million in claims for death, injury, or property loss. The Italians
and the Swedes dropped their suits against each other. Insurance underwriters paid out about $19 million toward the loss of the *Andrea Doria*.
The Italian government, which controlled the Italian Line's parent organization, the merchant marine trust Finmare, assumed the remainder of
the $30 million loss. The insurers for the Swedish-American Line,
which was owned by the Brostrom shipping firm, covered the $1 mil-
lion cost of restoring the *Stockholm*'s bow.

If any of the passengers who sued the Italian and Swedish shipping companies had refused to accept a settlement from the $5.8 mil-
lion fund posted by the two lines from their limited-liability reserves,
those parties could have demanded a full trial in which blame for the
accident presumably would have been resolved. But all the passengers
eventually reached accords, the Italians making 70 percent of the pay-
ments and the Swedes 30 percent under terms of the settlement, according to Brostrom.

The passenger claims were considered inflated since virtually every
claimant filed twice, seeking damages from both the Italians and the
Swedes. Nonetheless, many of the passengers were presumably vexed at
what they received.

Thure Peterson sought $500,000 for the death of his wife, Martha,
buried in the wreckage of Cabin 56. He settled for $10,000. Tullio and
Filomena Di Sandro sought $100,000 for the death of their four-year-old
daughter, Norma. They received $9,000. Ross Sergio, back in South
Bend, Indiana, having saved to bring his wife and four children over
from Italy, sought $300,000 for the death of Maria Sergio, age forty-

nine, and $50,000 apiece for the deaths of the children. He settled for a total of $37,500.

For the lucky ones, the claims were confined to lost property. Richardson Dilworth, the Philadelphia mayor, who had been unstinting in his praise of the *Doria* crewmen, nonetheless brought suit, together with his wife, Ann, for reimbursement from the Italian Line for personal articles that went down with the *Doria*. The Dilworths seemingly overlooked nothing, asking for $5,138 to cover their losses, among them 10 ties (which they valued at $75), 2 girdles ($70), and 6½ yards of raw Italian silk intended as gifts ($52). The terms of their settlement were not revealed.

The congressional committee that investigated the collision issued a series of recommendations, calling for better radar training for deck officers, greater observance of the recognized eastbound and westbound routes, and installation of bridge-to-bridge telephones, something that would have allowed the officers of the *Doria* and the *Stockholm* to speak to each other as the ships converged. Those recommendations were eventually adopted. But the most significant steps arising from the collision were the creation of the International Maritime Consultative Organization, a unit to promote safety measures, and its sponsorship of a Safety of Life at Sea Convention in London in 1960.

The last settlements in the passengers' lawsuits were reached in May 1959. By then it was clear there would never be a legal determination of blame for the accident. The American court proceeding had ended before a full trial could get under way. The Italian government conducted an investigation in which virtually all of the *Andrea Doria*'s 572 crewmen were believed to have testified, but the hearings were closed and the findings were not disclosed. The Swedish government decided against its own inquiry.

Life magazine sought an interview with Captain Piero Calamai in an effort to elicit some explanations beyond his testimony in federal court, but the Italian Line delayed in making him available, and *Life* finally gave up.

Look magazine interviewed the *Stockholm*'s Johan-Ernst Bogislaus August Carstens-Johannsen in March 1957, when he set out on a transatlantic trip as an officer of the newly repaired liner. "I did what was right and I would do the same thing again tomorrow if the emergency arose," he said.

While Carstens was in America for the court proceedings, his wife had given birth to a daughter, their first child. "Now that I have a family, I would like to spend more time at home," he told *Look*. "Maybe I will leave the sea. Perhaps I can become a helicopter pilot or navigator of an airplane."

CHAPTER 33

"I Could Have Changed Course"

Two ocean liners sighted each other on radar, each having ample time and an open ocean allowing them to carry out a safe passage with ease. And yet, as if destined to come together, they collided in one of history's most calamitous disasters at sea.

Who was at fault?

Both Piero Calamai, the captain of the *Doria*, and Johan-Ernst Bogislaus August Carstens-Johannsen, the third mate of the *Stockholm*, allowed their ships to approach each other at full, or nearly full, speed, with little margin for reacting to an unexpected maneuver by the other ship.

The *Andrea Doria* was 17 miles from the *Stockholm* when it made radar contact. The *Stockholm* was 12 miles from the *Andrea Doria* when the Swedish ship's radar picked up the Italian liner. The ships' officers drew opposite conclusions from reading their radar screens: the *Doria* concluded that the *Stockholm* was approaching on its right side, while the *Stockholm* concluded that the *Doria* was approaching on its left side. But in each case the angle of approach was small. The *Doria*'s radar operator estimated that the two ships would pass with a separation of about a mile if both kept to their courses. Carstens believed their separation would be about three quarters of a mile if neither changed course.

Calamai, running in fog, and Carstens, operating in what was evidently mostly clear weather and oblivious to the possibility of fog ahead, could have made early, decisive turns that would been obvious on each other's radarscope and would have allowed a wide berth for passage. But neither did so, each man confident there would be a parallel passing.

"Both vessels were to blame," Captain Richard Cahill, a fellow of Britain's Royal Institute of Navigation and a former professor at the U.S. Merchant Marine Academy, has written. "Where sea room is available a prudent mariner does not let another approach so close that some sudden and unanticipated move does not allow time to take effective evasive action."

That point was raised at the pretrial hearings in federal court when Charles Haight, the Swedish-American Line's lawyer, questioned Calamai about the period after his radar first spotted the *Stockholm* approaching 17 miles away and before he saw her lights and realized a collision was imminent.

"Is it not your practice when meeting other vessels to pass port to port [left to left] when circumstances permit?" Haight asked.

"Yes," Calamai replied.

"Was there sufficient deep water on your right to pass port to port?" Haight followed up.

"Yes," Calamai said.

"At that distance, about 17 miles, would there have been any risk of collision if the *Doria* had made a substantial change of course to the right so as to pass port to port, assuming that the *Stockholm* remained on a parallel course?" Haight asked.

"No, I could have changed course, but I did not deem it necessary because the radar indicated we were going to pass safely, green to green [right to right]," Calamai replied.

In reconstructing the *Andrea Doria–Stockholm* collision from the available technical data on their courses, Cahill concluded that Carstens had been incorrect in concluding that the *Doria* was continually to his left as the two ships approached each other. The *Stockholm's* radar may have been a degree or so off, and the helmsman, considered somewhat unreliable, may have misinformed Carstens as to when he was on course, Cahill believed. (In reflecting on the collision, the *Ile de France*'s captain, Raoul De Beaudéan, maintained that radar readings on the scopes of the 1950s possessed an uncertainty of 4 to 5 degrees.)

According to Cahill's reconstruction, if neither liner had deviated from its course, the *Stockholm* would have passed a quarter mile to the north (or starboard) of the *Doria,* not three quarters of a mile to the south, as Carstens believed.

But the liners did change course. The *Andrea Doria* began a turn of 4 degrees to the south (or portside) at about 11:05 P.M., and the *Stockholm* began a swing to its south (in the Swedish liner's case, to starboard) shortly afterward.

According to Cahill's computations, the *Stockholm* would have passed the *Andrea Doria* at a little more than four tenths of a mile to the north had she not changed course after the *Andrea Doria* swung

4 degrees to port. It was the *Stockholm*'s swing to its south—by about 17 degrees—that, in Cahill's view, brought disaster.

While concluding that Calamai and Carstens were equally to blame for accepting an inadequate passing distance, Cahill wrote: "It was not the port turn of *Doria* that brought about the collision but the starboard turn of the Swede. Once that maneuver was executed, the collision was all but inevitable."

Cahill's reconstruction disputed Carstens's contention at the federal court hearings that he made his turn to the right (to widen the passing distance) only after he spotted the *Andrea Doria*'s lights to his port side at just under 2 miles' distance.

What most likely happened, according to Cahill, is that "Carstens made the course change to starboard just before sighting *Doria* rather than just after" and that this would explain how the *Doria* was first sighted, emerging from fog, on the *Stockholm*'s port bow, showing its red sidelight.

Carl O. Nordling, a former professor at the Royal Institute of Technology in Sweden, also analyzed the data and agreed that the *Andrea Doria* was to the starboard side of the *Stockholm* as the two ships approached each other, not, as Carstens believed, to the port side.

Nordling estimated that when the two ships were 10 miles apart, the *Doria* was about 0.8 degree to the right of the *Stockholm*, not 2 degrees to the left, as Carstens stated, and that when the two ships were 6 miles apart, the *Doria* was approximately 2.3 degrees to starboard, not 4 degrees to port, as Carstens said. But Nordling concluded that the *Doria*'s officers also erred by estimating an angle of approach wider than it truly was, although they were correct in anticipating a right-side-to-right-side passage.

Nordling, like Cahill, was critical of both Calamai and Carstens for failing to make bold turns well in advance of their anticipated passing point.

"There can be no doubt that the officers in command on both ships deliberately took some improper risks," Nordling maintained.

John Carrothers, a former chief engineer with the Matson Navigation Company and watch engineer on the United States Lines, also reconstructed the maneuvers leading to the collision and he, too, concluded that the *Doria* was approaching to the right of the *Stockholm*, not to the left, as Carstens believed. Carrothers suggested that Carstens thought his radar was on a 15-mile range when it was really set to a 5-mile range, causing him to believe that the *Doria* was farther away than it really was (6 miles distant rather than the actual distance of 2 miles) when he made his late starboard turn.

The reconstruction by Carrothers was fed into a simulator used as a navigation teaching tool at the U.S. Merchant Marine Academy on Long Island. Captain Robert Meurn, a professor in the academy's department of marine transportation, invited *Andrea Doria* survivors attending a 1996 reunion held at the academy to enter the simulator, in effect placing them on the bridge at the spot where Carstens-Johannsen was watching the *Stockholm*'s radar. More than one survivor shed a tear when an image of the *Andrea Doria* appeared on that simulator, emerging from the fog.

Peter Padfield, a former British merchant marine officer who has written widely on technical matters involving navigation, has concluded that the two ships were indeed on converging courses, not on safe parallel paths, as the *Doria* and the *Stockholm* officers had believed. As Padfield put it, "They saw each other at 17 and 12 miles respectively and then steered to a collision point. . . ."

The two ships turned into each other in what mariners call a "radar-assisted" collision: Had neither ship possessed radar, no collision would have occurred. They would have passed each other safely—though less than a mile apart—having kept to their courses instead of turning in response to the conclusions they drew from their radarscopes.

There are other issues that raise questions about the performance of the officers on the two ships.

Carstens failed to call Captain Nordenson from his cabin although his radar showed another ship approaching, almost head-on, and he could not see that ship. It did not occur to Carstens that he could not spot the other ship's lights because it may have been shrouded in fog, even though he knew that the seas around Nantucket were often fog-bound and Nordenson had reminded him of that earlier in the evening by asking to be called in the event fog were encountered. Moreover, Carstens continued at the *Stockholm*'s full speed of 18.5 knots. When he finally did turn, at a point when the collision was a few minutes away, he did not sound a whistle to signal that maneuver, believing it was not required because he was running in clear weather.

Beyond all this, Captain Nordenson had charted a route placing the *Stockholm* in the path of westbound ships instead of taking the recommended eastbound path 20 miles to the south.

Captain Calamai cannot be faulted for having maintained close to his top speed (21.8 knots, down from a maximum of 23 knots) while running in fog during the previous 8 hours to maintain his schedule. Captains of transatlantic ships, under pressure to arrive on time, did not customarily reduce speed in fog when no one was near them, since they had radar. But Calamai's failure to slow down upon approaching an oncoming ship he could not see in a close meeting situation—or, as an alternative, his failure to utilize his speed to create a significantly wider separation between the two liners—represented a questionable decision.

The controversy over whether the *Doria*'s crew met its responsibilities to the passengers has no easy resolution.

Numerous accounts by survivors and *Stockholm* crewmen told of service personnel from the *Doria*—essentially kitchen workers and waiters—fleeing in the first lifeboats that went to the *Stockholm*. Captain Calamai and senior *Doria* officers either denied this happened or said that many of the crewmen in those lifeboats were working the levers that propelled them.

Those crew members who truly abandoned passengers might just as well have been employed in a Genoa restaurant and could not be expected to have had an allegiance to the code of the sea. Although there was evidently some confusion in the evacuation efforts, the *Doria*'s true seamen performed gallantly under great stress, something attested to by many passengers. Crewmen strung ropes to help passengers negotiate the listing decks, aided them in going down the ladders and ropes, and took many survivors to the rescue ships. Engine-room personnel worked furiously for more than 3 hours in an effort to pump out water and maintain electrical power in the face of intense heat from escaping steam. The efforts of the waiter Giovanni Rovelli to free Jane Cianfarra and Martha Peterson from the wreckage of Cabin 56 provided a heartening portrait of selflessness.

Announcements were made over the loudspeaker directing passengers to go to their evacuation stations and asking them to remain calm. Whether these were transmitted in an understandable manner is debatable, since many passengers reported hearing little or nothing in the way of instruction—at least in English.

Although there was no mass panic, the fear engulfing passengers may have resulted in their tuning out instructions. Beyond that, a sense of betrayal—a lovely ocean voyage became a terrifying experience—may have blocked out recollections of the crewmen's efforts to help.

Dr. Louis Linn, the New York psychiatrist who interviewed *Doria* survivors, was struck by the anger—even on the part of Italian-born passengers—at anything embodying the *Andrea Doria*. He saw this anger, in part, as "familiar expressions of the quest for scapegoats" common to those seeking "to master an overwhelming trauma."

Many passengers displayed a cultural bias against Italians, according to Dr. Linn.

"They expressed certainty that the accident was the fault of the *Andrea Doria* . . . ," he wrote in the *American Psychiatric Journal*. "This prejudice was based on the a priori acceptance that Swedes are dependable, faultless sailors and people of impeccable integrity and reliability, while Italians on the other hand are childlike and irresponsible, tending to pursue their pleasures instead of their duties."

Prejudicial attitudes against Italians—the mind-set that may have cast the *Doria*'s crew in an undeservedly poor light—were displayed, as well, by some of the people traveling on the *Ile*. The psychiatrist told of "contempt voiced by some passengers toward immigrant survivors because of their uncontrolled demonstrations of despair."

The notion that Italians were cowardly—that they would panic, in contrast to Anglo-Saxon or Nordic types—was nothing new. It had been voiced by crew members of the *Titanic*.

Appearing at the American inquiry into the *Titanic*'s sinking, a steward named George Crowe testified that as his lifeboat, containing mostly women and children, was about to depart, "there were various men passengers, probably Italians, or some foreign nationality other than English or American, who attempted to rush the boats." The commander of Crowe's lifeboat, Fifth Officer Harold Lowe, told the investigation that his boat contained fifty-seven women and children "bar one passenger, who was an Italian, and he sneaked in, and he was dressed like a woman." Lowe testified that he fired shots to prevent other Italian immigrants—presumably men—from getting into the lifeboat. His remarks incensed the Italian ambassador to the United States, prompting Lowe to issue a retraction stating that he did not really know whether the people menacing him were, in fact, Italians. "They were of the types of the Latin races," he said upon reconsideration, adding that "I did not intend to cast any reflection on the Italian nation."

Beyond the issue of who bore the larger measure of responsibility for the *Andrea Doria–Stockholm* collision, and the controversy over the conduct of the Italian crew, there remained the question as to why the *Andrea Doria* listed severely. The list, which continually increased, resulted in seawater flooding A Deck, known as the bulkhead deck since the tops of the bulkheads extended only that high. Once that deck was underwater, the *Doria* could not survive, whether it was one, two, or three watertight compartments that had been flooded, since the flooding from the bulkhead deck gradually extended to the other sections underneath it, further undermining stability.

The report by the House of Representatives' Merchant Marine and Fisheries Committee in January 1957, suggesting that the *Andrea Doria* listed so severely because it was unstable at the time of the collision—evidently as a result of insufficient ballasting—went unchallenged publicly at the time except for a brief rebuttal from the Italian Line.

The controversy was revisited in 1980 by a former public information director for Brostrom, the Swedish shipping conglomerate whose Swedish-American Line subsidiary owned the *Stockholm*. In his book *The House of Brostrom: Portrait of a World Company*, published in Sweden, the official, Algot Mattsson, told of a long, unsigned letter sent to Brostrom in 1957, purportedly by a senior employee of the shipyard near Genoa that built the *Andrea Doria*. The letter supposedly stated that the *Doria*'s design was faulty, that Italian officials knew this, and that bribes were paid to inspectors to certify the ship as seaworthy. Italian officials denied the allegations reported in the book, and the identity of the letter writer was not established.

Asked by the *New York Times* to comment on Mattsson's book, Gian Piero Battoni, head of the press office of the Italian Ministry of Merchant Marine, which in 1956 undertook Italy's closed inquiry into the collision, defended the seaworthiness of the *Doria*. And he said that the Italian investigation—its findings never made public—had "concluded unanimously that the collision between the two ships was the fault of the captain of the *Stockholm*."

At a symposium on the collision held at Genoa in 1988, former senior officers of the *Andrea Doria* attributed the starboard list to the massive damage inflicted by the *Stockholm*, to the *Doria*'s having been leaning to starboard at the time of the crash as a result of making a sharp turn, and to the placement of baggage on the starboard side of the Promenade Deck. They maintained that the *Doria* was not an unstable ship because of design or ballasting deficiencies.

As for efforts to correct the list in the hours following the collision, some maritime experts have questioned the engine-room crew's decision to pump water out of two starboard tanks in the double bottom to ease the tilting to starboard. That action, they suggest, may have only made the liner more top-heavy, further reducing its stability.

Officers of the *Andrea Doria* and the *Stockholm* have persisted in blaming each other for the crash and have acknowledged no wrongdoing or even poor judgment.

Speaking at the round table in Genoa, Eugenio Giannini, formerly the *Andrea Doria*'s third officer, told the audience, "The victims of that night will never weigh upon our conscience."

The *Stockholm*'s Johan-Ernst Bogislaus August Carstens-Johannsen has also professed a clear conscience. "I know what I saw and I know what I did," he said long afterward in a television interview. "I had everything under control."

PART V

The Memories

CHAPTER 34

"Why Did
I Get Spared?"

An event with disastrous consequences for many spawned professional triumph for some.

The ballet stars Nora Kovach and Istvan Rabovsky found their careers flourishing with a boost from the celebrity status conferred on *Andrea Doria* survivors.

The impresario Sol Hurok, who had managed the Hungarians since they fled Eastern Europe in 1953, phoned Ed Sullivan, who had already had them a few times on his enormously popular Sunday night television variety program. "Remember the Hungarians? They were so successful on your show. They just arrived from the *Andrea Doria,*" Hurok told Sullivan. A few weeks later, Sullivan brought them back, and they became regular guests. The dancers also won a booking on a bill with Judy Garland at the Palace. And a month after the collision, their fellow survivor Mayor Richardson Dilworth invited them to Philadelphia, presented them with the ceremonial key to the city, and arranged a visit to the Liberty Bell.

For some journalists, the *Andrea Doria* became a trophy of sorts emblematic of the rise in their careers.

"At midnight my life changed as suddenly as Cinderella's," Max Frankel would write of the night the *Andrea Doria* collided with the *Stockholm.* He had received an immediate raise—a $25 increase to about $80 a week—for his vivid page 1 article in the *New York Times* on night rewrite, but that was the smallest measure of his achievement. The following evening, he was back on rewrite while the *Times's* ace reporters were doing the big stories on the disaster, but a few weeks later, Frankel was rewarded with an assignment to cover the second Eisenhower-Stevenson presidential campaign. He was soon reporting from Vienna and then Moscow, and in 1986 he became the executive editor of the *Times.*

Harry Trask, the only newspaper photographer to capture the *Doria*'s final moments—having arrived on the scene late—returned to the *Boston Traveler*'s offices near the Common in time to make his 12:15 P.M. deadline. Asked by the paper's top editors what his film would show, Trask had no idea. "I'll tell you in about 6 minutes," he said. He began developing the plates, then emerged from the darkroom to report his photos were "just beautiful."

The following May he was awarded a Pulitzer Prize for news photography.

A quarter century later, when a granddaughter was born, she was named Andrea Doria Trask.

Don Hewitt, the CBS producer better known decades later for *60 Minutes,* and Douglas Edwards, the TV network's nightly news anchorman, saw their careers propelled by their exclusive film report of the *Doria*'s sinking, also the product of a late arrival.

For those not in the public eye, surviving the *Doria* brought demands for a moment-by-moment account.

When Bernie Aidinoff began work as a lawyer at Sullivan & Cromwell in August 1956, he was as sought after as the most senior attorney. "Everyone wanted to know what had happened," he would remember. "I had lunch invitations from just about every partner. I couldn't eat because I was so busy telling the story."

The *Andrea Doria* disaster soon became a source of TV entertainment.

Antoinette Misciagna, the sister of the tailor Leonardo Paladino, contacted *Strike It Rich,* a popular but mawkish show that invited unfortunates to tell their tales of woe. Upon answering a few easy questions, a hard-luck contestant qualified for gifts from viewers whose phone calls lit up an electronic "Heart Line."

The Paladinos' life savings from their sale of property in Bari had gone down with the *Doria,* together with their clothing, so *Strike It Rich* was delighted to have Leonardo, although he spoke no English. A friend of his sister stood beside him to provide the identification of a song, and the "Heart Line" began to glow.

Dresses were donated for the Paladinos' three daughters, a shoe store on Fifth Avenue guaranteed that the family would be well shod, a clothing store on the Lower East Side donated a topcoat for Leonardo, and another Manhattan clothing store gave him a suit and, more important, a job as a tailor. He worked there for a year and a half as the family built a new life in America.

I've Got a Secret asked the Coast Guard to permit a guest appearance by Lieutenant Harold Parker Jr., who oversaw the *Doria* search-and-rescue operation from headquarters in Lower Manhattan.

A senior aide to Admiral Cy Perkins, commander of Coast Guard units in the eastern United States, thought the disaster had received enough publicity without having a Coast Guard lieutenant appear on a game show.

"That's one of my favorite shows," Admiral Perkins told the aide. "I want him to go on it."

Parker stumped the panelists although, as he recalled it, his appearance in a Coast Guard uniform provided an inkling of his secret.

"They said, 'You must have something to do with the *Andrea Doria*. Were you the radio man in charge? Were you out on the scene? Did you fly the rescue airplanes?' They didn't guess what it was because I was so damned young-looking in those days. They never figured out that I coordinated the rescue."

And 43 years later, the *Doria* reemerged as mass entertainment in a *Seinfeld* episode when George was turned down for an apartment he coveted because the tenants' association gave preference to a long-ago survivor of the *Doria*.

But there were serious matters to be dealt with by survivors in the first weeks following the collision.

As soon as Father Thomas Kelly reached his family's home in Chicago, he was met by a limousine taking him to an interview on a popular local news show. He was eager to appear—a representative, in effect, of the Chicago Archdiocese. He had great affection for Italian people and wanted to assure the Italian Americans of Chicago that while the rescue operation seemed disorganized at times, many *Andrea Doria* crewmen fulfilled their obligations magnificently.

As months turned to years, the survivors went about their lives. But for some, the trauma—and the guilt for having survived when family members or friends were lost—would never be expunged.

Linda Morgan pondered the randomness of her survival while her half sister, eight-year-old Joan Cianfarra, sleeping a few feet away, had perished.

"Why me?" she thought. "Why did I get spared and she didn't?" She wanted to return something to society, a payback for surviving, and considered becoming a nurse. But she realized that would not resolve anything for her.

While she tried to cope with losing her half sister and her stepfather and seeing her mother severely injured, Linda had to weather painful reminders of that night on the *Doria*.

Her autograph book recovered from the *Stockholm*'s bow had been a memento from her days as a Campfire Girl in Spain. When her miraculous rescue made headlines and brought her the sobriquet "The Miracle Girl," the Campfire Girls presented her with a life-saving badge.

It struck Linda as an absurd though well-meaning gesture, since she had saved no one. The Campfire Girls also gave her a new autograph book, but four decades later she still had her original book with the red and gold cover, words of good wishes inside from Bernabe Polanco Garcia, the Spanish seaman who saved her, and from Dr. Ake Nissling, the *Stockholm*'s physician.

When Linda graduated from boarding school four years after the accident, her father, Edward P. Morgan, persuaded her to travel on an ocean liner once more, hoping that would help her overcome an understandable fear of the sea. She yielded to his wishes, booking passage on the *Queen Elizabeth,* accompanied by her boarding school roommate, Heller Halliday, the daughter of the actress Mary Martin.

Linda was extremely nervous throughout the trip; each time the engine rhythm changed during the night, she awakened. And she was subjected to two unsettling moments as a result of her father having told someone on the *Queen Elizabeth,* without her knowledge, about her *Andrea Doria* ordeal.

During the *Queen Elizabeth*'s evacuation drill, the officer who was to show passengers in Linda's group how to fasten their life jackets turned the instruction session over to her. "Let's have Linda demonstrate how this works," the crewman said. "She's been in an accident before." But Linda had never donned a life vest while imperiled, having been swept from her cabin while she slept.

The second disturbing incident on the *Queen Elizabeth* came when Linda and her friend were suddenly invited to have lunch in the captain's quarters. "We sat and chatted with the captain," she recalled. "We couldn't figure out what the hell was going on until a seaman knocked on the door and said: 'It's okay, we've gone over it.'" The passengers had just been informed on the loudspeaker that the *Queen Elizabeth* was passing over the spot where the *Andrea Doria* went down. The captain had invited the girls to lunch because he didn't want Linda to hear the announcement, but his assistant spoiled the strategy.

That crossing of the Atlantic was an exceedingly unhappy experience for Linda. Over the next 40 years, she never again boarded an ocean liner.

Linda's mother, Jane Cianfarra, never fully recovered from the trauma resulting from the severe injuries she and Linda suffered and the deaths of her husband, Camille Cianfarra, and her other daughter, Joan Cianfarra.

Mrs. Cianfarra's broken right hand did not heal properly following surgery, and despite a second operation she was never able to close her fist. Leg injuries left her with a slight limp that threw her back out. She underwent psychotherapy for a few months, although skeptical about its benefits, then discontinued treatment when asked to talk about the *Doria*. "She was an emotional mess," her daughter recalled.

Mrs. Cianfarra was hired by the *New York Times* in January 1957 to cover fashion news, having contributed articles to the paper while Camille Cianfarra was reporting from Italy and Spain, but she left in June, injuries impairing her ability to work. She went back to journalism soon afterward, filing reports from the United Nations for the *Nation* magazine from 1958 to 1962, having married its publisher, George Kirstein, in September 1957.

She enjoyed sailing at their winter home in St. Thomas, although uneasy on the water at night or in fog. In the summer of 1968 she was completing a handbook, *Family Under Sail,* a guide for women interested in boating. But summertime brought back memories. "It was always a very hard period in her life around July," Linda remembered. On July 25, 1968—the twelfth anniversary of the *Andrea Doria*'s collision with the *Stockholm*—she died in her sleep at her home in Mamaroneck, New York, at age fifty-two. Death was attributed to heart failure.

Two months before her mother died, Linda Morgan married Phil Hardberger, a lawyer, and she hoped that at age twenty-six she had shed the tag "The Miracle Girl." She happily took her husband's name. It would not be so easy for newspaper reporters seeking survivors' reminiscences for *Andrea Doria* anniversary stories to find her.

Linda Morgan Hardberger and her husband settled in Texas, where she became a museum curator, and they raised a daughter. Like her mother, Linda enjoyed boating, and in summers the Hardbergers sail off the coast of Maine. Living an active life reflected her philosophy: "Events are random. You can't be terrified of stuff all the time. You have no control over it."

But the terror of that night on the *Andrea Doria* could be evoked at a wholly unexpected moment. One day in 1979, the Hardbergers were at the movies, watching *The Black Stallion*. When a ship was hit by a mine in the movie, Linda jumped out of her seat and fled the theater.

She did not see *Titanic*.

"I find the fascination of the whole thing bizarre," she says. "I'm totally amazed at the interest in the *Titanic*. The movie was fiction; there was very little truth in that. I don't get it. I don't understand it. It's a tragedy and doesn't need to be romanticized. It doesn't need to be fooled with. It just needs to be left alone."

On a few occasions, acquaintances learned of Linda Morgan Hardberger's connection with a shipwreck, although sometimes the association was not quite grasped. "Several people have asked me if I was on the *Titanic*," she says.

She presumes that the tale of her rescue will be in the headlines again someday.

Flying to New York City one summer's day to do research for her museum work, she envisioned her obituary if her plane had gone down.

"I could just see it: 'Miracle Girl Dies in Plane Crash.' That's going to be in the headline, I just know, if I'm going to live to eighty-five."

Linda Morgan's ordeal had an unexpected emotional impact on another survivor, the songwriter Mike Stoller.

For a while following the collision, Stoller felt generally fearful. He was afraid to fly, and his sense of immortality, a common enough sentiment for young persons, had been lost at age twenty-three. But the trauma faded away with time.

Then, on the twenty-fifth anniversary of the *Andrea Doria*'s sinking, Stoller flew to Boston for a broadcast remembrance. When a woman who had been on his lifeboat told the story of Linda Morgan, he began to cry. He had never met Linda and had no idea why he had been affected so.

A few days later, Stoller went to Montreal to collaborate with the writer Mordecai Richler on a musical based on Richler's novel *Duddy Kravitz*. While he was salmon fishing with the Richler family, Stoller related the Linda Morgan episode—and he began to weep once more. During the following week, he told the story to others, and each time he cried.

Although Stoller liked being on the water—he and his wife, Meryl, had an 18-foot boat at their summer home in East Hampton, Long Island, and took their children fishing—he stayed away from ships.

Meryl experienced claustrophobia that lasted several years. She refused to enter self-service elevators and feared going below ground to take a subway. When she got on a bus, she sat near the driver so she could see how it was being operated. Having switched from the ocean liner *Olympic* to take the *Doria*, she never again changed a plane reservation. She feared being on the water far from land. The Staten Island ferry was about as adventuresome as she would be.

The Stollers were later divorced, and more than a decade after the collision, Mike Stoller finally was back on an oceangoing vessel, a one-night trip from Grenada to Martinique on a Greek cruise ship called the *Jason* with his second wife, Corky Hale. But when ocean spray entered the cabin through an open porthole, it triggered repressed memories. Stoller dreamed that water was pouring through the porthole, the ship in danger of sinking.

Eventually overcoming his fear of ocean liners, Stoller appeared with Hale, a modern-jazz harpist, pianist, and singer, on Christmas cruises of the *QE2*. They lectured on songwriting and the art of performing to passengers no doubt familiar with the 1990s Broadway revue *Smokey Joe's Cafe,* a reprise of the songs of Leiber and Stoller.

Kathy Kerbow Dickson, the student at Park College in Missouri who had been dancing when the ships collided, also experienced acute anxiety at an unexpected moment. A year and a half after the collision, having returned to her native Texas, she was attending a function in a ballroom. Suddenly, and inexplicably, she was seized by panic. She ran out of the room—just as Linda Morgan Hardberger had fled a movie theater when a ship exploded on the screen. Kathy came to realize she had experienced a flashback to the moment in the *Andrea Doria*'s ballroom, seconds before the collision, when she glimpsed the lights of the *Stockholm*.

The passing of more than four decades could not shake the fear of water from Leonardo Paladino and his wife, Giovanna. Leonardo refused to go to the beach, and when he stepped into the shower at his home on Long Island, he felt uneasy—"kind of stiff," as he put it. Mrs. Paladino would not venture a visit to the Statue of Liberty, lest she have to ride on a boat once more.

But Elisabeth Hanson reveled in water sports. For some years following the collision, the Hanson family had a season's ticket to an outdoor pool in their hometown, Urbana, Illinois. Every July 26—the anniversary of the *Doria*'s sinking—Mrs. Hanson jumped off the high diving board to affirm the gift of life given herself, the child she was carrying on the *Doria* (a healthy boy born full-term), and the two sons and a daughter she had tossed into the sea.

Fifteen years after surviving the *Doria*'s sinking, Mrs. Hanson was part of a group that took state legislators on canoe trips down a scenic river to lobby against its being dammed up to create a reservoir. On one trip, the politician in Mrs. Hanson's canoe grabbed an overhanging willow branch to protect her from it, forgetting that it was attached to a very stationary tree, causing the canoe to tip over. Mrs. Hanson would reflect that if she had mentioned her experience on the *Andrea Doria* just then, the politicians who hoped to preserve the river might have viewed her as a jinx to their cause.

Joan Dier, who had been watching *Foxfire* when the ships collided, experienced sleepless nights afterward and feared being in the dark. But she surmounted her anxiety, married, raised three daughters, and looked back on her ordeal as "a maturing experience."

"It made me grow," she reflected. "I felt satisfied with myself. I didn't melt into a puddle of tears. I dealt with reality as an adult." And it strengthened her belief that "God is always with me."

Charles Alfano, the barber from White Plains, New York, who survived only because his roommate insisted they leave their lower-level cabin to take in late-night partying, had never been a religious person. He used to leave money on the kitchen table for his wife, Lena, to place in the collection box when she went to church, but seldom accompanied her. After surviving the *Doria,* he became a churchgoer. He carried with him the image of the Italian immigrant girl who was always holding an orange, and her father—both dead in the next cabin—while his life was spared.

Raymond Goedert, a young priest back in the summer of 1956, became an auxiliary bishop of the Chicago Archdiocese. "I think we kid ourselves as priests," Goedert said years later. "We talk of the joy and happiness of heaven. I was faced with the prospect and found that I was not all that happy to go. I was willing to wait."

Father Richard Wojcik, who had occupied a cabin next to Thure and Martha Peterson and had escaped death only through the happenstance of a Scrabble game on a higher deck, pondered the lessons taught. "God writes straight with crooked lines," he believes. "It looks like an abandonment, it looks like an end, and it was a beginning. Life takes strange turns, but you're not surprised by them anymore. You go with the flow."

The first few years after the accident, images from the *Doria* floated through Father Wojcik's mind in the stillness of night. When he saw *Titanic,* the memories returned in the scene when all was silent just before the young woman portrayed by Kate Winslet blew a whistle upon spotting a lifeboat in the distance. At that moment, Father Wojcik's hands began to sweat.

He took his parents on a fiftieth-anniversary cruise to the Caribbean, but only after reflecting once more on the *Doria.* "I had to convince myself it was an accident. There was nobody out to get me. It was the perfect accident—everybody did the wrong thing at exactly the right time and it produced the maximum evil effect. There's nobody out to get you. If you think that way, you become psycho."

The trauma that endured for many became complicated for some by survivors' guilt. For Linda Morgan, the loss was immediate—two members of her family. For Frank Russo, it was the loss of family friends. For Eugene and Freda Gladstone, it was a missed opportunity to save strangers.

Tonya Paladino, age two; Felicia, three years old; and Maria, four (left to right), with their parents, Leonardo and Giovanna Paladino, at St. Adelbert's Church in Elmhurst, Queens, giving thanks for their survival.
(Courtesy of Leonardo and Giovanna Paladino)

Russo did work for a while in the market Giuseppe and Antoinette Guzzi had owned in Easton, where they had promised him a job. Then he made his way in America. He and his wife, Patricia, raised five children and opened a pool-installation company in Florida.

Even with the passing of the decades, Russo retained a feeling of sadness and a measure of guilt. "I miss the Guzzis," he says. "It makes me feel bad. They had money, they could have traveled first class. They traveled third class to be with me. Had they been upstairs, they would not have been killed."

He found consolation in the thought that "it was an act of God."

Eugene and Freda Gladstone underwent treatment at psychiatric hospitals, having been unable to cope with the emotional turmoil of their chaotic escape from the *Doria* down a cargo net. Gene later wrote a memoir at the urging of his therapist, a means of coming to terms with his torment.

A Romanian Jew, he came to Canada in the 1930s. At the end of World War II, he learned that his father, mother, and sister had perished in the Holocaust. In his memoir, Gladstone wrote of his guilt feelings for having survived while the rest of his family were killed by the Nazis. And he likened that to his remorse over having forgotten to summon aid for fellow passengers stranded in an *Andrea Doria* elevator as he rushed topside in those first moments after the collision.

"What right have I to live while they are all dead?" he wrote of his family members. "I know there was nothing in the world I could have done to save them, but I believe I shall always worry that there might have been. Just as those passengers trapped in the elevator between decks on the *Andrea Doria* will haunt me forever with their cries for assistance."

Theresa Buccilli, the young Italian immigrant who had huddled in a corner of her third-class cabin, paralyzed by fear and waiting for the end, only to be saved by a crewman, also suffered severe psychiatric distress.

She had been adopted, as planned, by an uncle and aunt and had settled in at their home in a Cleveland suburb. On October 16, 1956, they watched a television production *SOS from the* Andrea Doria. When it ended, Theresa screamed, leaped from her chair, and cried, "I'm afraid, I'm afraid. I'm going to die. Somebody save me."

Over the next few days, she became unable to go to her job as a packer at a sweater factory. She hid in her room, developed headaches, was unable to sleep, and insisted that a doctor she saw was trying to poison her. Eight days after her breakdown, she was admitted to the psychiatric section of Marymount Hospital in Cleveland.

She underwent seventy-five electric shock treatments but showed no improvement, then was discharged in February 1957 when her adoptive father ran out of funds. Her family filed suit against the Italian and Swedish shipping lines, accusing both of negligence leading to the collision and responsibility therefore for Theresa's emotional trauma. Her lawyers sought $250,000 in damages for the twenty-three-year-old woman but accepted an award of $70,000, evidently the only settlement stemming from mental illness among the hundreds of claims that were filed.

The money enabled Theresa Buccilli to continue psychiatric treatment. On the advice of her psychiatrist, she spent the summer of 1958 in Italy, reuniting with her former fiancé, a tailor, whom she had left upon her family's urging that she go to America. They married and settled in her native village of Tracco. She raised three children, and though she underwent periods of unexplained sadness, she found peace in the quiet environment.

Betsy Drake, outwardly calm in the hours awaiting rescue, suffered emotional distress in the months to come. "Betsy had simply stopped functioning, either as an actress or in any other field in which she had once been interested," the actress Rosalind Russell once said. "It was pathetic to see her wasting away like that."

Drake had spent time aboard the *Doria* with Camille Cianfarra and his wife, Jane. Although the actress escaped unscathed, she was no doubt troubled not only by her own harrowing experience but also by the death of the *Times* correspondent and his daughter Joan and the severe injuries suffered by Linda Morgan and Jane.

Believing that a return to acting might help her emotionally, Cary Grant obtained a role for his wife in the 1957 movie *Will Success Spoil Rock Hunter?*, a satire of the television industry starring Jayne Mansfield and Tony Randall. But Drake turned to hypnotism to deal with her trauma and later left acting for a career in psychotherapy. She specialized in the problems of children and adolescents and led psychodrama groups at UCLA.

Her marriage to Grant, already stung by his romancing of Sophia Loren on a Spanish movie set, resulting in Drake's hasty departure for America on the *Andrea Doria,* did not survive. Drake and Grant were separated in 1958 and were divorced 4 years later.

The *Andrea Doria* disaster took an emotional toll on one family that had never even boarded the liner.

Cabins No. 52 (occupied by Linda Morgan and Joan Cianfarra) and No. 54 (taken by Camille and Jane Cianfarra) had originally been booked by Ray Flook, who was returning with his wife, Veronica, and their daughters, Karen, six, and Maria, four, to their Delaware home after he had worked as an engineer for Fiat in Turin, Italy. But the Flook family canceled its reservations in favor of an earlier crossing aboard the Italian Line's *Giulio Cesare.*

In her book *My Sister Life: The Story of My Sister's Disappearance,* published in 1997, Maria Flook saw the death and injury visited upon the Cianfarra family in those two cabins as symbolic of her own family's destruction by an emotionally distant mother and a father who passively submitted to the two daughters' rejection. Just as Linda Morgan would forever be separated from her half sister, so the Flook sisters would see their lives forever haunted after Karen left home, at age fourteen, and slid into prostitution.

Their mother had kept the canceled vouchers for the *Andrea Doria* cabin, and—lamented Maria—would torment the children with them.

Maria recounted how her mother often extended an end-table drawer and displayed the vouchers. "You girls would have died," she told them. "We couldn't have saved you. Ray and I would have been dancing in the Belvedere Lounge. There's always a big party on the last night of the crossing. Little girls would have been in bed."

For some survivors, mementos of the *Andrea Doria*'s final voyage were no objects of torment, but souvenirs of having been caught up in high drama.

Bernie and Cissie Aidinoff kept the keys to their cabin and Jerry Reinert framed the white shirt he had worn, its collar tinged by the orange of his soggy life jacket.

Cissie Aidinoff would tease her husband with another reminder of that night, quoting his words of reassurance during those hours when they awaited rescue. "Any time we had one of those arguments that neither spouse can win, or should win, she would just say, 'The ship cannot sink,' and the argument ended," Bernie Aidinoff remembered.

A few years after the collision, Aidinoff wrote a letter to the Italian Line saying he had been on the *Doria* and wanted to see the newly built *Leonardo da Vinci,* which he understood was the *Doria*'s successor. That ship, which went into service in 1960, was indeed a replacement for the *Doria.* But Aidinoff received what he remembered as a "snide" response saying the *da Vinci* had no relationship at all to the *Doria* and that if he wanted to visit the liner, he could see the ship on a Sunday when visitors were required to pay a $10 boarding fee that benefited Merchant Marine personnel.

Aidinoff passed on the offer.

For some survivors, the *Andrea Doria* is remembered in fellowship.

In the early 1990s, Vincenzo Della Torre, a chef on the *Doria* during its final voyage, began playing host to annual reunions of survivors at his Italian restaurant on Long Island, replicating the buffet served on the final day at sea.

On the twenty-fifth anniversary of the *Doria*'s sinking, Donald and Jean Ruth of Woodmere, Long Island, were guests at the home of Alfred and Beverly Green in the Westchester suburb of Rye. The couples were partaking in their annual gathering—a thanksgiving dinner in the middle of summer.

The Ruths would almost certainly have died in their smashed cabin if not for the Greens' having invited them for a drink in the Belvedere Lounge, where the couples were toasting the final night at sea when the ship began to shake. "If it had not been for the Greens' persuading us to have that last drink," said Donald Ruth on the twenty-fifth anniversary, "we'd still be on the ship today."

Forty-four years later, Jerry Reinert with the white shirt he was
wearing when he was evacuated from the *Andrea Doria*.
(Courtesy of Jerry Reinert)

Anthony Grillo, three years old when he was tossed by his mother
into a blanket held aloft in a lifeboat, remembered the *Andrea Doria* by
creating a Web site devoted to the ship's history and the collision.

Melanie Ansuini and John Vali celebrated their survival in an enduring manner. Melanie, a teenage immigrant, had been dancing with
John, whom she met aboard the ship, when the ballroom rocked. After
Melanie plunged into the sea from a ladder, John hauled her into a
lifeboat. They returned to New York together on the *Ile de France*, and
a year and a half later, they were married. They settled in California,
and when their first child was born, they remembered their good fortune once more. They named their daughter Doria.

CHAPTER 35

"The Poor Man Was Destroyed"

The captain of the *Ile de France* savored the hero's mantle. In the months following the French liner's rescue of 753 passengers and crewmen, Raoul de Beaudéan received more than a thousand messages—thank-you notes from survivors and even requests for autographs and pictures—and he was awarded membership in France's Legion of Honor. But he was touched most by presentation of a simple gold medallion with his name and that of the *Ile* engraved on one side, created by the Rome newspaper *Il Tempo* and paid for with contributions from the Italian people.

In October 1957 the U.S. Maritime Administration presented its first peacetime Gallant Ship Awards to the *Ile de France*—the first foreign vessel to be so honored—the *Cape Ann,* and the *Private William H. Thomas,* and conveyed a letter of commendation to the tanker *Robert E. Hopkins.* In ceremonies aboard the *Ile* while she was docked in New York, the captains of the rescue ships accepted bronze medallions created by the American sculptor Jo Davidson depicting a ship steaming full ahead. The Gallant Ship Awards, for the saving of life or property in disasters or other emergencies, had previously gone to only nine ships, all for action under fire during World War II.

The day after the *Doria* sank, President Eisenhower had paid tribute to "all those, of whatever nationality" who participated in the rescue. But no Gallant Ship Award went to the *Stockholm,* which had taken aboard more than five hundred survivors. The unresolved determination of blame for the collision presumably made it awkward to honor the Swedish seamen.

Thirteen Coast Guardsmen and the captains of the Navy destroyer escort *Allen,* the *Thomas,* and the *Cape Ann* were honored by the Italian ambassador to the United States, Manlio Brosio, in ceremonies at the

Lieutenant Roger F. Erdmann, Lieutenant Philip G. Ledoux, and Lieutenant Commander L. F. Lovell (left to right), the captains, respectively, of the Coast Guard cutters *Hornbeam, Legare,* and *Evergreen,* at the Italian embassy in Washington, D.C., where they received commendations in January 1957 for their part in the search and rescue. (*U.S. Coast Guard Magazine*)

Italian embassy in January 1957. But the Italians ignored the rescue efforts of the Swedes.

De Beaudéan continued as captain of the *Ile* until reaching the French Line's mandatory retirement age of fifty-five in spring 1958. By then the *Ile* was nearing the end of her years. She departed Le Havre for the last time in the winter of 1959, bound for Osaka, Japan, to be cannibalized for scrap. The following July, her forward funnel toppled onto the captain's quarters in an explosion orchestrated in Japan by Hollywood for *The Last Voyage,* a film about a doomed ship starring Dorothy Malone and Robert Stack.

The French Line, angered over the renowned liner's ignoble demise, insisted that the legend *Ile de France* be removed from her bow when the scene was shot. And so the glamour ship of the 1920s and 1930s, troop carrier of World War II, and savior of *Andrea Doria* passengers, ended her life as the celluloid *Claridon.*

The Swedish-American Line provided a public vote of confidence to Captain Gunnar Nordenson and Third Mate Johan-Ernst Bogislaus August Carstens-Johannsen of the *Stockholm* by assigning them to the new liner *Gripsholm* in May 1957. But there was one hitch. The

Lieutenant Harold W. Parker
Jr., who coordinated the Coast
Guard's search and rescue operation, receiving a commendation
from Manilo Brosio, the Italian
ambassador to the United States.
(*U.S. Coast Guard Magazine*)

Gripsholm was built at the Ansaldo yards near Genoa, the same shipyard that built the *Andrea Doria*. The dockworkers at Genoa announced
they wouldn't work if Nordenson and Carstens came there to take the
Gripsholm on her maiden trip. So the Swedish-American Line had to
send another captain to bring the ship out of Italian waters.

Nordenson retired after two years in command of the *Gripsholm*
and died in Göteborg, Sweden, in 1981 at age eighty-eight. Carstens
became a captain on various ships, later owned his own shipping company, retired to the Swedish town of Kullavik, and stood by his account
of the events leading to the collision. "You can't build up a story around
an accident like this," he told a television documentary interviewer more
than four decades later in recounting his federal court testimony in
1956. "One question you would get ten times a day and every day just
to see if I understood it, if I changed anything, but I don't think I did."

Following the reconstruction of her bow at the Bethlehem dry dock
in Brooklyn, the *Stockholm* resumed transatlantic trips in December
1956. She was sold in 1959 to an East German firm that renamed her
the *Volkerfreundschaft* (People's Friendship). On the night of January 20, 1983, serving as a ferry between the East German port of Ros-
tock and the Swedish coast, she collided with a West German submarine
and suffered damage to her port propeller. But this time there were no
casualties.

The former *Stockholm* was later converted into a floating hotel by a Norwegian company and was eventually sold to the Nina Cruise Line of Genoa, the home port of the *Andrea Doria*. In 1993 she was decorated in Italian marble in a $100 million renovation and renamed the *Italia Prima*. Only her hull remained from her years as the *Stockholm*, but she retained her distinctive bow and familiar white trim, embellished now with a blue racing stripe. A picture of the *Stockholm* in the aftermath of the collision—her bow a mass of wreckage—was hung aboard the *Italia Prima*, a tribute to a troubled past. With the arrival of a new century, the old *Stockholm* continued to carry on as a cruise ship. But it had been given yet another identity. Owned now by West Indies Cruises and called the *Valtur Prima*, it made seven-night cruises out of Montego Bay in the winter of 2001, including stops at Havana and Isle of Youth, Cuba.

By the close of the 1950s, when the *Stockholm* was sold to the East Germans, the era of the luxurious North Atlantic liner was approaching its end. On August 13, 1957, Britain's ninety-two-passenger *Bristol Britannia*, the world's largest, swiftest, and quietest prop jet commercial airliner, made her maiden flight to New York's Idlewild International Airport. In October 1958, the Boeing 707 inaugurated true jetliner service over the North Atlantic.

Two months after the *Andrea Doria* sank, the Italian Line ordered her replacement, the *Leonardo da Vinci*. By July 1960, when that liner made her maiden voyage, airlines were carrying almost 70 percent of transatlantic travelers. But the Italian government, under pressure from seamen's unions, pressed ahead on a grander scale, backing construction of the *Raffaello* and the *Michelangelo,* each larger than the prewar Italian superliner the *Rex*. Heavily subsidized by Rome, the twin liners debuted in 1965. By then, airlines had 95 percent of the North Atlantic passenger traffic.

On one winter's trip in the 1960s, the *Queen Elizabeth* carried two hundred passengers and twelve hundred crew. But the French and the English, like the Italians, refused to surrender. The *France* was introduced in 1962 and the QE2 in 1969.

For the Italians, it was all over by the mid-1970s.

The *Raffaello* and the *Michelangelo* had become known as "makework" ships, providing jobs for shipyard workers and crewmen but never turning a profit. By the late 1960s, with transatlantic ocean travel continuing to ebb, they were often employed on Caribbean and Mediterranean cruises. But at 45,900 gross tons each, they were too large for many ports and often had to anchor offshore, then bring their passengers

The *Stockholm*, its bow restored, undergoing sea trials in the fall of 1956.
(Bethlehem Steel Corporation)

in on small boats. In 1975 the twin superliners were taken out of service and moored at La Spezia, south of Genoa. Two years later, they were sold to the shah of Iran for use as military barracks, then fell into disrepair. The *Raffaello* was sunk by an Iraqi missile at its berth in the Iranian port of Bushire in February 1983. The *Michelangelo* was sold by the Iranians to Pakistani scrappers in 1991.

The *Leonardo da Vinci* made her last run between Genoa and New York in June 1976, closing out the Italian Line's transatlantic service. On July 4, 1980, while at anchor off La Spezia, she was gutted by a mysterious fire that began in her chapel and burned for four days. Valued at $1 million as scrap, she was stripped by wrecking crews. By 1982, the last of her remains had been cut away.

The *Andrea Doria*'s sister ship, the *Cristoforo Colombo,* was shifted in 1973 from the North American transatlantic run to the Italy–South America route. Four years later, she was sold to the Venezuelan government for use as a dormitory serving workers at a steel factory. In 1980 she was purchased by Taiwanese scrappers, who finished her off.

Piero Calamai had been scheduled to become the captain of the *Cristoforo Colombo* following the round trip that the *Andrea Doria* would never complete. But the Italian Line did not give him command of that ship. He was placed on shore duty following the collision and remained deskbound until retiring at the end of 1957.

Carmelo Grillo, the Italian Line official whose wife, Angela, and three-year-old son, Anthony, survived the *Doria*'s sinking, long remained troubled over Calamai's fate.

Having attended the federal court hearings at which Calamai and the other Italian and Swedish officers testified, Grillo felt that the American reporters favored the Swedish side.

But Grillo's anger was reserved mostly for the Italian Line. "My feeling was the damage done to Captain Calamai was done mostly by Italian ship management, their own people did it," he said decades later. "Instead of saying, 'Okay, Captain, now you're going to become the captain of the *Cristoforo Colombo*,' they put him in mothballs."

"The prize for the worst marketing concerning the *Doria* affair should be awarded the Italian Line's press office," Eugenio Giannini, the *Doria*'s third officer, maintained three decades later. "The Swedes, on the contrary, showed their ability to exploit the mass media."

Calamai's nephew Mario Galassi painted a depressing picture of the *Andrea Doria*'s captain as he lived out his years. "The poor man was destroyed in his last days," Galassi told a 1979 forum on the collision held at the U.S. Merchant Marine Academy in Kings Point, New York. "He never appeared in public. His mind was always on that night. You could see he was a finished man."

"Never has one word been written in his favor," said Galassi. "What really happened will never be heard."

Guido Badano, the second officer junior on the *Andrea Doria* and later the captain of the *Cristoforo Colombo*, remembered Calamai as "a gentleman—a good seaman, a good captain, a good man."

"The day of the *Andrea Doria* disaster began his long agony," Badano reflected. "He lived with his family in Genoa, but he was like a ghost. He died asking if the passengers had been saved."

It is questionable whether Calamai would have taken command of the *Cristoforo Colombo* had it been offered by the Italian Line. Soon after the *Andrea Doria* went down, her captain pondered his life's calling. "When I was a boy, and all my life, I loved the sea," he said. "Now I hate it."

Piero Calamai died at his home in Genoa on April 9, 1972, at age seventy-five. He had never returned to the sea since that summer's day when he lost the *Andrea Doria*.

PART VI

The Shipwreck

CHAPTER 36

"It's Got the Mystique"

They call her the Mount Everest of deep-sea diving.

Her starboard side embedded in the ocean floor at a depth of some 250 feet, the *Andrea Doria* poses a supreme challenge for divers, just as the Himalayas entice the most ambitious of mountain climbers. For the past four decades—and now in ever-larger numbers, drawing upon sophisticated diving equipment—adventurers and fortune-seekers have been visiting (and, some say, violating) a cold, dark, and exceedingly dangerous world where, in a sense, it is still the summer of 1956. And, as the *Doria* fades into history, her superstructure crumbling but her mementos of the good life at sea hardly exhausted, her death toll mounts with the passing summers.

"The *Andrea Doria* is not a place for the faint of heart," says Dr. Robert Ballard, the oceanographic researcher who discovered the *Titanic* in 1985 and reached the *Doria* aboard a submarine almost a decade later.

"On a good day, I could take you down with no problems," observes Dan Crowell, the captain and owner of the *Seeker,* a boat that takes as many as two hundred divers a summer on a 10-hour, 100-mile trip to the *Doria* from Montauk Point, Long Island. "But the *Andrea Doria* will give you all the rope you need to hang yourself." Over the summers of 1998 and 1999, five men died while diving to the *Doria,* all of them brought to the wreck site by the *Seeker.*

Beyond the *Doria*'s superb artwork, the maroon-and-gold-banded first-class china and the silverware, still there for the grasping, riches are said to abound—jewels and wads of currency supposedly in the purser's safe. But the perils match the prospect of grand rewards.

Unpredictable and swift currents stir up muck that blinds diving lights and threatens to sweep a diver into the open sea. "The visibility was so bad that we landed on the wreck's port side like a plane making

an instrument landing in dense fog," Ballard wrote in recalling the day
he arrived at the *Doria* on a filming expedition aboard the nuclear-
powered submersible NR-1.

The *Doria*'s interior is choked with electrical wiring, the hull laced
with commercial fishing nets and a web of monofilament fishing lines
invisible to divers, all of these easily ensnarling a diver's tank or fin
until the air supply runs out. A diver can become disoriented in a shipwreck lying on its starboard side, its walls now ceilings and floors. The
water temperatures are in the 40s—even during June, July, and August,
the *Doria* diving period—a formidable challenge for the finest of diving
suits. And the seas south of Nantucket are a breeding ground for the
blue sharks attracted by fish swarming around the wreck.

The pressure at 180 feet below the ocean's surface (the depth of the
Doria's upturned port side) and the deeper interior of the ship limits
divers to 20 minutes or so at the wreck, and requires a slow ascent with
frequent stops in order to avoid decompression sickness, whose best-
known consequence is the potentially crippling and sometimes fatal
"bends."

As Bill Campbell, a veteran diver from Rhode Island, has put it,
"The *Doria*'s got the sharks. It's got the depth. It's got the current. It's
got the mystique. It's got the whole ball of wax."

The *Andrea Doria* lay undisturbed for only 28 hours.

Peter Gimbel, a twenty-eight-year-old explorer and photographer—
the son of Bernard Gimbel, the chairman of Gimbel's department
store—and Joseph Fox, a twenty-nine-year-old book editor, both amateur divers, went down to the *Doria* the day after she sank to take
black-and-white photos for *Life* magazine.

Wearing frogman gear and descending along the mooring line of the
buoy placed by the Coast Guard cutter *Evergreen* to mark the *Doria*'s
grave, they explored the port side. Carrying an underwater Leica camera and using fast film in the dim light, Gimbel photographed Fox
examining one of the portside lifeboats rendered useless by the *Doria*'s
list. Then they peered through the portholes, spotting luggage, furniture, and blankets. After they had been down for 13 minutes, Gimbel
felt a tap on his shoulder and saw that Fox was frantically trying to
open a reserve air valve. Assuming that his partner was being overcome
by carbon dioxide, Gimbel inflated Fox's rescue pack, grabbed him
under the arm, and guided him to the surface. Fox emerged with nothing more than a severe headache.

Later that summer, Gimbel dove to the *Doria* with an editor from *Life* and several experienced divers from California to shoot color film for the magazine. They came away, meanwhile, with the first souvenirs. Robert Dill, one of the divers, brought back the solid-mahogany riser on which the *Doria*'s helmsman was standing when the collision occurred, converting it into a coffee table at his home.

In the summer of 1964, Robert Solomon and H. Glenn Garvin, businessmen from Silver Spring, Maryland, mounted a salvage effort from a surplus Coast Guard cutter they named *Top Cat*. Their divers brought up the bronze statue of Admiral Andrea Doria from the first-class lounge on the Promenade Deck, cutting it away at the ankles. Three years later, the statue was standing in the patio of a Florida motel owned by Garvin. "Nobody offered us a nickel for it," he said.

An Italian television producer-director and amateur oceanographer named Bruno Vailati led a major exploration of the *Doria* during a two-week period in 1968, the divers based on the chartered fishing trawler *Narragansett*. But the diving team had a grander ambition. It hoped to raise the *Andrea Doria,* a dream envisioned ever since the liner went down. One would-be salvor had proposed filling the hull with air-laden Ping-Pong bills, only to learn that the air pressure at that depth would flatten them. Another entrepreneur suggested using ore barges as pontoons. The Vailati team thought it could flood the *Doria* with foam that would harden and displace the heavier water inside the wreck until the ship gradually rose. It never obtained financial backing for the plan, but undertook the first extensive photographic survey of the shipwreck for a documentary, *Fate of the* Andrea Doria. Vailati likened the interior of the *Doria* to "a dream world"—beautiful fish darting, handsomely carved tables bolted to what was once the floor but now hanging at right angles.

The expedition almost suffered the first casualty of *Doria* exploration when a 9-foot blue shark tore at the fin flipper of Al Giddings, one of the divers, as he ascended. Vailati, close by with a spear, stabbed the shark in the back, but it didn't seem to feel anything. Then he stabbed it in the gills, a sensitive area, and it took off.

In the summer of 1973, a pair of former Navy divers from San Diego, Don Rodocker and Chris DeLucchi, led a team of twenty-six in a quest for riches, utilizing a technique called "saturation diving," in which divers spend time in a pressurized mixed-gas atmosphere each day. When they weren't exploring the wreck, the divers lived inside a compartment called "Mother," a steel cylinder 13½ by 5 feet tethered to the *Doria* and attached by an umbilical to the support ship *Narragansett,* the same boat the Italian expedition had chartered in 1968. By resting in that chamber, which was equipped with food, cots, and piped-in music, the divers avoided the time-consuming and dangerous decompression ascents they would otherwise have had to make after each dive.

While the team had been preparing for the dives at a dock in Fairhaven, Massachusetts, an elderly woman approached a brawny and tattooed Navy master diver named George Powell, who was supervising the topside operation. "Do you think you can get my sister's rosary beads?" the woman asked. "She was in Cabin 358 and they're in the drawer by her bed."

The operation continued for 23 days, the bulk of the diving carried out by Rodocker and DeLucchi, who cut a 4-foot-square hole in the hull as their entrance point. But the divers were plagued by the swift currents and found the wreck in much worse shape than they had anticipated. Rodocker came within 10 feet of the gift shop, only to find mud circles on the corners of the windows, evoking the image of snow on glass panes in wintertime. He could not see anything on the inside. Above him, a pile of debris was supported precariously by small timbers that had fallen. Rodocker realized that if his equipment touched the debris it could collapse, so he left the area without venturing closer to the shop. The divers' most valuable find was a bottle of French perfume, but it could hardly earn back the expedition's costs, estimated at upward of $150,000. If the divers ventured into Cabin 358 for those rosary beads, they didn't mention it afterward.

Peter Gimbel, otherwise known for a fine documentary film on the great white shark, remained fascinated with the *Doria*. In 1975 he led a diving expedition aimed at corroborating speculation that a watertight door between the *Doria*'s generator room and the deep-fuel tank compartment had been removed or left open, allowing seawater from the pierced fuel storage area to seep into the generators. The divers could not find the supposed missing-door area, but came away with superb film for the documentary *The Mystery of the* Andrea Doria.

In August 1981, Gimbel and his wife, Elga Andersen, a former actress and diver, spent $2 million on a thirty-person expedition to check out the missing-door theory once more but also to attempt salvage of a *Doria* safe. Just about every day that month, the divers descended in a yellow pressurized bell from their boat, *Sea Level 11*. They spent at least 12 hours daily exploring the wreck, then ascended inside the bell each evening to the boat deck and transferred through an airlock to pressurized living quarters, avoiding lengthy decompression procedures after each day's work.

The divers failed again to confirm that a watertight door had been missing. But they came upon a large hole in the bottom of the generator room, evidently opened by the pivoting of the *Stockholm* while interlocked with the *Doria*. The hole was large enough for a diver to swim through, but the team could not estimate its size because of the darkness. According to Gimbel, the discovery of the hole proved that seawater had entered the generator room directly from the ocean, rendering the issue of the missing door irrelevant and revealing that three watertight compartments had been breached, one beyond the tolerable limit. (Those were a cargo hold, the deep-fuel tank compartment, and the generator room.) But a photograph of the sinking *Doria* that appeared in *Marine Engineering/Log,* a professional journal, in 1956 suggested that very thing. So the Gimbel discovery was less spectacular than it seemed, although providing corroboration of the damage inflicted by the *Stockholm.*

That expedition produced thousands of feet of film for a 90-minute television documentary, Andrea Doria: *The Final Chapter,* but it made newspaper headlines for something far afield from aesthetics or oceanography—the recovery of the 3½-ton Bank of Rome safe.

Gimbel's divers cut the safe from its moorings in the first-class foyer with acetylene torches and brought it to the New York Aquarium at Coney Island, placing it inside the shark tank. The sharks were to provide security, while the tank's salt water would presumably prevent further deterioration of the safe and its unknown contents. But the safe didn't stay with the protective sharks for long. It was transferred to a tank with cooler water when it began emitting gas bubbles, apparent evidence of bacteria growing in the warm water and perhaps eating away at currency.

While Gimbel worked on putting the documentary film together, the safe remained at the aquarium. He finally opened it the night of August 16, 1984, on a ballyhooed international television hookup in front of a few hundred guests, U.S. Customs agents who had kept the safe under seal, shotgun-toting private guards, and more than a dozen New York City police officers.

Just as the show went on the air, a thunderstorm erupted, drenching the writer George Plimpton, serving as the emcee, and interrupting some of the televised transmissions. And the climax was just as soggy. Gimbel found not a single strand of jewels. The safe contained only low-denomination U.S. and Italian bills, some of them waterlogged and decaying.

Gimbel marketed the bills as souvenirs rather than turning them over to the American and Italian treasuries in exchange for new bills at their face value. He hired paper conservators to restore the currency, mounted the bills between pieces of acrylic with a "certificate of authenticity" accompanied by a history of the *Andrea Doria,* and touted them as gifts in a Christmas catalog. When the *Doria* went down, a 1,000-lire note was worth about $1.60. Twenty-eight years later, it was worth one third of that. The price for a catalog gift set containing a single bill: $299.

The televised safe-opening was incorporated into Gimbel's hour-and-a-half documentary on the 1981 expedition.

Writing in the *New York Times,* the critic Walter Goodman noted how a few of the Italian bills were displayed in the documentary "along with a little lecture on their fine points by Mr. Gimbel, who appears to be under the impression that he has discovered artifacts from the reign of Diocletian."

"We are not told how much the contents are worth," Goodman observed, "but this writer can report they do not add up to 90 minutes."

In the summer of 1993, an expedition led by John Moyer of Vineland, New Jersey, entered the Winter Garden and brought up the first significant pieces of salvaged artwork, two 1,000-pound ceramic panels by the Italian artist Guido Gambone depicting mythological scenes. Having made many dives to the *Doria,* Moyer was awarded exclusive salvage rights by a federal judge in New Jersey who agreed with his contention that the *Doria* was an abandoned vessel. According to traditional salvage law, a sunken ship is open domain for salvors after it has been declared a derelict by insurance companies who obtain ownership when they pay all claims.

Moyer gained the right to recover valuable artwork from the *Doria* without interference, but has allowed recreational divers to continue removing items such as china that can be carried away by hand. In addition to the Gambone panels, the Moyer team has brought up Admiral Doria's pedestal and ankles, left behind when the rest of the statue was cut away in 1964.

Today the *Andrea Doria*'s funnel lies amid the rubble on the ocean floor. Huge sections of her decks are a mass of debris. Her steel hull, draped by sea anemones, is intact, but defaced by rust holes and large cracks beyond those left by the *Stockholm.* Her lifeboat davits are heavily barnacled. Silt lines the crumbling public rooms.

Only the most experienced divers venture to her.

Many of the 1 million to 3 million recreational divers in the nation descend only to a depth of some 60 feet, breathing compressed air. The recreational diving limit is about 130 feet, but *Doria* divers go almost twice as far down. They are certified for "technical diving"—descents with custom-gas mixtures, most commonly trimix, a combination of oxygen, nitrogen, and helium. This mixture, first used by the Navy and later commercially, reduces the threats of the disorienting phenomenon nitrogen narcosis as well as decompression sickness and allows dives that are deeper and longer than those relying on regular compressed air.

But as Steve Bielenda, the owner of the *Wahoo*, a boat that takes many divers to the *Doria* from Long Island, has observed, "If you're a certified diver, it doesn't make you qualified to dive the *Doria*. It's like using Mount Everest for a training ground."

Since the *Doria* lies in international waters, diving to the wreck is not regulated. The U.S. Coast Guard places no restrictions on access. But even with trimix, when a diver experiences a physical or equipment problem in darkness at a depth of more than 200 feet, he is in major trouble.

As Joe Jackson, a diver from Cincinnati, tells it, "It's just another big wreck until you get inside, and there are nine thousand different things to entangle you. Stairways become hallways, and the current just rips you off the wreck."

Divers usually enter through Gimbel's Hole, an opening cut into the Foyer Deck by Peter Gimbel's crew in 1981, when it removed the Bank of Rome safe. The opening, about the size of a garage door and some 180 feet below the ocean surface, allows access to a corridor, at a depth of about 205 feet, leading to the first-class gift shop and dining room, the prime areas for recovery of dinnerware and other souvenirs.

In the first twenty-five years after the *Andrea Doria* sank, not a single diver died exploring the wreck. But as the ranks of souvenir-hunters have grown some of the divers perhaps less than ready for their expensive and sophisticated equipment—the death toll from the *Andrea Doria–Stockholm* collision has climbed.

July 1, 1981—John Barnett of Pound Ridge, New York, was found dead near the *Doria*'s bridge with air remaining in his tanks, leading investigators to believe he may have gone into convulsions and stopped breathing. He was forty years old.

July 15, 1984—Francis Kennedy of Wrentham, Massachusetts, ran out of air during his ascent. He was thirty-seven.

August 1, 1985—John Ormsby of Key West, Florida, is believed to have panicked, swimming into electrical cables and becoming so entangled it took divers two days to cut him out. He was twenty-seven.

July 15, 1988—Joe Drozd of Stonington, Connecticut, cut himself free of a line entangling his air tanks, then became disoriented, spit out his regulator, and drowned. He was forty-two.

July 2, 1992—Matthew Lawrence of Miami Lakes, Florida, dived with tanks containing inadequate air and died 14 minutes into his descent. He was thirty-two.

July 15, 1992—Michael Scofield of Soquel, California, apparently became lost inside the wreck and passed out. He was thirty-six.

July 12, 1993—Robert Santulli of Port Jefferson, New York, panicked at a depth of 210 feet, struggled with another diver, allowed the regulator to fall out of his mouth, and drowned. He was thirty-three.

June 24, 1998—Craig Sicola, a building contractor from Surf City, New Jersey, having dived alone in search of china, rose to the surface too quickly and was found dead with three pieces of china in his bag. He was thirty-two.

July 8, 1998—Richard Roost Jr., a dive shop owner from Ann Arbor, Michigan, who helped train police divers, was found floating in the first-class lounge less than 20 feet from an exit. He may have become lost and hyperventilated, causing him to pass out. He was forty-six.

August 4, 1998—Vincent Napoliello of Brooklyn, a financial adviser at a Wall Street securities firm, who had been making annual dives to the *Doria* since 1992, was found dead, floating on the ocean surface, after exploring the wreck. He was thirty-two.

July 22, 1999—Christopher Murley of Cincinnati, the owner of a telephone installation company, apparently suffered a heart attack while swimming along a line leading to the *Doria*. He was forty-four.

July 28, 1999—Charles McGurr, an auto body mechanic from Brick, New Jersey, was reported missing after last being seen above the *Doria*'s port side. Divers recovered his body outside the Winter Garden. It was not clear whether he had passed out and floated down there or had gotten stuck. The dive was a present he had given himself for his birthday. Five days earlier, he had turned fifty-three.

When Peter Gimbel announced plans for a diving expedition in 1981, Linda Morgan Hardberger was asked by a reporter for her sentiments.

"Very personally, I find the whole exploration rather distasteful," she said. "The *Andrea Doria* is kind of my Forest Lawn. I can understand their feeling, but I sort of wish they'd leave it alone."

Two decades later, pondering the heightened popularity of the *Andrea Doria* for divers in search of souvenirs—twelve of them having perished—"The Miracle Girl" of the summer of '56 held to those thoughts. "It's a gravesite," she said.

The collision of the *Andrea Doria* and the *Stockholm* had taken the lives of Linda Morgan's stepfather, her half sister, and forty-nine others. As the years pass, as the sea takes its toll on the *Andrea Doria,* so does the *Doria* exact a toll on those who venture to see her in ruin.

Appendix

A total of 1,660 passengers and crewmen survived the sinking of the *Andrea Doria* 45 miles south of Nantucket Island. Forty-six people died.

The *Doria* was carrying 1,134 passengers and 572 crew members. Forty-three passengers died in the wreckage of their cabins or, perhaps, when they were swept into the sea at the moment of impact. Only two of these forty-three were accounted for—Camille Cianfarra, flung from Cabin 54 to Cabin 56, and Martha Peterson, an occupant of that cabin, both of whom died there. All *Doria* crewmen survived.

Two *Doria* passengers died aboard the *Stockholm*—Jeanette Carlin, who was catapulted onto its retreating bow, and Carl Watres, who succumbed to a heart attack. Norma Di Sandro, the four-year-old who suffered head injuries when her father tossed her from a *Doria* deck into a lifeboat, died two days later at a hospital in Boston.

Julia Grego, a passenger, died six months later of spinal injuries suffered in the collision.

Five *Stockholm* seamen were killed. Three were swept overboard, another succumbed to injuries on the liner, and a fifth died shortly after being evacuated by helicopter to Nantucket Island.

The fifty-one people who lost their lives in the collision or its immediate aftermath:

The *Andrea Doria*

Paul Anderson	(hometown not listed)
Agnese Baratta	Rome
Margherita Pontecorvi Baratta	Rome
Laura Bremmerman	Fort Worth, Texas
Jeanette Carlin	New York City
Margaret Carola	New York City
Camille Cianfarra	New York City
Joan Cianfarra	New York City
Giuseppe Cirincione	Albany, New York
Rosalia Cirincione	Albany
Christina Covina	(hometown not listed)

Giuseppe DeGrandi Jr.	Port Chester, New York
Lucia DeGrandi	Port Chester
Theresa Del Gaudio	Salerno, Italy
Angelina Diana	Hartford, Connecticut [American destination]
Biaggio Diana	Hartford
Victoria Diana	Hartford
Maria Di Luzio	Tuckahoe, New York
Concetta Di Miche	Waterbury, Connecticut
Norma Di Sandro	Providence, Rhode Island [American destination]
Josephine Ferraro	South Bend, Indiana
Angelina Gonzales	Santa Stefano di Quisquina, Sicily
Marie Grechi	Cremona, Italy
Antoinette Guzzi	Easton, Pennsylvania
Giuseppe Guzzi	Easton
Amelia Iazzetta	New York City
Marie Imbelloni	San Francisco
Anita Leoni	Rome
Domenico Palmeri	Agrigento Province, Sicily
Francesca Palmeri	Agrigento
Martha Peterson	Upper Montclair, New Jersey
Giovanina Russo	New York City [American destination]
Maria Russo	New York City
Michael Russo	New York City
Vincenza Russo	New York City
Anna Maria Sergio	South Bend, Indiana [American destination]
Domenica Sergio	South Bend
Giuseppe Sergio	South Bend
Maria Sergio	South Bend
Rocco Sergio	South Bend
Michelina Suozzi	Potenza, Italy
Ferdinand Thieriot	Burlingame, California
Frances Thieriot	Burlingame
Carl Watres	Manasquan, New Jersey
Rose Zumbo	Cosenza, Italy
Vincenzo Zumbo	Cosenza

The *Stockholm*

Alf Johannson	Göteborg, Sweden
Carl Jonasson	Göteborg
Karl Osterberg	Skara, Sweden
Sune Steen	Göteborg
Evert Svensson	Göteborg

Sources

Interviews and Correspondence

M. Bernard Aidinoff, Lena Alfano, Charles Annino, Philip Ansuini, Emery Antonacci, Guido Badano, Robert Boggs, Frank Brown, Johan-Ernst Bogislaus August Carstens-Johannsen, John Casten Jr., David Corey, Joseph Coviello, Loomis Dean, Kathy Kerbow Dickson, Lars Enestrom, Nora Kovach Farago, Max Ferrill, Hank Fisher, Raymond Goedert, Robert Goedert, Kenneth Gould-thorpe, Joe Griffith, Carmelo Grillo, Paul Grimes, Elisabeth Hanson, Linda Morgan Hardberger, Boyd Hempen, Claude Hess, David Hollyer, Louise Hollyer, Carol Johnson, William Johnson, Thomas Kelly, Ernest LaFont, Louis Linn, Yvonne Magnusson Reinholdsson, Stan Mastin, Ray Maurstad, Ernest Melby, Robert Meurn, Stig Oscarsson, Giovanna Paladino, Leonardo Paladino, Harold Parker Jr., Istvan Rabovsky, Alan Rassner, Harry Rea, Jerome Reinert, Ake Reinholdsson, Val Robbins, Frank Russo, Leon Scarborough, John Smith, Meryl Stoller, Mike Stoller, Robroy Todd, Robert Wallace, Neale Westfall, Richard Wojcik, Richard Worton.

Newspapers

Baltimore Sun, Boston Globe, Boston Herald, Cape Cod Times, Chicago Tribune, Easton Express-Times, Long Island Press, Miami Herald, National Observer, New York Daily Mirror, New York *Daily News, New York Herald Tribune, New York Journal-American, New York Post, New York Times, New York World-Telegram and Sun, Newsday, Philadelphia Inquirer, St. Louis Post-Dispatch, Wall Street Journal, Washington Post.*

Articles and Pamphlets

"*Andrea Doria–Stockholm* Collision: Round Table." Presentations by the former *Andrea Doria* officers Guido Badano, Giovanni Cordera, and Eugenio Giannini, Genoa, Italy, October 6, 1988.

"*Andrea Doria–Stockholm* Tragedy." Mariners Weather Log, National Oceanic and Atmospheric Administration, Washington, D.C., January 1957.

Bell, F. C. "The Mystery of *Andrea Doria*." *Journal of the Institute of Navigation,* April 1971.

Brean, Herbert. "Case Hangs on Old Law of Sea." *Life,* October 15, 1956.

"Camera in a Sea Tomb." *Life,* August 13, 1956.

Carrothers, John C. "The *Andrea Doria–Stockholm* Disaster: Accidents Don't Happen." *U.S. Naval Institute Proceedings,* August 1971.

"Death of a Superliner." *Marine Engineering/Log,* September 1956.

Friedman, Dr. Paul, and Dr. Louis Linn. "Some Psychiatric Notes on the *Andrea Doria* Disaster," *American Journal of Psychiatry,* October/November 1957.

Gebhardt, Neil. "A Night of Terror." *Titanic Commutator,* Titanic Historical Society, Winter 1991.

Hardy, A. C. "The Motor Liner *Stockholm.*" *Shipping World,* March 3, 1948.

"Italian Government Decorates Coast Guardsmen for *Andrea Doria* Rescue." *U.S. Coast Guard Magazine,* February 1957.

Lord, Walter. "The Hours of Fear as People Lived Them." *Life,* August 6, 1956.

MacLeish, Kenneth. "Divers Explore the Sunken *Andrea Doria.*" *Life,* September 17, 1956.

McMahon, Bucky. "Everest at the Bottom of the Sea." *Esquire,* July 2000.

Nordling, Carl O. "The Course to Disaster." *Voyage—The Journal of Titanic International,* Spring/Summer 1996.

Roman, Ruth. "What I Learned from the People of the *Andrea Doria.*" *Parade,* September 9, 1957.

Ryan, Cornelius. "Five Desperate Hours in Cabin 56." *Collier's,* September 28, 1956.

"Sculptures, Plaques, and Other Valuables Lured Two Young Divers." *Popular Mechanics,* January 1975.

"Ship Disaster: 24-Hour Log of *Times* Coverage." *Times Talk,* August 1956.

"Ships in the Night: Red Cross Relief Operations Following Collision of the *Andrea Doria* and *Stockholm.*" American National Red Cross, New York Chapter, 1956.

Sutton, Horace. "Night of July 25: *Stockholm* and *Andrea Doria* Collision." *Saturday Review,* October 6 and November 3, 1956.

———. "One by Sea, One by Land: *Doria-Stockholm* Debacle." *Saturday Review,* September 1, 1956.

Taylor, Captain Brown. "*Andrea Doria:* Soldier of the Sea." *U.S. Naval Institute Proceedings,* September 1971.

Tortori-Donati, Dr. Bruno. "The Tragedy of the Sinking of the *Andrea Doria* Witnessed by the Ship's Doctor." Review, *Annali di Medicina Navale,* Genoa, Italy, March 1979. Translation in *Journal of the Royal Naval Medical Society,* London.

"Transatlantic Liner *Andrea Doria.*" *Shipping World,* January 14, 1953.

Trask, Harry, interviewed by John Hollis. "Harry Trask: Eyewitness to History." *Voyage—The Journal of Titanic International,* Spring/Summer 1996.

Young, Robert. "Collision in the Night." *USA Today,* July 1981.

Books

Ballard, Robert D., with Rick Archbold. *Lost Liners: From the* Titanic *to the* Andrea Doria, *the Ocean Floor Reveals Its Greatest Lost Ships.* New York: Hyperion, 1997.

Barnaby, K. C. *Some Ship Disasters and Their Causes.* South Brunswick, N.J.:
   A. S. Barnes, 1968.
Berger, Meyer. *The Story of the* New York Times, *1851–1951.* New York:
   Simon & Schuster, 1951.
Bliss, Edward Jr. *Now the News: The Story of Broadcast Journalism.* New
   York: Columbia University Press, 1991.
Brinnin, John Malcolm. *The Sway of the Grand Saloon.* Bronxville, N.Y.: Dela-
   corte, 1971.
Cahill, Richard A. *Collisions and Their Causes.* London: Fairplay Publications,
   1983.
———. *Disasters at Sea: Titanic to Exxon Valdez.* London: Century, 1990.
Catledge, Turner. *My Life and the* Times. New York: Harper & Row, 1971.
De Beaudéan, Raoul. *Captain of the* Ile. New York: McGraw-Hill, 1960.
Flook, Maria. *My Sister Life: The Story of My Sister's Disappearance.* New
   York: Pantheon, 1997.
Frankel, Max. *The Times of My Life and My Life with the* Times. New York:
   Random House, 1999.
Gentile, Gary. Andrea Doria: *Dive to an Era.* Philadelphia: Gary Gentile Pro-
   ductions, 1989.
Gladstone, Eugene W. *In the Wake of the* Andrea Doria: *A Candid Autobiog-
   raphy.* Toronto: McClelland & Stewart, 1966.
Harris, Warren G. *Cary Grant: A Touch of Elegance.* New York: Doubleday,
   1987.
Heiskell, Andrew. *Outsider, Insider: An Unlikely Success Story.* New York:
   Marian-Darien Press, 1998.
Hoffer, William. *Saved! The Story of the* Andrea Doria—*the Greatest Sea Res-
   cue in History.* New York: Summit Books, 1979.
Lord, Walter. *A Night to Remember.* New York: Holt, Rinehart & Winston,
   1955.
Marriott, John. *Disaster at Sea.* New York: Hippocrene, 1987.
McAuley, Rob. *The Liners: A Voyage of Discovery.* London: Boxtree, 1997.
Mikes, George. *Leap Through the Curtain: The Story of Nora Kovach and Ist-
   van Rabovsky.* New York: Dutton, 1955.
Miller, William H. Jr. *Picture History of the Italian Line.* Mineola, N.Y.: Dover
   Publications, 1999.
Morgan, Edward P. *Clearing the Air.* Washington, D.C.: Robert B. Luce, 1963.
Moscow, Alvin. *Collision Course: The* Andrea Doria *and the* Stockholm. New
   York: G. P. Putnam's Sons, 1959.
Nelson, Nancy. *Evenings with Cary Grant: Recollections in His Own Words
   and by Those Who Knew Him Best.* New York: Morrow, 1991.
Padfield, Peter. *An Agony of Collisions.* London: Hodder & Stoughton, 1966.
Sindell, David. "SOS from the *Andrea Doria.*" In *The Verdicts Were Just:
   Eight Famous Lawyers Present Their Most Memorable Cases,* edited by
   Albert Averbach and Charles Price, pp. 138–148. New York: Van Rees
   Press, 1966.

Stanford, Don. *The* Ile de France. New York: Appleton-Century-Crofts, 1960.

Wade, Wyn Craig. *The* Titanic: *End of a Dream.* New York: Penguin Books, 1986.

Videos

Andrea Doria: *The Final Chapter.* Independent United Distributors.

Sea Tales: The Sinking of the Andrea Doria. New Video Group.

Shipwreck: Fatal Collision. CineNova Productions.

Wrath of God: Collisions in the Mist. Towers Communications.

Documents

U.S. District Court, Southern District of New York, miscellaneous files, Petition of Italia Societa per Azioni di Navigazione as owner of the steamship *Andrea Doria* for limitation of liability (A. 189-102) and Petition of Aktiebolaget Svenska Amerika Linien, as owner of the motorship *Stockholm,* in a cause of exoneration from or limitation of liability (A. 189-73), Boxes 119 to 130, National Archives and Records Administration, Northeast Region, New York City.

U.S. House of Representatives, Committee on Merchant Marine and Fisheries. "Report on the *Andrea Doria–Stockholm* Collision." Washington, D.C., 1956.

Internet

Grillo, Anthony. "*Andrea Doria:* Tragedy and Rescue at Sea." www.andreadoria.org

Index